JAMES PARTRIDGE OBE is the founder of Face Equality International, an alliance of NGOs and charities around the world working together to campaign for 'face equality' and to challenge disfigurement prejudice and discrimination. From 1992 to 2017, he was founder and chief executive of Changing Faces, the leading UK charity supporting and representing people with disfigurements. He is a founding director of Dining with a Difference, a disability consultancy company.

James writes and presents widely on disfigurement, disability, inclusion and social entrepreneurship in the UK and internationally and has been variously honoured for his work: an OBE from Her Majesty the Queen in 2002, an honorary fellowship from the Royal College of Surgeons of Edinburgh, and honorary doctorates from the Universities of Bristol and the University of the West of England, as well as a number of national awards, such as the Third Sector award for Most Admired Charity Chief Executive in 2010 and the Beacon Prize for Leadership.

Over the last thirty years, James has served on many committees and panels, such as the UK's National Institute for Clinical Excellence, bringing disability, human rights, user and lay perspectives to bear on a range of subjects. His first book, *Changing Faces: The Challenge of Facial Disfigurement* was published by Penguin in 1990. James is married, has three grown-up children and six grandchildren, and lives in Guernsey.

'This is a wonderful book from a wonderful person. Always honest, never dull, it tells the engrossing story of one man's journey through life with facial disfigurement. More than that: it shows how someone can change society, and leave us all better off as a result.'

Professor Tom Shakespeare FBA
(London School of Hygiene and Tropical Medicine)

'Required reading for anyone seriously interested in the human condition. Partridge writes for those personally battling the forces of Face-ism and Stigma, and for policy makers and medical professionals on the psychosocial support that people 'Facing It' require if they are to live their lives to the full. And as the world's leading authority, he outlines what societies need to do to systematically tackle facial stigma and discrimination – all of this grounded in his deeply lived experience of the `Not-Perfect Face in a Perfect-Face World.'

Susan Scott-Parker OBE,
founder of business disability international (bdi)

'An excellent resource for people with facial differences, and for people without. James Partridge has used his personal situation to better the world – helping people with facial differences be seen, be accepted, be free from discrimination and love ourselves. This book will change lives – I am all the better for finding James and Changing Faces, and I know readers will feel the same.

Carly Findlay OAM, writer, speaker and appearance activist

'Fizzing from start to finish with candour, humour and passion ... James Partridge charts his journey along the path to self-acceptance, self-esteem and confident living ... There is much in this book to help those longing to thrive with a distinctive appearance, as well as food for thought for health care professionals and policy makers ... and the monumental effort needed to remove the stigma and discrimination currently experienced by people living with not-perfect faces.'

Professor Nichola Rumsey OBE (University of the West of England)

FACE IT

FACE IT

Facial Disfigurement and
My Fight for Face Equality

JAMES PARTRIDGE

First published in 2020 by Pebble Press

Copyright © James Partridge

The moral right of James Partridge to be identified as the author of this work has been asserted in accordance with the Copyright, Designs and Patents Act 1988.

All rights reserved. No part of this publication may be reproduced or transmitted in any form or by any means, electronic or mechanical including photocopying, recording or any information storage or retrieval system, without prior permission in writing from the publishers.

Every effort has been made to contact copyright holders. However, the publisher will be glad to rectify in future editions any inadvertent omissions brought to their attention.

ISBN 9781912892808

Also available as an ebook
ISBN 9781912892815

Typeset by seagulls.net
Cover design by Simon Levy
Cover photo by Garlinda Birkbeck
www.garlindabirkbeck.com

Project management by whitefox
Printed and bound by Clays

In gratitude to my mother who said, ridiculously, and made me believe, that all the pain would not be in vain and would have meaning one day.

CONTENTS

INTRODUCTION   1

PART 1: THE PERSONAL

1. Growing Up with a Near-Perfect Face   9
2. Losing Face   13
3. Seeing *IT*   27
4. Fixing *IT*? First Questions   37
5. Re-entering the World   41
6. Fixing *IT*? Second Thoughts   47
7. Going Solo to University   53
8. Facing My Fault   57
9. Discovering Stigma   61
10. Restarting Life   71
11. Reconstructing *IT*   87
12. Building a New Me   101
13. Looking Back and Moving Forward   121

MEZZANINE: Living Full-on – and Finding My Voice   125

PART 2: THE PROFESSIONAL

14.	Inventing Changing Faces	141
15.	Faces: The Principles of Effective Psychosocial Care	161
16.	Making Faces Available to Everyone	191
17.	The Professional – A Conclusion	197

MEZZANINE: Going 'Political'   199

PART 3: THE POLITICAL

18.	'Face-ism' Unmasked	213
19.	Where Does Face-ism Come From?	223
20.	The Vision of a World that Respects Face Equality	247
21.	The Campaign For Face Equality in the UK to Date	257
22.	What Can We All Do to Create Face Equality?	303

FACE IT – SUMMING UP   325

LAST WORD   329

Annex 1: A Reflection on Face Transplantation	333
Annex 2: 'At Long Last, A Newsreader Who Made Us Face Reality'	351
Annex 3: The International Media Standard on Disfigurement (2020)	355
Annex 4: A Logo With Meaning	359

Acknowledgements	361
Notes	365
Credits	373

*July 1970, six months before the accident.
I took my face entirely for granted.*

Autumn 2019, my 'very-not-perfect face'.

INTRODUCTION

For the first eighteen years of my life, up to 1970, I used the comment 'I'm not just a pretty face, you know' with no irony whatsoever.

I lived in and with a near-perfect face which I prized and used to my advantage. It was a face that was central to the high hopes I had for being 'successful' in the perfect-face world into which I was emerging as a young adult.

Today, I use 'I'm not just a pretty face, you know' very deliberately precisely because of its irony. Usually it's when someone appears to praise me for something; I'll surprise them, disarm them even, but in a gentle way: 'Not just a pretty face, you know.'

I lost that near-perfect face on a wet December night in 1970. For ever. That moment was the start of living with IT, as I called my very-not-perfect face. I had to face IT: I'd blown my chances completely. I could have zero expectations of anything good.

I didn't want to face IT at all. FACE IT tells how eventually, after much pain and angst, that changed. Now, fifty years on, I live with my very distinctive face with pride. It's a hotchpotch of scars, skin grafts and weird asymmetry (thanks to brilliant surgery). I even often say, again with much irony and stroking my chin, 'I'm very attached to my face.'

And that surprises some people, because our global society has become ever more obsessed by perfect-face thinking. Without great looks, you're destined for failure...

And my smiling is also a surprise to some. How come?

It is said that a camel smiles because it knows the hundredth name for God. My reasons are much more earthly, but perhaps no less profound for being so.

I am smiling for three main reasons, which I will elaborate on in this book.

First, I smile because largely by trial and error, I discovered a way of living successfully despite, or, more accurately, because of my outstanding face, which enabled me by the late 1970s to get work, and to find love and happiness. I know I'm a very lucky man.

Second, I smile because, after a series of coincidences in the late 1980s, I had the opportunity to write about the lessons of my adjustment, and how I'd risen above the facial stigma that surrounded me. And that led, thanks to much generosity, to my turning these lessons into practical, empowering help for children, young people and adults with unusual faces from any cause – congenital, hereditary, traumatic, cancer-related, dermatological or neurological. I have been honoured to do that work.

And third, I am smiling because I am pleased to be at the forefront of the campaign for 'face equality', which is going global. It will win. It will bring an end to the injustice, stigma and discrimination that people with facial disfigurements experience every day around the world – a very ambitious goal, but one to which many are now committed. This matters to me above all, and makes me smile the most.

Those three reasons for smiling are the basis for FACE IT's three parts. But before I explain how the book unfolds, a word about the vocabulary I'm using, because this is important.

If you were to ask members of the public about my face, they might well say that I have a facial disfigurement. It's in common parlance, and although 'disfigurement' is an unappealing 'dis' word, I will generally use it throughout the book whenever I am discussing the disadvantages that people with facial disfigurements have to live with in the early twenty-first century. I see it as the best *collective* term for 'the visual effect' of any condition, marks or scars

INTRODUCTION

on people's faces, like those with facial burns, a cleft lip and palate, a Bell's palsy, psoriasis and many others. And I think 'facial difference' is an acceptable alternative because it is specific to the face and 'difference' suggests some variation from the usual.

However, I will avoid euphemisms like 'visible difference'. Although that term is very inclusive, as every single member of the human race is visibly different, it is not definitive enough for people with disfigurements to use to make their case or get justice – just as 'differently abled' as a euphemism for 'disabled' people is not helpful.

I did wonder about using the word 'imperfect', as in 'people with imperfect faces', but decided not to because it irks some people who think it too judgemental.

On many occasions in the book, I have needed to use an adjective to describe my face or that of other people. I dislike 'disfigured' as an adjective. Instead I will use a range of more positive adjectives like unusual, distinctive, distinguished, outstanding, not-perfect, less-than-perfect, and even wonky!

Incidentally, if you want to describe me, I'm a man with burn scars on his face. Which is objective and informative, as it should be. There's much more on our common language in the third part of the book.

The other introductory point I need to make is that this book is quite deliberately about the significance of the human face. The face is the canvas that is on show to everyone you meet and on which you paint your moods, your personality and your experiences. It is what people think of when they think of you or me – it represents our identities. And it is what we see in the mirror and call 'me', our self-image, in our internal conversations.

Most important of all, your face is where people look when they meet you or see you in the street or the park or on social media, and make instant face-value judgements about you.

If you have a face that stands out, the impact it has on you as a person, your social identity and your social encounters is likely to be profound and lifelong and cannot be underestimated. This book is about all that and more.

Which is not to deny in any way that there are many conditions, injuries, etc. that affect the appearance of a person's hands and body, like arthritis or limb amputation. These conditions can be very psychologically and socially distressing too, although the visual effects can sometimes be covered up with clothing and other devices. However, in my view, those effects are qualitatively and quantitively different and probably lesser to having a distinctive face.

This book is about living with a not-perfect face in a face-perfect world – and about why and how that world needs to change. In line with my three reasons for smiling, I have divided this book into three parts:

- The Personal – I have often been asked, in the last twenty-five years especially, to write a personal account of what I went through and how I adjusted. This is a no-holds-barred account.
- The Professional – In the twenty-five years from 1992 that I led the UK charity Changing Faces, we pioneered and provided emotional support and life-skills training for many people with less-than-perfect faces. I describe in lay language how this help was developed and what it means for you if you are in need or are a health professional.
- The Political – Making life better for people with distinctive faces around the world is not just about empowerment, important as that is. We also have to eliminate the stigmas and injustices of the societies in which we live and create human rights for all, irrespective of the shape, complexion or irregularity of their faces. Face-ism is what we face, and it must go. Face equality is what we need.

Between the parts are what I'm calling 'Mezzanines' – passages or intermediary floors that carry you to the next 'level'. In the first I

INTRODUCTION

describe my transition from living as a private citizen with an unusual face to becoming a public face campaigning for those who have distinctive faces.

In the second Mezzanine, I include ten brief stories of people who have faces of distinction and (NB: not 'but') are each in their own way outstanding. Why ten? It could have been 500, even 5,000, but in the interest of length, I had to limit myself. Ten perspectives from people with distinctive faces are sufficient to show our common cause very well.

So, where to start? At my beginning…

PART 1

The Personal

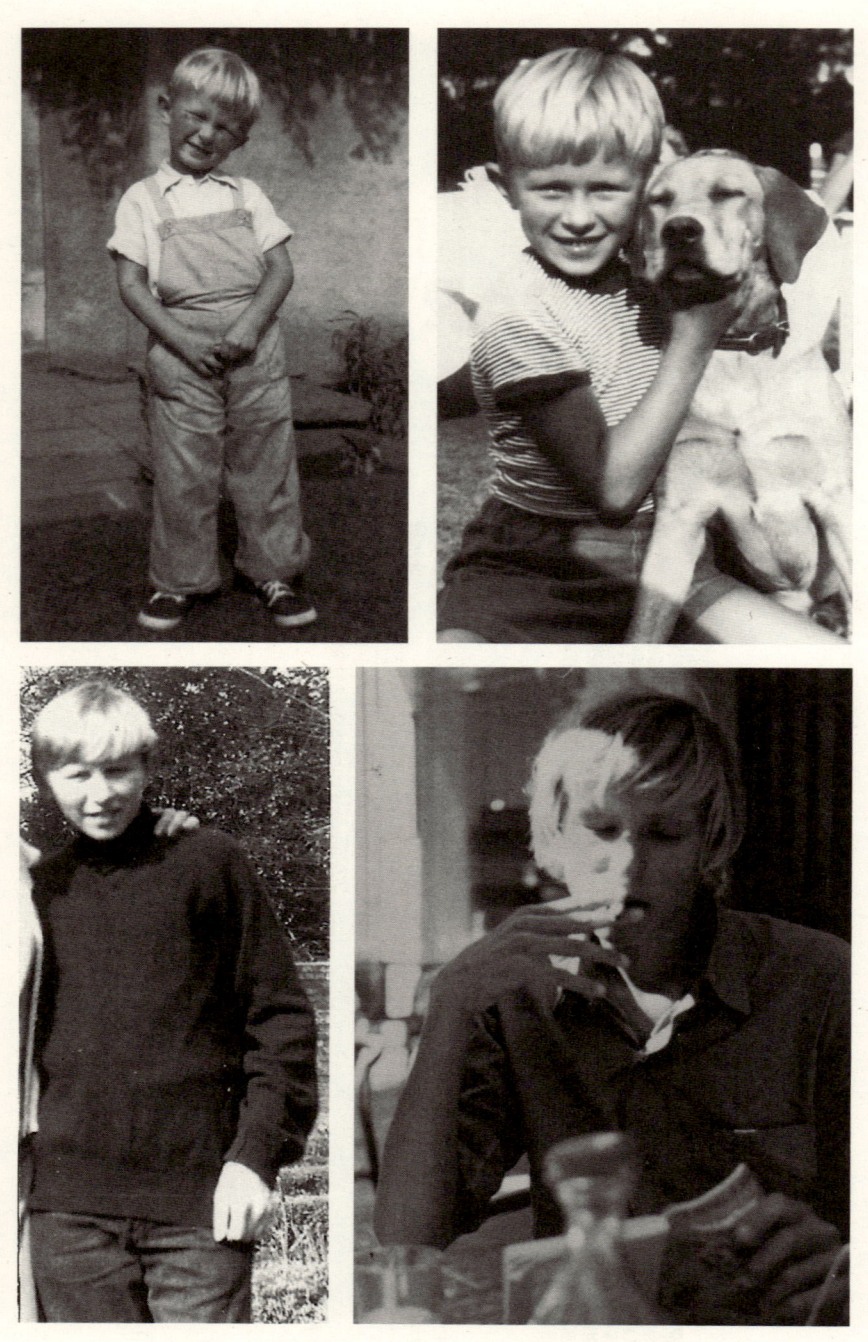

*Me at various stages growing up: aged five (top left),
seven (top right), thirteen (bottom left) and seventeen (bottom right).*

1.
GROWING UP WITH A NEAR-PERFECT FACE

I was born in the English West Country, in Chipping Sodbury Maternity Hospital in late October 1952, and spent my early years living in small villages outside Bristol, where my father worked. It was a carefree childhood shared with my sister, who was two years younger. We went to local play groups and primary schools.

At eight years old, I entered one of the Bristol public (private) schools, Clifton College, as a boarder, and that was to be where my life mostly played out for the next ten years, from 1960 to 1970. Clifton is a liberal Christian school; at that time it was for boys only and had a large Jewish community embedded in it. We had a good traditional education underpinned by a strong pastoral house system.

These were years of huge social and political change, which was slowly reflected in how the school itself changed. We lived through JFK's assassination, the freezing winter of 1963–64, the coming of the Beatles and rock 'n' roll, flower power, Carnaby Street and long hair, the Windrush generation, the US civil rights movement and the assassination of Martin Luther King, Britain devaluing the pound, and much more. Lessons and chapel services reflected, often very awkwardly, the throwing over of 'old values'. We were encouraged to read widely and learn about new movements, including the rise of charities like the Samaritans and Toc H. Looking back they were fascinating formative years and, despite the boys-only nature of the education, Clifton definitely shaped my values in a civilised way.

The school was also highly focused on 'games' – sports, especially rugby and cricket, were all-engrossing, and I thank my genes for enabling me to be a half-decent competitor in both of those and in cross-country running, squash, fives and rackets. The competitive streak I developed at school has stood me in good stead – though sometimes, apparently rather excessively!

Academically, I was bright and was pushed into the year ahead – a bad move in retrospect, because I was just not mature enough to enjoy it, a prime example being when I was expected at fourteen and a half to sit O level English literature with the set texts on First World War poetry and novels. It gave me an inferiority complex for several years.

But as I approached the end of my secondary education in 1970, I had achieved reasonable A level grades and some positions of leadership in the school, and could have been described as a confident person with an exciting future ahead.

I knew I had much going for me. And I knew my face was a crucial part of that good fortune.

My face was not yet fully formed, but I liked it very much and traded on it without scruple, especially to attract young women – as on a Spanish hitchhiking holiday during the summer of 1970. I was aware that I was able to convey a certain confidence and charm through it. I don't think I was brash or arrogant about it. And I call it 'near-perfect' because there were definitely better-looking young men in my peer group! But I believed that my good looks were an absolute prerequisite for a successful life.

By the end of my very last term at school, on Thursday 3rd December 1970, to be precise, this is what life looked like for me.

I was a confident and well-liked eighteen-year-old and had just finished the hardest exams I could possibly take in maths to get into

Oxford University. I had completed them to the very best of my ability. I had a chance... and if I didn't get a place, I had three other universities lined up to choose from.

A gap year of travelling beckoned... and I believed that my life would fall nicely into place – there seemed to be nothing in my way.

That Thursday evening, after the Oxford entrance exams, I went with a young teacher and several others to a local pub, the Cotham Porter Stores, and we mused: what did we expect our lives would look like?

I recall being guarded, partly because I knew I still had some growing up to do, but mainly because I didn't want to seem to boast. Actually, I thought I had it made.

My expectations were already formed, if not very precisely, and they went something like this: I hoped to get to Oxford the following autumn. I planned to let my hair down (literally) over the next nine months in a gap year of travelling in North America, doing half a ski season in the Laurentians outside Montreal (where my half-sister lived), exploring Iceland with classmates and more European excesses.

I'd arrive in Oxford in October 1971 a much worldlier young man, and my years in Oxford would see me grow up successfully, enjoying my chosen subjects (economics and politics especially), making strong friends and playing hard too. The rest of my life would pan out from there... maybe business, accountancy or the civil service...

A lot of that hinged on the confidence I had in my good-looking face. I took it entirely for granted. It would enable me to look the part: smart, accomplished, relaxed, confident – and I'd be seen as such. Pretty much perfect.

With a face like that, I could not fail.

Which is not at all how it turned out.

2.
LOSING FACE

GONE IN A FLASH

Two days later, on Saturday 5th December 1970, I was starting to live out that golden plan.

I didn't have to go to Saturday morning school for the first time in ten years. I listened to some music, Dylan's latest, played a very hard-hitting game of squash and some five-a-side football with others enjoying the same freedom, and then watched a great game of school rugby. By 6 p.m., I was meeting up with the same young teacher who was organising a weekend trip to North Wales in his Land Rover with the guys who were going to Iceland the following summer.

We set off at about 6.30 p.m. with a little drizzle falling, and before we got on to the motorway I took over the driving, just as I would in Iceland.

Just outside Usk, thirty minutes later, a new section of road was being constructed. A sign told me – or did it *warn* me? – that a dual carriageway was ahead. I started to accelerate.

But I then realised that it was not as simple as that, because the road turned sharply left in order to join the dual carriageway. There were a couple of arrow signs. But the corner was far sharper than I expected (and I know it's still sharp today, though better signposted, because I've been back to look).

I was driving into it faster than was safe, and although I tried to brake and slow down, the corner kept coming.

In a few microseconds, everything changed.

The Land Rover, still going too fast, careered and crashed onto the driver's side, my side, and skidded across the dual carriageway – and, seconds later, during which I had time to think we'd need to get a crane to set it upright again, IT EXPLODED IN FLAMES.

The petrol tank cap had come off and sparks ignited the fuel. An inferno.

There were shouts, swearing, 'Get out of the back'...

I had a millisecond to think about all that I loved about my life – so much – and then I felt an immense surging desire to LIVE.

Struggling to undo my seat belt... so little air... desperate... I had to use my left hand to push myself up from the flames that were all around me... HURRY... and then I was free and crawling out of the back of the vehicle. OUT.

'Thank God, I'm out – a bit singed, I think.' My face felt battered, puffy, painful...

All over in less than thirty seconds. Just a nasty little accident, a bit of a shock. Drive on.

My clothes were on fire but someone quickly patted them out. (I can still smell the burning of my denim jeans.)

I stood in the road with the others, shocked, wondering what next, how we could continue our journey.

I had *no* idea – but the woman in the car behind did.

Lily Lewis had trained as a nurse. She took one look at me and one of the others and knew that we needed to get to hospital rapidly.

She draped a clean handkerchief over my face and wrapped me in her big white fur coat. I was bundled into her car, and she and her fiancé, who had been going for a night out in Usk, sacrificed their evening to save me by driving us – fast – to the nearest hospital.

My face was feeling more and more swollen, as if badly bruised, and though it was dark, I could tell I was oozing blood and more.

We drove in frozen shock. Stunned by what had happened. Not knowing the people who had swept us away from the accident, but grateful for their care.

Conversation in the car was muted and tinged with uncertainty and optimism. 'You'll be fine.' We eventually got to a hospital – I sensed some concern and was bundled into an ambulance for a faster journey to another larger hospital. When we got there, I was surprised that walking in was impossible. A wheelchair, clanking doors, weird smells...

I was starting to realise that something quite serious had happened. Stupid idiot.

I was helped onto an operating table, my clothes were cut off, dignity gone, pain screaming in all directions. Big lights glaring down. Relief, pain, injections...

'Can you see?' someone asked. I forced open my eyes through heavy lids. 'Yes, a bit blurred.' (Crucial information about my sight, I later discovered.) I looked at the faces staring down – they looked worried. Who were they? Where was I? Oh God. Then out.

That half an hour was the end of my 'pretty much perfect life'.

I returned to consciousness sixteen or so hours later. I could not see anything at all. My face was very swollen – apparently twice what it had been before. It felt enormous, and very heavy indeed. I'd had a few bruises on my face in the past (from playing rugby and cricket) but nothing like this. I later discovered that it was not just swollen but covered all over with open wounds, and a huge scab developed over the coming days.

Moving was impossible too. Pain was everywhere. I had heavy bandages on both my hands and both my legs. Is this normal to deal with singeing, I wondered?

I could hear people around me. 'How are you feeling?' – a funny question. 'Sore but OK' – the familiar stiff upper lip I'd learned in other predicaments was still in evidence, but it seemed a bit irrelevant now. I was NOT OK.

'What happened?' I asked. The nurse said I'd been in a nasty accident, had some burns to my face, hands, body and legs, and I'd be out in a few weeks. She said nothing about what I might look like… and I figured she probably couldn't know, given I was covered in bandages. Maybe the medics would give me a clearer idea.

'Are the others OK?' I asked. 'Yes,' she said, but not much more. Years later, I heard from Tony, who was in the vehicle too, that he too had received facial burns, and Julian had burns to his legs, I think. The others had been very shaken but were uninjured. Tony had very vivid memories after forty years, but I had to admit to him that I had blanked out the fact that he had also experienced facial burns. I knew deep down that my stupidity had hurt many people, but owning up was very painful.

My parents arrived what seemed like a few minutes later. MY GOD. RED ALERT. I sensed them enter the room. My father said, 'Bad luck, old chap, you look as if you've been in the wars.' A typical understatement from him, but what did he mean by 'look as if you've been in the wars'? What could he see that I couldn't?

My mother asked if I'd like a drink – typical practical hands-on care from her, straight away. She fussed around and got me to suck some warm water (yuck) through a straw which I could not see. They said they'd got a call at home late 'last night' from the hospital and had come down immediately.

This *is* serious. Maybe not just singeing? What does singeing, or perhaps minor burns, do to a face, my face? My hands and legs were all heavily bandaged and didn't feel part of me at all. What is me? Where is me? I couldn't see anything. I drifted in and out of sleep.

A day or maybe two passed in darkness; time was impossible to gauge. I had no idea then just how close my entire system was to collapsing in those first critical seventy-two hours. Blood transfusions and plasma replaced the pints and pints of blood and liquids I'd lost and was still losing. I was heavily sedated and my bottom became a pincushion for needles injecting painkillers and antibiotics.

There were short waking moments when they tried to feed me and wash me. Zero privacy from here on. I lay immobilised, virtually naked, and wondered what was happening in what was rapidly becoming 'my past life' of school...

Then, one morning, I woke and could see some tiny edges of light in the total darkness that had enveloped me, a blurred light... a window, a face, a room... IMPORTANT. SIGHT.

My facial swelling had eased and I started to see. Relief. But as soon as I could see, I started to see how others were responding to me. Little did I know that this was just the start of what would become a lifelong task of dealing with others' reactions.

When my parents arrived, I was able to see their obvious relief about my sight, but I could also see the profound concern etched on their faces, however hard they tried to conceal it. Were my injuries somehow much more serious than I thought? I couldn't figure it out and didn't really want to ask or know. No mirrors available.

The nurses and doctors didn't give anything away. Behaved just as they would, I thought, towards someone who was a bit sick. They said I'd be better in a few weeks. And I believed them.

And then, a day later, I witnessed, for the very first time, something very disconcerting.

The ward had a wooden door with a little glass panel in it, through which medical staff could keep an eye on me without disturbing me. I knew my fifteen-year-old sister, Alison, was coming to see me, so I kept looking at the spyglass.

And then suddenly, there she was – and I saw her wince and recoil. Only a fleeting moment, which she probably assumed was unseen. She came in with my parents, all caring and wishing well. She had been forewarned – and so had I, by her instinctive reaction.

Up until then, my parents had shown concern, but had given nothing away to suggest anything out of the ordinary. And the medical staff looked at my face 'normally' too.

But, try as she might once in the room, Alison just could not do so. She could not hold off indicating to me what I yearned to know – but dreaded, too.

My precious face was not just a little damaged. It was...

Destroyed.
Capital D. Large font size.
Bold.
Very bold.

Here's Alison's memory:

> *I don't remember what they said or who told my fifteen-year-old self about the accident. A house mistress at boarding school, probably – 'Your brother's had a car accident – a car fire – he's in hospital – he's OK – your parents will take you to see him on Saturday.'*
>
> *It set a tone – it was a matter of fact – it was the 'it's all right' version that threaded through all conversations about your accident, your face, your future, you. It was a version that froze me into silence.*
>
> *On the way – a car journey to Chepstow – your first hospital. Stilted conversation – 'Not as bad as it looks – might be a bit of a shock. How's school – the last hockey match?'*
>
> *Arriving – 'Take a look through the window of the side ward before you go in,' they said. Somersaulting stomach – wrong room, wrong person, distortion, disgust, disbelief, dis-everything.*
>
> *Entering – where was your blonde blue-eyed healthily tanned being, ready to take up your groomed-to-succeed Oxbridge career? Where are you inside this bandaged body, crusted black-scabbed face, tufted charred hair? But you noticed the brown of my skirt – you must be there somewhere – a sneak of a sibling tease.*
>
> *Leaving, without words, what could we say anyway though?*

Over the next days, I got to know the orange corridor snaking from the car park to the burns unit, the tidal transition across the Rubicon between two worlds, as the smell of burns, infection, disinfectant, tea and dressings became familiar greetings.

Our footprints erased it all as we left with our untold stories from the inside, of nightdress and tent fires engulfing children, depersonalised body parts – the eyelid, the ear, the finger, the leg – your body dissembled to manage the enormity of the mess. Washed back out down the orange corridor, denying what I knew.

Teenage worlds juxtaposing uncomfortably – words of unmade sentences – out, outside, outsider, outed, outer, out and out... scared, scarred, escape, scapegoat... fear, phantom, phantom fingers. My Jackie *mag struggling to hold its previously unrivalled, unquestioned grasp on my teenage psyche, with its poster pull-outs of Davy Jones and David Cassidy, top tips on how to manage unwanted blemishes, and find-out-if-he-loves-you quizzes.*

I knew by the time she left after that first visit that the messages of 'It's all right' and 'It will come right in the end' were fantasies. But I was too sedated to make any sense of it.

I was told that I was to be moved to a London hospital that specialised in my sort of injuries – 'You'll be out in no time'. I got the same 'It'll be all right, I'm sure' from teachers and friends from school and even close relatives. Weirdly, the school chaplain arrived with communion (last rites?): 'We are all praying for you to make a speedy recovery' and 'It'll be all right, I'm sure'.

I knew deep down that they were all pipe dreamers. I said, 'Don't ever say it won't happen to you' to everyone. The unimaginable *had* happened to me. I knew my life had been changed completely in a millisecond.

Nothing was 'all right'. I could tell from my visitors' reactions that my face especially was clearly NOT 'all right'. It wasn't right at all.

From the moment of my sister's wince onwards, and especially once I was refused a mirror, I started to think of my face as IT.

My lifelong study of other people's reactions had begun: some visitors couldn't look at IT at all, staring out of the window, at the floor, anywhere. One visitor left hurriedly.

And I began to avoid asking any more questions about IT because I was scared of what the answers might be. I just tried to live in hope. I connived with my parents and the medical team in a conspiracy of avoidance because I knew that the reality of IT was too awful and demoralising – and even a few moments of humour could not help.

Maybe everyone imagined that it was better for me to very slowly discover the extent of my wounds, but I think they misjudged me. It annoyed me. Because it made coming face to face with IT so much harder.

I don't think the doctors should have gone along with my seeming reluctance to know. I was in a foreign land without a guide. They had the knowledge. It could have helped me. As it was, I was left in the dark, literally.

And it wasn't just me. Here's my sister again:

There seemed to be a conspiracy of all's-all right, we all played it; perhaps we didn't know what else to do. It really was not all right though, and the noise in my head of silent disallowed questions crowded in: Why you? What happened? How can you even be alive? What next? When, how? What can 'they' do? How will you look? Will you still be you? What will 'ordinary' be like after? What will 'after' be like? Is there an 'after'? What is my place in the 'after'? What will 'better' look like? Will you still go to uni? Will we go out, go anywhere? How long will it all take?

   I still don't know how much our 'it's-all-rightness' protected us, allowed us to manage the day-to-day, month-to-month, year-to-year, and protected you too. I don't know whether it would have helped to delve for answers where there weren't any. Probably not right away – denial's a great thing – but it would have been nice, I think, to have unfrozen the lost words a bit earlier.

LOOKING AT THE DAMAGE

Ten days after the accident, I was transferred in an ambulance with a little girl, Margaret, who'd also been badly burned, from the Chepstow Hospital to a specialist facial burns unit in south-west London: Queen Mary's, Roehampton. I was told the surgeons there had lots of experience and I'd soon be out and able to get back to my life.

It was a tortuous five-hour journey in the days before the M4 motorway was built, with every corner and bump causing me pain. I'd apparently driven past Queen Mary's before but it could have been on the Moon. My life was no longer under my control. From a happy-go-lucky school-leaver, I was now a totally dependent patient with a very uncertain future – and with a face that nobody wanted to talk about, but which I knew was a BIG problem.

My arrival at Queen Mary's was to create a little more certainty, however. The good news – stunning news, actually, had I been in a fit state to appreciate it – was that I had been offered a place at University College, Oxford without an interview. I'd apparently done very well in the maths papers and was offered a place on the strength of them.

The bad news was much harder to bear. The very engaging young house officer who admitted me asked me all sorts of questions, including what sports I liked. We found a common enjoyment of squash and I said I looked forward to beating him soon. He seemed not very sure about when… Worrying.

Then he said that Queen Mary's had a policy of not covering up burns with bandages, so he would arrange for those on my hands and legs to be taken off immediately. A surprise, but a welcome one – or so I thought.

Burns patients the world over will know about the 'wonders' of saline baths. Warm salty water apparently helps dressings to 'float off' wounds. 'Float' is sadly a total euphemism, because certainly in those days, dressings stuck firmly and had to be prised off. Absolutely *excruciatingly* in salty stinging water!

Unknowing at that time, I found myself within an hour of arrival being lowered on a steel bed into a vast bathtub and my bandages started to be taken off – revealing the appalling damage to my hands and body and legs. RAW FLESH EVERYWHERE. Raw unhealed wounds all over my legs, my torso and hands. I knew immediately that IT was going to be the same, if not worse.

I gasped inside at the extent of it and at my already wasted body; muscles disappeared, no strength… and my left hand a dreadful mess of twisted fingers and huge gashes down both sides… Why? 'It was necessary to do an escharotomy to save the hand.' GOD, serious.

(Question: what is an escharotomy? I could not at that time reach for the dictionary but, pronounced es'kärot'əmē, it became one of my first medical terms: 'a surgical incision into necrotic tissue resulting from a severe burn. The procedure is sometimes necessary to prevent oedema from generating sufficient interstitial pressure to impair capillary filling, causing ischemia,' from *Mosby's Medical Dictionary*, which I did not have to hand.)

I was placed in a side ward, isolated – and within a few minutes, in burst a very lovely nurse! A night nurse… 'Just call me Potty!' Nurse Pottinger was a wonderfully positive presence. She was on duty that first night (and many others), and had a moment of genius for which I will always be grateful.

Whilst all the other nurses and doctors were fussing over my wounds – and I was worrying more and more about IT – she saw that all she needed to do was wash my hair. Yes, such a tiny gesture, but with her gentle touch and massage, she made me feel, just for a few hours, clean and valued. She had an irresistible humour, always positive and funny. Amongst her many other gifts, she discovered my penchant for pink blancmange after operations – but washing hair was her greatest...

Potty, I salute you! In that tiny action, up close to IT, you told me that IT was not completely impossible to look at and, indeed, with clean hair, I felt better – and even you said I 'looked better'. It sounded unlikely, but was a glimmer of hope.

DISAPPEARING FROM VIEW

That was mid-December. Christmas came and went in weird dreams and somewhat strained family gatherings... January 1971 is a blur in my memory but my hospital notes, rescued years later from the incinerator pile (yes) tell of weeks of sedation, pain control, raging infections, operations every two or three weeks, recovery, sedation, infections, pain...

But I was starting to learn about healing. I had to do a lot of it in order to get the 40 per cent of my body that had been burned covered again – either by natural process, or by scarring or with the help of a 'skin graft'.

My learning was slightly enhanced, after much prompting, by one of the nurses, who gave me an article from an old *Nursing Times* which had a diagram of the human skin and its layers. It wasn't much help, but my parents found it mildly illuminating.

February came in, although I was oblivious, sedated for pain and my life reduced to a dull fog by the blessed sleeping pills. There was very little that I could do – the board game, Chinese checkers, was prescribed to get my horribly damaged fingers to work again, but it was immensely painful to force the burned and damaged tendons and scarred skin to pick up the little pieces. Such were the trivial challenges that now seemed incredibly difficult.

My brain had virtually seized up. Damage around my eyes meant that I couldn't focus on a book or newspaper or concentrate for more than a few minutes. I relied on the radio for intellectual stimulation, and most afternoons, I tried to do *The Times* crossword with my mother, usually failing... failing, falling away... fewer and fewer visitors too.

And, piling on those problems, always in the back of my mind, was the nagging question: what does *IT* look like? It had gained asterisks in my mind by now.

I clung on to little snippets of hope, and I even held every word of one of the pop songs of the day close to my heart: 'Thank your lucky star, there's someone somewhere much worse off than you are,' sang that great songwriter, Labi Siffre... I hummed along. Could it be true that I should be thanking my lucky star?

I now shared a ward with an unexpected group of new friends – a pig farmer who'd fallen into his boiling pig swill, another who was a self-confessed drug addict who'd collapsed into an open fire under the influence, and several who'd fallen asleep in bed with lighted cigarettes. All of us had fallen, it seemed. I was falling out of life as I'd known it. They were unlikely companions but we found a common cause and a painful black humour to sustain us: 'It's no skin off my back if you do that, nurse,' etc.

My past life seemed literally to have passed away. School life and my friends drifted into oblivion. I felt left behind and they seemed unreachable. In the 1970s there was no texting, email or Facebook to keep me connected. Nothing came bar the odd letter.

The Moon landings were big news too. And they provided me with a big challenge.

I determined that on 6th February 1971, the day that the second set of men, Apollo 14's crew, walked on the Moon, I would make my first unaided walk after two months of healing. With my legs swathed in rubberised bandages to prevent all the skin grafts from peeling off as the blood rushed into my now-vertical legs, I staggered in a circle around my bed. I wobbled horribly, not least because I had grown an inch in my bedboundedness.

I collapsed back, exhausted. My legs felt completely weak and wasted. I watched Alan Shepard hit golf balls hundreds of yards on the Moon, but knew I was weeks from even walking ten yards. Only three months ago, I'd have done it in five seconds. I was a mess.

Eventually, a few days later, I found enough strength to stagger around my ward... 'a few small steps for this man'...

I was terrified about the next trek though – from the ward into the world beyond. Because I knew the time was coming when I would be well enough to leave – and so would reluctantly have to leave – the safety of the cocoon that was the burns ward and expose *IT* to others' eyes.

But first, I had to meet *IT*.

3.

SEEING *IT*

MY FACE DAY

March 1971 began with me still, three months on from the accident, in the male burns ward in a building now demolished in Roehampton, south-west London, completely out of sight and, to all intents and purposes, a forgotten young man except to my family and a few loyal friends.

The run-up to my seeing *IT* seemed to drag on for ages. Throughout January and February, I had asked intermittently to see 'the damage' but was constantly and firmly rebuffed – 'Not quite yet', 'Better when you're better', whatever that meant.

But secretly, I was starting to feel the surface of *IT*, because my right hand had partially healed up; so by running my hand over my face – not in sight of nurses or doctors – I could begin to get an impression, despite all the gauze and scabs.

I was still 100 per cent bedbound, so no chance of stealing out to the bathroom (where, as I later discovered, there were no mirrors either).

Then a physiotherapist accidentally left a shiny finger splint next to my bed and I was on it in a second, secreting it under the bedclothes and then stealing a look at a very blurred image of *IT*. Not much help, but it surely couldn't be that bad? But then I recalled my old physics master's frequent rejoinder: 'Surely always introduces a weak argument'.

When the agreed day for looking in the mirror – my 'Face Day' – finally arrived, the whole process seemed to be a huge problem, adding to my agony. I could sense the kindness and protectiveness of everyone around me, but what were they shielding me from? *IT* *must* be even worse than I could possibly imagine.

My mother, who had been to see me every single day of my ordeal over the last three months, arrived as usual; several nurses arrived too, and fussed around me – including, I was glad to see, one particular nurse in whom I had particular faith. I trusted her touch and calm.

Eventually, at 2.15 p.m. (curious how I recall the precise time that day), I was handed an unremarkable thin rectangular object with a shiny surface: a mirror – The Mirror.

I had played this moment over and over in my mind, but now when it arrived, I waited for advice. But I then saw that none of those around my bed appeared to have done this before either. They were all in the same uncharted territory. Just as terrified.

No choice, take the initiative. I suggested spontaneously that it might be better *not* to show myself the whole of *IT* all at once. Right? Good idea? I looked around for confirmation. None came. So here was the moment of truth, stripped down to its rawness.

It was down to me. I very deliberately and slowly drew the mirror across *IT*… from the left side ('The better side?' 'Yes') across the bridge of my ruined nose… *Oh God…* to my right eye, three-quarters closed, jagged with scars and skin grafts… and then, *oh dear God*, to my gaping mouth and jaw…

I gasped but had no breath… and finally to my right ear (totally unrecognisable as an ear).

And then the whole thing. *IT*.

My stomach churned and I felt faint. I looked at my mother, saw how worried she was. I lied – 'I thought it would be much worse' – and then, 'Not as bad as I had feared.'

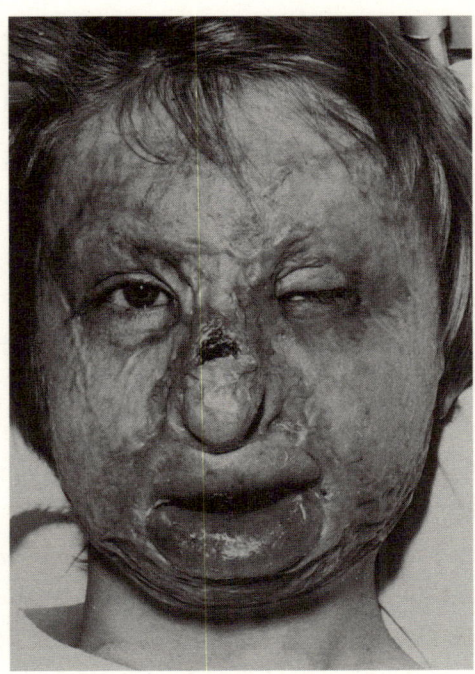

June 1970 – my seventeen-year-old face and May 1971 – my new, unrecognisable one, almost a year later.

I was shattered, and yet even in those first tiny seconds, I knew instinctively that I *had* to take ownership of *IT* for one simple, immediate reason: so as to manage the reactions that I saw in the shocked faces and minds of the people around the bed. People who cared so much for me.

If I disowned *IT*, they – the people I'd come to rely upon for so much – would be even more devastated than I was.

IT was my fault and my responsibility. I lay back, exhausted.

The photo at the bottom of the previous page (which is the mirror image, and therefore represents what I saw) was actually taken two months later, but will give you a hint of roughly what I saw.

By way of comparison, there is the mirror image of what I had been looking at just three months earlier above it, a fresh, bright, young, stainless, hopeful face.

Now *IT* – scabs, distortion, redness and hopelessness.

The black and white photo is grim enough, but in real gory technicolour, *IT* was far starker than that. It was vivid, bloody, scarlet red, streaked with scabs and gauze and unhealed wounds. The distortion of my eyes and my gaping lips were even more evident. My chin had disappeared.

My hospital notes do not contain photos of what I actually saw in that Mirror Moment. In fact, there are very few. Perhaps they really didn't want me to see any of *IT*, even later.

But I don't need to see the photos to remember the image I saw, which is forever imprinted on my mind's eye.

My mother left at about 4 p.m. and I assured her I'd be all right. Just letting *IT* sink in. And I'd like the mirror left close enough so I could look again.

I lay there, watching the three other men in the ward; I wondered how they were thinking about their futures. All of them had severe burns, but none seemed to have the major facial burns I had just seen.

I'd only ever met one man who looked like I did now. He'd come in to see me a month or so before my Face Day, probably sent in

SEEING *IT*

by the nurses to cheer me up. Sadly, he did exactly the reverse. Just made me more worried.

He had rescued a child from a blazing tent four years earlier and had been burned down to his waist all the way round – including his hair and face. He seemed ridiculously and unbelievably at ease with his grafted, leathery and distorted appearance. I'd asked if he was due to have more surgery. 'Oh no, they've done a remarkable job, don't you think?' WHAT?? I struggled to say the little word 'Yes', so shocked was I by his looks.

Now, as darkness set in, I started to realise that this was my fate, too. I wept inwardly, sobbed silently, trying not to draw attention or give away anything of how I was feeling to those I didn't want to be open towards. Stiff upper lip seemed a difficult reaction given a complete absence of a top lip, but that, I knew, would have to be my public stance. I could only envisage unstiffening in private on some far-off day, and then only to a very few people.

And so began my long, long struggle to face up to *IT* and live in *IT* and with *IT*.

I already knew that my avoidance of using the right descriptive word for *IT* was typical – and not very psychologically healthy if it persisted. But the fact was that I had no other word for *IT*. What I had thought of my self-image was now *IT*, not Me.

IT could not possibly be Me. From that day forward and for a long time, if I ever had to refer to *IT*, I refrained from talking of 'my' face. Inside me, it was *IT*. To others, I talked about my injuries, scars or skin grafts.

The Mirror was face down on the cabinet next to my bed and I wrestled with myself. I occasionally took another look, but when I did, what I saw frightened me. I already had enough knowledge of how burns healed (scars and all) to know *IT* was a tangled mess and would remain so.

I was amazed too at how, after just over three months, I had very little memory of what my old face had looked like. What I had been. The old 'Me' had gone. But *IT* wasn't Me. I had no identity.

But if that was worrying, far worse was the fact that the eyes that looked at *IT*, my eyes, had belonged to another face, and the aesthetic, prospect and moral judgements of those eyes now kicked in. And those judgements were brutal.

Aesthetic judgement: '*IT* is revolting, ugly, ruined'. Every fibre of my being told me *IT* was a thing I could never like nor be proud of. Ever. I recoiled from *IT*. Shuddered. Revolted.

Prospect judgement: I *instantly* assumed that because of *IT*, I had lost all hope of a future. That face would never be my fortune. *IT* was a passport to failure. A disaster.

Moral judgement: the only moral judgement that I knew about facial scarring was that people with *IT*s have unlikeable and morally dubious personalities. Best to avoid.

The 'face values' that I had grown up with told me insistently and continually through that night that not only were my scars and distorted visage ugly and unappealing, but they also made me less of a human being, less worthy of being liked and respected.

I could not help myself imposing that profound moral judgement on myself. In my own eyes, my worth had catastrophically nosedived to a shadow of its former value. I was now a lesser human being. My self-respect shrank to minuscule.

And the dreadful thing was that I knew my friends, and maybe even my family, were likely to think and believe the same. Certainly anyone who didn't know me would share those judgements. 'Brave chap but, frankly and very sadly, he's destined to a life on the edge of society, with very few enjoyable moments.' Immediately, I knew that others' expectations about me had shrunk to nothing.

Not that they would own up to thinking that. But I did think it. However much I tried to deny it. All because of *IT*, my ghastly thing.

I could not articulate all that during the long night of 18th March 1971, but I went over and over, round and round those thoughts in the days and weeks that followed, and could find absolutely no way out of them.

SEEING *IT*

I was now trapped in *IT*. Imprisoned. A life sentence to live on the margins, one of the uglies destined never to be successful in anything. Sad.

I mark the day of my accident, 5th December, every year publicly, but my Face Day, 18th March 1971, is forever remembered privately as my day of bleak discovery.

FACING THE WORLD

On 19th March 1971, I woke up to my new life with *IT*. Throughout that day and for the next week, I tried to look at my face with some degree of appreciation, but I could find absolutely nothing appealing. I could only see wounds, scars, vivid redness, distortion… and could understand why those few people who came to see me winced or literally put on a brave face, tried not to show it. One had fainted – possibly due to the heat, possibly not.

Hospitals have a wonderful separateness from the outside world – 'wonderful' in that those who are being treated for illness or injury are able to recover out of sight. No prying eyes or rubbernecking. I was certainly glad of this privacy. Ward G at Queen Mary's had become my home for the last three months and as my visitors dwindled, so my interactions with the nursing, medical and physiotherapy staff became increasingly trusting and familiar. They accepted me unconditionally, and I needed that more than ever. None of them winced.

It was a blissful cocoon. But I knew it was a temporary haven. I had to take *IT* out of the safety of the burns unit into the world sometime soon, a world that I simultaneously wanted to rejoin and was absolutely terrified about. I could already feel the prying and judging eyes on *IT*. And I could sense that all around me were worried too.

I knew I had to put on a brave face. I was determined not to show all my inner gloom, because I owed it to everyone who'd supported me not to buckle, not to show fear.

And so, a few days later, I decided – which sounds a very positive thing, but it was definitely my inner voice telling me firmly: 'DO IT' – that I should try to walk out of the cocoon… into the hospital corridor and down to the visitors' café that was apparently twenty-five yards away. In my collapsed life, it represented 'the world'. Very small steps for this irrelevant man.

With my mother close at hand, I tottered through the swing doors, along the shiny lino hallway, looked through windows at the beautiful garden beyond and shuffled down the slope towards the restaurant. Only half a dozen people passed by but their looks were impossible to avoid, rapier-like and inquisitive. My self-consciousness screamed in pain but I kept on, eyes down.

I just wanted to hide *IT*. Hide. But, somehow, we got into the café and I sat down as my mother went to get some tea. I felt as if everyone was either looking at *IT*… stealing little glances, whispering, 'Ooh, look at that,' taking another look, hoping I wouldn't see – or were avoiding looking altogether. I wanted the floor to open up and swallow me.

My mother came back with the tea and the straw I needed. I couldn't put words to my feelings. *IT* did not show them either. *IT* couldn't show anything except pain. I sipped the sweet tea and made small talk… the weather, the plans for my first discharge from the hospital the coming weekend, little bits of news from the outside, anything to avoid talking about *IT*.

Somehow, I got back to the ward, brave face still on, and collapsed, exhausted. Shrank into myself, self-pity close to taking hold of my whole being.

That tiny escapade was the start of what I came to call 'my re-entry' into the world. I had no idea if I could do it successfully. I just knew I had no choice but to try. Even if it took me weeks, months, even years to achieve.

Re-entry was much in the news too, with the Apollo spacecraft returning from the Moon landing. I was struck by one phrase in the

SEEING *IT*

BBC's coverage: all the Apollo missions depended for their success on whether the heat-resistant tiles on the tiny craft would be able to withstand the heat of re-entry into the Earth's atmosphere. I wondered if, having lost so much skin, I had any 'heat-resistant tiles' left to protect myself from others' reactions to me... Ironic, eh?

But my other, bigger thought was that if man could go to the Moon, then surely plastic surgery could get *IT* looking normal – perfect – again. Quickly. I needed to find out.

4.
FIXING *IT*? FIRST QUESTIONS

As an eighteen-year-old in March 1971, I'd heard about but knew virtually nothing about plastic, reconstructive or aesthetic/cosmetic surgery. But I knew I had to find out. It might be my salvation.

The questions sounded simple: what could plastic surgery actually offer me? Discovering the answer, however, was not easy. My first port of call was the surgeon who'd done all my operations so far. Known to his patients as 'Mr Evans', and to the nursing staff as 'the big chief', he was actually a man of short stature from the old school of medicine who had the very highest standards and ran a very hierarchical clinical team. Everyone, from senior nursing staff downwards, came to attention as soon as he appeared for his weekly round on the ward, which was always spruced up in the hours before he arrived.

Jim Evans had been trained by the founder of plastic surgery, Sir Harold Gillies, at Rooksdown House in Basingstoke during the Second World War. He had been transferred to Queen Mary's, Roehampton in the early fifties. He and colleagues like Patrick Whitfield took patriarchal care of a steady flow of medical students and young trainee surgeons (housemen and registrars). He trained them well. Some, like Tim Milward, went on to be presidents of the

British Association of Plastic Surgeons, which Gillies had founded in the late forties. Many others, like John Gowar and John Clarke, became pre-eminent leaders of their profession in later years.

I knew absolutely none of that history and nobody told me. I saw little of Mr Evans in the early days – just fleetingly, once a week, as he made his ward round. He sent his young doctors to do the mundane tasks and inspections. But a few days after my excruciating trip to the hospital café, I managed to stop him in his tracks in his whistle-stop tour of my ward with the stark question: 'Please, sir, what can plastic surgery do for me?'

His response was very hard for me to read – 'We'll certainly be able to get you looking better, but it may take some time.' On the one hand, it was very guarded about plastic surgery's capability and the next steps he had in mind, but on the other, it was quite optimistic.

He was the expert and I just didn't have the stomach or words to ask any follow-up questions. I meekly said, 'Thank you, Doctor...'

I lay back after he left. No quick fix. Absolutely not. My stomach churned.

The next week, just prior to my discharge from the burns unit, I asked again. 'So where would you start?'

'Our plan (*ah, you do have a plan*) is firstly to do a Wolfe graft from under your left arm to create a new covering for your nose.'

'A what?'

'A Wolfe graft is a full-thickness skin graft, different to what you have been having to date.' What? All gobbledegook.

Getting realistic facts about what surgery could do to *IT* started to become an urgent need. But I had to live in ignorance for another couple of months with that little glimmer of optimism keeping me going.

I returned to the hospital for my first plastic surgery in early May 1971, for the promised Wolfe graft. Which worked 'incredibly well', everyone said. My nose, so terribly scarred, was re-covered from a graft from under my left arm – a big painful incision there and a long

FIXING *IT*? FIRST QUESTIONS

scar still remind me. It made a bit of difference, I suppose, but let's be honest, not that much.

But then, I wasn't surrounded by that type of honesty. I had to be grateful for what had been achieved, hiding my disappointment. My nose was *not* back to what it had looked like before. I had no option but to lower my expectations of what was achievable with *IT*. Oh God.

As I left hospital a few weeks later, *IT* looked like this.

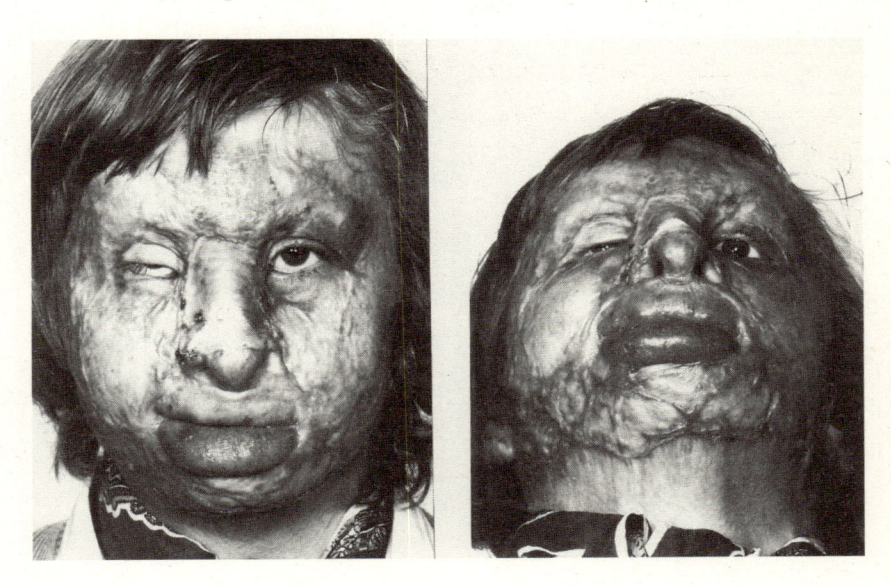

That hospital visit for reconstructive surgery (the first of many) also gave me the information I'd been seeking — but not wanting. I left with the knowledge that *IT* could and would *never ever* be recovered to look as it did before.

Indeed, one of the young surgeons involved in that operation, John Gowar, admitted as much to me one evening. He showed me a graft he'd had on his arm years back — 'a remarkably good result'. Yes, maybe, but definitely *not* what I had hoped for. I didn't tell him so. Hold your tongue. Swallow hard. Take in your fate.

And I could see that my hands and legs, which had also received some reconstructive surgery, would never ever be the same again.

The rest of my body had been severely burned too, and I was still physically very incapacitated, with unhealed wounds on my legs where the grafts threatened to 'float off'. My hands were also still very sore – my left had only one finger functioning at about 40 per cent, the others and the thumb virtually useless, stiff and very sensitive to touch. So, although I was by then out of hospital, I was virtually housebound and not at all independent.

5.

RE-ENTERING THE WORLD

LEAVING THE COCOON

Looking back to April 1971, the day came when I was finally 'let out' of the burns unit, a release in some ways but very scary to leave the cocoon too. I shuffled into my parents' car and my mother drove me home. Up the stairs, along the landing to my bedroom. It was as if I was entering it for the first time. I collapsed wearily onto my bed.

All around were the signs of my old life. But I felt very different. I sat up and looked aghast at some of the trivia that I had collected in the past – yes, trivia, because I had changed. But they were treasures too, reminding me of the person I had once been.

I got up and looked at *IT* in the mirror in which only a few months ago, I had proudly prepared my handsome face to meet the world. Now as I looked at *IT* and into my eyes, I felt an emptiness deep down, a sadness sweeping over me, not for the first time but certainly very strongly, enough to make me cry, out of sight of everyone.

Numb too. Unable to put any shape or words to my circumstances or prospects. Everything had to be focused on the next hours. Because there was to be a family gathering for Easter. I had to be prepared for the questions (even 'How are you?' was difficult to answer), the looks, the unspoken angst. And I knew I had to put a brave face on. It was my fault, all this.

That gathering and the following weeks were agonising, with some moments of excruciating pain. My half-sister in Canada had come to stay and her little girls, aged four and six, tried not to look at *IT*, too much for them to take in. One of my nephews wanted to eat in another room because my face repulsed him – and he didn't want to eat the ham because it looked like one of my wounds.

Everyone was committed to unspoken denial – at least in my presence. I knew they all thought I'd 'blown it'… blown all my prospects… but I might go to Oxford, and even if I went to Oxford after all, what then?

I imagined everyone thought that in those few seconds of carelessness I had thrown away a life that could have been successful, happy, even rich and fulfilling. 'Oh, what a shame – a life so full of promise ruined.' I yearned to turn the clock back and retrace my steps, to drive round that corner without incident. If only that were possible. But there was no way back. I was trapped in my reality. It was my fault. I hated it. And I was ashamed.

Shame threatened to drain my self-belief. Shame cast dark clouds over my aspirations. How could I possibly rise from the internal misery of knowing I had self-destructed?

And just as those around me avoided talking about my prospects, so I tried to bury my shame in the deepest recesses of my brain.

And yet, I was daily reminded by what I imagined my parents and anyone we met were thinking. In my effort to deny my shame, I found myself overreacting – probably heroically – to the looks of anyone who came to visit. As if to prove everyone wrong. As if by behaving in an unnaturally confident way, I could convince them that their instant judgement of 'What a shame!' would go away. Which it wouldn't, of course.

But my being 'brave' about *IT* did at least distract attention from my own inner turmoil… and so enabled me to con myself that shame would not dog me for life. It sort-of worked. But the façade was very hard work to sustain and was really only paper-thin – and shame crept back into my mind.

RE-ENTERING THE WORLD

INTO THE PUBLIC EYE

Being stuck at home and hobbling around had one advantage. I didn't have to meet the public's gaze. My self-consciousness was excruciating, and I dreaded going out or anyone coming to see *IT* and the me that was behind it somewhere.

Far from being a confident eighteen-year-old undergraduate-to-be, I faced every single social encounter with fear. *IT* was no longer just another face in the crowd; *IT* stuck out like a sore thumb. Every single encounter with another human being, even total strangers, had to be negotiated. I was back in kindergarten – and without a clue how to socialise with *IT*.

How to survive?

My first visit to a pub with an old friend was beyond painful. He came to see me at home and then rather suddenly suggested that we go to the pub for a drink. No time to object, we walked around to the local and suddenly I was in public… or rather, *IT* was.

We sat in a corner and I tried to ignore the barrage of staring mixed with looking away and, I thought I could sense, whispering behind hands. My friend kindly tried to assure me that nothing was going on. 'All in your imagination.' We drank and chatted. It was as normal as possible and at least I was not on my own, friendless. I was sheltering in his goodwill. It was very generous of him. I tried to relax into the beer. And it sort-of worked.

To make public places slightly less daunting, I got hold of one of my father's old trilby hats and started wearing it – and dark glasses too. They protected me a little from the intrusiveness of others' eyes, but the downside was that everyone could see I was on the defensive. I could at least travel on public transport, although curiously, it felt as if even more people were looking at me, if that were possible. But at least I had some armour on to protect me from the stares – the only armour I could think of.

My first visit to a football match did not go well either. Although I was again with the same good friend, an alcohol-fuelled element of the crowd spotted me and I gasped for breath as a couple of tasteless remarks floated my way. Perhaps they thought I couldn't hear over the crowd's cheering, but I could. 'Cor, who's the ugly one then?' That one little tedious insult from a drunk fan threatened my self-esteem profoundly for years and I avoided matches and crowd situations in general.

Even being with my parents in supposedly sophisticated places like quality restaurants did not insulate me from others. On one occasion, we were eating a delicious meal at a top London restaurant when the head waiter rather sheepishly came over to ask if we would mind moving to another table. Another diner had reported that the sight of me was putting her off her food.

My father's assertiveness was immediate: 'She can move if she wants to. We are not moving an inch.' It was a massive vote – and I loved his protectiveness. My close family gave me freedom to start to find my new me, but we all lived in the here and now, just about surviving.

Even the very simple everyday chores like going shopping locally were daunting. I knew I was liable to meet people who knew me or who'd heard of my accident. I suspected they would not know how to react to me – I wouldn't know how to react to them either. Double-edged embarrassment. Best avoided. I'd cross the road if I saw them – and sensed they did the same. Or go to another shop. Or avoid shopping altogether.

Throughout the summer of 1971, my reality was becoming ever clearer. *IT* was the cause of agonising self-consciousness and very unpredictable reactions from other people which I feared would be life-long. The impact on me and my self-worth was severely diminishing.

I was met by startled looks, staring and avoidance amongst the public – or by sympathy and what felt to me like patronising kindness.

Then there were the comments and questions. 'What happened to you?' and a whole set of variations on that theme. Some asked if I was in the armed forces. Things might have been very different had I been able to wear a uniform, I mused. As it was, I wheeled out my painful explanation: 'I was in a car fire...' not adding, in my shame, 'My fault...'

There was not a single minute when out of my bedroom that I did not feel 'on show', wrestling with my sky-high self-consciousness, fighting to retain my sanity and self-belief. Every minute, every hour, every day when in the public eye. Feelings of loneliness and isolation went hand in hand with being in the spotlight, in the headlights. I longed to be anonymous again. I'd have given anything for just an ordinary face, nothing flash.

But there was one upside that first summer with *IT*. I was invited to a disco party in July, at the home of some old family friends. July 1971, such a great time for music and dancing! But, of course, I expected to be excluded because of *IT*.

It was tempting to go, but I dithered. Who would be there? What would I say or do? How would they react to my face? Easier not to go. But eventually, after much discussion, I decided to go – just for a couple of hours.

I can remember my intense angst as I walked up to their front door, music playing loudly, party already in full swing – the Stones' 'Brown Sugar' was top of the charts.

I was so nervous. The door opened, friendly faces and voices meeting *IT* in the porch. I was warmly welcomed and made comfortable in a chair in a corner – walking was still not easy... and then, within a few minutes, a girl whom I'd called my girlfriend not that long ago came over, got us some drinks, sat down and talked to me with such ease. She asked a little about my state, but then we moved on to her and her life and hopes – did I lead her away? I think not... it was just easier to talk about her.

It only lasted perhaps twenty minutes but, on an evening when I felt lots of sympathy (which I didn't really want but could not easily reject), she was a minuscule sign of hope... and if I hadn't actually flirted with her, we'd definitely engaged and enjoyed doing so.

And then, a little later in the evening, the DJ put on 'I Can't Let Maggie Go' by Honeybus, a favourite of mine when I was with her... and she came over and found me and got me on the dance floor, wobbling, holding me; for a few minutes, we danced just as we had in the past. 'She flies like a bird in the sky, She flies like a bird and I wish that she was mine.'

It was probably a completely forgettable moment for others, but for me, being on that dance floor for three minutes, was a tiny flicker of light – and so *absolutely* memorable. She'd given me a little moment of magic. And then she kissed me and was gone, snapped up by other young men. I looked away.

It was a tiny chink of hope. I *had* floated, just for a second or two. It could happen.

Back to reality. I left the party with head held reasonably high. Friends were going to be crucial. Old ones who could bear to see me again (as the hosts of that party had been prepared to, thankfully) were one sort, but I knew I was going to need new friends. Unknown territory.

And the biggest test was around the corner. Going up to university, to Oxford no less, knowing nobody, to a college I'd not even been to for interview. I quaked inside.

6.
FIXING *IT*? SECOND THOUGHTS

LOTS OF SURGERY NOW?

In August 1971, I had another consultation with Mr Evans. He asked how I was doing and I said, 'Fine, going to university in October,' which is what I thought he wanted me to say. He did. Without a moment's questioning, he moved straight on to examine *IT*. Doing OK, he thought. I groaned inside. We planned that I should come into hospital in the Christmas vacation for surgery on my eyes.

In ten minutes, I was out of the clinic and back into the hospital corridor. He hadn't asked me about my life, but then I hadn't offered any information about it either. Mainly because I knew Mr Evans had no way of influencing the maelstrom of doubt and fear that I was going through outside the cocoon. And he had nobody on his team to call upon to help me; only the hospital chaplain, perhaps.

But in the corridor, I met two people who did ask more.

A social worker, Carol, had shown some interest in my circumstances a few months earlier. Now she stopped and asked caring questions and I did say it wasn't that easy out there, but that I was looking forward to going to university (liar). She wished me well.

And then a few minutes later, one of the younger plastic surgeons who'd been treating me also asked me how I was doing – and I said my surgery seemed to be going slowly but with reasonable results.

He asked if I had thought of taking a further year off to have much more plastic surgery done before university. It could be very transformative, he said, and might well make a big difference to how I looked. Would I like to see some of his photographs?

I was shocked. He wasn't to know, but going up to Oxford in October had been a big personal goal from the moment I'd heard I had a place ten days after my accident. I asked him to explain more.

He suggested that a series of reconstructive procedures could rebuild my chin and straighten my eyes, and some large grafts could smooth out my forehead and other anomalies… and I could become an expert at using skin camouflage creams so that people really wouldn't be able to tell that I'd had such major burns. He said that he was increasingly involved in cosmetic surgery and had seen some remarkable transformations.

It was an upbeat message and I wanted to believe him. Perhaps surgery really was the answer. And he was telling me implicitly what I already suspected: that I would have a very difficult time at university 'looking like that'. He raised my hopes that there might be a solution… but should I put my life on hold in its quest? Could I bear the pain that would inevitably be involved? I'd been through a lot already. Maybe another chat with Mr Evans?

But after he left me, as I walked on, I could feel myself beginning to fume inside. Was he really suggesting that without a lot of surgery, with 'a face like that', my chances of having a good time at university, or indeed success in life, were much reduced?

I knew that this was a distinct possibility and was internally railing against the beauty trap – the widely held belief that good looks are essential for success in all aspects of life. Here was a young surgeon seemingly endorsing that idea. I did not like it!

He also seemed oblivious to the fact that he was dragging me into the trap with him: the only answer was to have lots of surgery. Doubting my ability to live with *IT*.

And he was going against the very cautious messages from Mr Evans about the aesthetic limits to his art – borne out by looking at and talking to my fellow patients.

By the end of a hundred-yard corridor, I had rebelled. No, what I needed was help to accept and to live with *IT*, not unrealistic hopes that surgeons could make it look less ghastly.

An immensely important hundred yards. I was making a major decision. Unless my surgeon said differently, I was most definitely going up to university – if for no other reason than to prove to that young surgeon that I could wear *IT* with some sort of success.

I sought out Mr Evans – he was surprised to see me again so soon – and asked him directly for an honest prediction of what I would look like after the long programme of reconstructive surgery that he had hinted at. He was very hesitant – it would all depend on how my skin healed, how well the grafting blended in and lots of other variables. He thought we should start with my eyes, then look to do something to my chin and then 'We'll see.'

Was that honest? Yes, I decided, definitely. I knew already I would never ever have a face that resembled my long-lost and much-loved one.

Was he ambitious for *IT*? Maybe not. Confident? Yes, but not complacent. Lots of caveats.

But such a stark contrast to the certainty and hope presented by his young colleague.

Which to believe? I hated the confusion that had been sown in my head. And yet it was also a significant moment in my journey towards accepting *IT* and finding a future.

My irritation with that young surgeon unexpectedly fired me up (I love those burn analogies!) to take up my place at Oxford University in October.

I chose, very deliberately, to accept the advice of my old-school but, I decided, very wise surgeon. Although he might not be able to magic back my old looks, I knew he would use all his skills on *IT*. I trusted him. I would have to learn to live with *IT*. Somehow.

Curiously, out of that confusion, I felt a tiny surge of determination as I left the hospital that day, more than I had done for nine long months.

WHAT ABOUT SKIN CAMOUFLAGE?

Surgery was not the only option available to me. That summer, I was encouraged to look at 'cosmetic camouflage' – what I now refer to as 'skin camouflage'. This involves the application of waterproof and long-lasting creams of varying colours and textures that can be blended by a trained eye.

I learned how to use skin camouflage creams thanks to the advice of a beautician on the high street of the town where we lived. I went to see her with trepidation and much scepticism. I'd never worn make-up except in school plays, and couldn't imagine it would be of any use. But actually, the skill with which she sought the right colour for my skin and then taught me how to apply the cream was hugely comforting.

Massage was much less common in those days, but she also showed me how to massage the scars. So I came away more in touch – literally – with my scars, but most importantly, I came away knowing that I could hide them a little more effectively. I got on a bus to get home and felt just a tiny bit less noticeable.

As an eighteen-year-old man, I never imagined I would wear make-up. But I did secretly. I wore it in places where I was not known and when I wanted to make an impression that was not dominated by my very livid scars.

FIXING *IT*? SECOND THOUGHTS

GETTING READY

During the summer of 1971, the vivid redness of *IT* lessened marginally. The nose was slightly less unsightly. Although I now knew that neither surgery nor camouflage were going to make my life much easier, my determination had risen a fraction.

My sunglasses became a fixture as I sought to negotiate the public gaze because my overwhelming emotion was of being impotent, powerless to control the reactions *IT* produced – reactions that I knew were often entirely genuine (like sympathy) or questions which were not intended to be intrusive but which I nevertheless dreaded. I'd already been made aware of the unpredictable nasty ones: the staring (which is never pleasant) that becomes hostile, the 'ughs' from passers-by, the sniggering behind hands and the drunken lout's abuse. These hurt me to the core. As did behaviours that I took for not wanting to know me, discounting my existence, denying that I had value.

However, I was becoming a student of those reactions, trying hard to analyse what *IT* prompted and why – and critically, whether there were things I could do to influence the reactions I received. A rational approach of applying my intellect to the problem of *IT*.

But could I do anything to prevent any of these? I was in the dark, no guidebook or mentor around. And as long as I was in the dark, I was horribly disempowered and at the mercy of those I met.

7.
GOING SOLO TO UNIVERSITY

The day came in early October 1971, ten months after the accident, for me to walk into the unknown. With *IT* and my dark glasses and as much courage as I could muster, I entered the porters' lodge at University College, Oxford. I insisted on going solo, doing it alone – my mother waited in the car.

The head porter looked me up and down. A millisecond was all it took. Douglas Millin, as a former regimental sergeant major, took me into his care – with a few tasty swear words (dealing with his embarrassment) and much compassion, he gave me my keys and welcomed me.

I knew instantly that here was an ally. I was in safe hands. It would not be quite the cocoon that was the burns unit, but I had a chance. A big moment. What I didn't know then was that Douglas set the tone for the whole college: 'This man is to be accepted wholeheartedly.' Oxford colleges have scouts who clean students' rooms and keep the college smart. Mine were a lovely diligent couple who never gave me a moment of doubt either. 'Univ' quickly became 'home'.

My first few days were extraordinarily welcoming and strange – little moments stick in the mind, like telling my story in the beer cellar to a small group of new acquaintances, all of whom seemed to have had the sort of gap year I'd dreamed about – work and travel to exorcise the trappings of school. They listened and, amazingly, warmed to me.

But despite all the apparent bonhomie and camaraderie of those early weeks and my success at making new 'friends', inside I felt increasingly alone with *IT*. The staring was – or seemed to me in my ultra-sensitive state – constant and ever-intrusive, the questions were far too frequent, the avoidance all too obvious. Even a lack of eye contact, which I had never really noticed as important before, now struck me as indicative of people's discomfort or embarrassment on meeting me.

As many of my fellow students paired up into relationships in those early weeks, I knew that mine was to be a lonesome time. I even suspected that some people avoided my company for fear that it might taint their beautiful worlds. But others commented on how confident I appeared – 'How do you pull it off?' How indeed! Entirely by trial and error…

I made a few male friends and drank a lot of Guinness. A barwoman in the King's Arms treated me as just another customer – quite a regular one for some weeks! 'Hello, luv, what can I get you?' And I loved her for it.

How *did* I do it? By talking to myself through every single social situation. And I mean a real 'talking to' – my inner self-talk was so loud and insistent that I worried people could hear it. 'Ignore that look. Keep smiling. Go on into that room.' Very strong instructions to dampen my acute and very disabling self-consciousness.

Possibly because I carried with me lessons from sport in my earlier life, I found my loud inner voice was invaluable – and almost impossible to dispute. In school cross-country runs, I had countered fatigue with an inner 'Go on' and had distracted my mind from pain – the inner mind is a fundamental part of any sportsman's armoury. Now I was using that self-same self-talk to deal with another barrier, and it worked.

I was discovering by trial and error that taking *IT* anywhere required preparation – if I didn't do it, I floundered in self-consciousness and the result was horrible. I had to reprogramme my mind and behaviours accordingly.

A simple action like walking down the High Street had to be undertaken with explicit internal intent: 'Keep your eyes looking ahead, do not let your chin drop, sanction the staring without reacting to it.' Don't show your inner uncertainty. Sounds easy? Not at all so.

Or before going into a pub, I would say strongly to myself: 'Look confident even if you don't feel it' and 'Don't be put off by people turning away' and 'Introduce yourself, because nobody's going to speak to you otherwise.'

I had had no advice or support as to how to do this, but I found it worked surprisingly well. People couldn't see, or said they couldn't, my screaming self-consciousness. One new close friend – an important person! – allowed me to explain my new theory to him. He thought there might be something in it. But neither of us really had a clue.

I was glimpsing very blurrily a breakthrough by applying my analytical faculties: I was starting to be able to predict, like having a sixth sense, what reactions *IT* was likely to produce in any given situation. And that was giving me the idea that if – and it was a big IF – I could figure out a way to deal with them – even pre-empt them, prevent them from happening – especially if they came from young children (so painful), then maybe, just maybe, I could exist.

8.
FACING MY FAULT

From the very early hours after I came round after my accident, the issue of whether I was responsible for what had happened was in my mind, though pushed to the back for the most part.

By the autumn of 1971, I knew I needed to find out whether I really had been as stupid as I thought in causing the accident in the first place. I blamed myself deep down for failing to drive round that corner. I knew I had to go back. I dreaded it because it could confirm my incompetence, but it had to be attempted.

Was steering round that corner really so difficult to do? How on earth could I have made such a horrendous error? And if I could drive round it now – scars, damaged hands, *IT* and all – would that help?

A few friends advised me not to do this yet because they feared it would make me even sadder, even more self-blaming, but I insisted that driving round that corner was part of the exorcising of the deep emotional wound I had sustained. It would help me to 'move on', in the modern idiom.

So I pestered the guy whose Land Rover I had ruined to take me back – he'd bought another one so I wanted to attempt what had been my undoing. I sensed his anxiety and reluctance. But eventually he agreed, and I went and did it in the early autumn of 1971.

The offending corner was innocent enough as we drove towards it, but we both recalled that at the time, in December 1970, the road on to the dual carriageway was being changed, and being a Saturday evening, there were no road-making crews in the area, just a few 'sharp corner' signs.

But, critically from my point of view, the blue sign saying 'dual carriageway ahead' was still there, suggesting that drivers could expect to accelerate — which is what I had done. However, now that the road works had been completed there were very large 'sharp corner' signs that told all drivers, even inexperienced ones like me, not to be fooled into accelerating.

We got out of the Land Rover and walked around the corner and I just looked and looked – no sign of skid marks any more. Nothing to show that this had been a danger spot. Nothing to show that this was where I had blown my life away.

But the misleading road sign was there – as I had seen in my mind's eye during all those weeks in the burns unit. Which was crucial. My accident was explainable. I could just about understand how I could have made such a stupid mistake.

A young driver, dusk descending, misty rain in the air, poor visibility…

Very foolish, but maybe not a mistake that was completely unforgivable.

Maybe I was not so stupid.

Three short but very significant conclusions.

I stood still to be sure – and then I got back into the vehicle and drove round the corner. It was quite tight and difficult, but this time I got round it unscathed. Done.

We drove on to find a pub lunch. And then went on to say a great big hugging 'Thank you' to Lily Lewis, the nurse in the car behind whose actions had saved my life.

She gave me hope, too, in her lovely Welsh lilt: 'Oh yes, that's a wicked corner.'

At last I had some defence in the court of my brain, a counter to the nasty finger-pointing inner demon who claimed the accident was *entirely* due to my incompetence, my lack of concentration.

FACING MY FAULT

It was a tiny defence, but I clung to it. There *were* extenuating circumstances. Which didn't completely explain the accident or excuse my weakness or lessen my fault, but at least I could raise the case that it wasn't *entirely* my fault. I wasn't concentrating enough, but…

My self-blame began to fade and my story of how the accident had happened became more plausible. I *had* been fooled by the bad signage on that road.

Friends also commented that the very act of going back to that corner was admirably brave. I didn't like the brave epithet but, on this occasion, I enjoyed the positive reinforcement.

Finding a plausible explanation for what had happened to me mattered hugely. It put a rational counterargument into my head when feelings of shame crept up unwanted to threaten my recovery.

But proving to others that I could make something of my life with *IT* was another matter. 'What a shame, life ruined' would take years to erase.

9.
DISCOVERING STIGMA

University College, Oxford isn't designed to be a convalescence and rehabilitation centre. It was and is one of the country's premier academic institutions. And it soon became apparent to me that I was liable to fail to meet its demands. My brain had to be switched back on.

Hospitalisation, sedation and pain had had a nasty fogging effect and, having been very tuned in to mathematics only ten months previously, my short-term memory seemed to have been erased completely. Tutorials in three new subjects, politics, philosophy and economics, were immediately a nightmare. And if I imagined the tutors were going to be sympathetic and make allowances, I was horribly wrong. They had absolutely no intention of treating me with any leniency whatsoever.

So, I had to relearn how to read, read, read… and, most of all, concentrate. It was painful and I struggled in every subject, especially philosophy. I had to spend hours and hours in the amazing, silent (soporific) libraries of Oxford reading some very, very dry tomes. And I scoured the local bookshops for easier-to-read versions so that I could make sense of the new subjects.

And that's how I came to be in the basement of Blackwell's bookshop in the Broad one early November afternoon in 1971, walking past the sociology shelves en route to the politics section. Out of the corner of my eye, I caught a title that leapt off the display shelf: *Stigma: Notes on the Management of Spoiled Identity* by Erving Goffman.

I picked it up and peered inside. On the very first page of the foreword, it said:

> *I sit and look at myself all day and cry. I have a big hole in the middle of my face that scares people even myself so I can't blame the boys for not wanting to take me out... Ought I commit suicide?*
>
> *Letter to Miss Lonelyhearts from Desperate*[1]

WOW. I shuddered and quickly found a corner of the bookshop to read on.

It was mesmerising and uncannily accurate. The first few pages were all about people exactly like me, who, in Goffman's words, were labelled and made to feel inferior because of their face or some other characteristic.

What a find! At last, after nearly a year, I could start to properly reflect on my position.

Even in those first few minutes of reading, I could feel myself standing back from *IT*'s immediacy, objectifying my situation, putting it in context. I was not alone. Someone had studied 'our' plight academically – those of us with 'a spoiled identity'. Yes, me.

Half an hour later, I bought *Stigma* without looking the shop assistant in the eye, not wanting to see her nod of 'Yes, you need to read that'.

I stole it back to my room – yes, 'stole', because I knew I now had something very precious which I wanted to keep absolutely secret, and not let anyone else know that I had found out about. But even on the walk back to my room, my head was held higher.

DISCOVERING STIGMA

Despite other tutorial pressures, I read the whole book that evening and kept going back for more in the days that followed.

Stigma was written in 1963 and rapidly became a classic sociology text. Goffman was a key figure in 'labelling theory' which, in the early seventies, was gathering momentum and support. It argued that a person's self-concept is socially shaped and reshaped though his or her encounters in their community and culture – and that we all take on labels from others because we are continually testing, evaluating and retesting how people judge us.

Those judgements can mark out some people as 'deviants' because of their behaviour (like criminals), personal characteristics (like a facial disfigurement or a disability) or ethnicity. Goffman expounded this theory with a number of books and in *Stigma*, he explored how people who are defined as deviant manage their day-to-day interactions.

Goffman gave me the analysis I desperately needed to help me understand how and why I was condemned to my lot, both by other people's awkwardness and lack of acceptance *and* by my own judgements, rejecting myself because of my conditioned dislike of *IT*. Those instant judgements I had found myself applying when I first saw *IT* were condemning me.

In Goffman's terms, my entire identity, not just *IT*, had been 'spoiled' by the accident. My scars were marks that not only rendered me unusual, odd, an outsider, alienated but also, critically, degraded me to a lower moral order. And I was imposing that judgement on myself, too. This was the root of my aloneness.

Stigma described how people like me lived with their 'deviance', sometimes trying to conceal it (e.g. with sunglasses or hat), and through other strategies to manage their spoiled identity. It gave me a concrete structure on which to hang my struggle with *IT*, but there wasn't much good news in it – certainly no magic wands. According to Goffman, people just had to find a modus vivendi and eke out their lives with their unavoidable label.

I buried the book away deep in my belongings. And for many years not a single person drew my attention to it – even sociologist friends! Perhaps because it was just an academic tome. Or perhaps because they felt the guilt that we *all* feel about the labels that are so quickly and unwittingly attached to marginalised people – and are so hard to remove.

STIGMA: AN OVERVIEW
WITH COMMENTS IN ITALICS FROM MY 1971 SELF

Goffman traces the term 'stigma' to the Greeks: it refers to 'bodily signs designed to expose something unusual and bad about the moral status of the signifier'.[2] Although Christians adapted it, in stigmata, to be a sign of holy grace, the word stigma still implies disgrace, but in a more sophisticated way than in the original Greek usage.

In social encounters, Goffman suggests that when we human beings meet a stranger, first appearances allow us to categorise and anticipate what they will be like by assessing their 'social identity'. But if we don't get to know the person, we use what Goffman calls their virtual rather than actual social identity, two concepts which may be very different – the virtual being based on our assumptions of what they are likely to be like.

Using the visual evidence they present to us (e.g. a scarred face), we may well reduce them – by attaching a stigma – to 'a tainted, discounted' person, and so assume they are discredited; even if visually, the stigma isn't immediately evident (i.e. concealed).

Stigmas are not only attached to physical features (Goffman also referred to 'abominations' and 'deformities', which I found very difficult to accept applied to me). They can also attach to what are perceived as character failings, such as dishonesty and addiction, and to 'tribal' signs 'of race, nation and religion'.

Goffman's conclusion was crystal clear:

an individual who might have been received easily in ordinary social intercourse possesses a trait than can obtrude itself upon attention and turn those of us whom he meets away from him, breaking the claim that his other attributes have on us. He possesses a stigma, an undesired differentness from what we had anticipated.[3]

By this point in the thesis, I was finding the use of 'we normals' distinctly uncomfortable. I was no longer one of the 'we's. I was now a non-we, an outsider.

We [normals]… believe the person with the stigma [me] is not quite human. On this assumption we exercise varieties of discrimination, through which we effectively, if often unthinkingly, reduce his life chances. We construct a stigma theory, an ideology to explain his inferiority and account for the danger he represents… We use specific stigma terms such as cripple, bastard and moron in our daily discourse as a source of metaphor and imagery, typically without giving thought to the original meaning. We tend to impute a wide range of imperfections on the basis of the original one.[4]

Goffman writes of the person with stigma: 'We may perceive his defensive response to his situation as a direct expression of his defect'[5] – and as just retribution for something they or their parents or their tribe did, and hence a justification for the way we treat them.

But the really interesting analysis for me was when Goffman turned to what the stigmatised person thinks and does. I was amazed to read that some stigmatised people are oblivious to and completely unrepentant about the stigma applied to them, but he's right. However, that is a rarity.

Goffman goes on:

The stigmatised individual tends to hold the same beliefs about identity that we do; this is a pivotal fact. His deepest feelings about what he is may be his sense of being a 'normal person,' a human being like anyone else, a person, therefore, who deserves a fair chance and a fair break... Yet he may perceive, usually quite correctly, that whatever others profess, they do not really 'accept' him and are not ready to make contact with him on 'equal grounds'.[6]

Yes, that was my overriding sense: a sympathetic 'poor you' making allowance for my defect, treating me as a second-rate person.

Further, the standards he has incorporated from the wider society equip him to be intimately alive to what others see as his failing, inevitably causing him, if only for moments, to agree that he does indeed fall short of what he really ought to be. Shame becomes a central possibility, arising from his perception of one of his attributes as being a defiling thing to possess, and one he can readily see himself as not possessing.[7]

*Yes, I knew that onrush of self-hatred very well; it could overwhelm me and obliterate my sense of having a valid self. It occurred most forcefully in the presence of exceptional people whom I admired and perhaps wished to be friends with. But I sensed that *IT* meant I would never be viewed as their equal.*

The central feature of a stigmatised individual's situation in life... is a question of what is often, if vaguely, called 'acceptance'. Those who have dealings with him fail to accord him the respect and regard which the un-contaminated aspects of his social identity have led them to anticipate extending, and have led him to anticipate receiving; he echoes this denial by finding that some of his attributes warrant it.[8]

DISCOVERING STIGMA

Is that what I was doing? Conniving in my labelling?

Goffman's analysis of everyday encounters, what he calls 'mixed contacts', was also incisive: 'The stigmatised individual may find that he feels unsure of how we normals will identify and receive him.'[9] *Definitely!*

> He is 'on [show]' having to be self-conscious and calculating about the impression he is making to a degree and in areas of conduct which he assumes others are not… Also he is likely to feel that the usual scheme of interpretation for everyday events has been undermined. His minor accomplishments, he feels, may be assessed as signs of remarkable and noteworthy capacities in the circumstances.[10]

Precisely. Others' expectations of what I could do had changed, diminished, lowered.

Goffman then asks how the stigmatised person responds to their situation. *Good advice coming?*

> He… [starts] on a new 'moral career',[11] the process by which he learns what society thinks of someone with his deviance and then how to adjust to having it.

Goffman considers that their options include the following:

1. He can try to correct the objective basis for his failing, such as through surgery, but these corrections may be less than 100 per cent successful and may have other consequences – and sometimes this turns into an obsessive search and further stigmatisation. *I knew by then that surgery could improve *IT* only up to a certain point, but there was no magic fix available. Option number one not looking promising.*

2. He can try to repair his failing by deliberately devoting hours to mastering activities that are considered beyond his capability. *I was hardly going to become an amazingly attractive lover or a star on stage with *IT*. Option number two uninspiring.*

3. He can also use his stigma for what Goffman calls 'secondary gains', as an excuse for his inadequacies and any mishaps that come his way – and if he then has surgery that removes his stigma, he can feel bereft of the hook on which to hang his woes. *Yes, I could certainly see that option as plausible: I could blame *IT* for all manner of failings and live on benefits and hand-outs – and dismiss surgery in case it did remove *IT* as my excuse. But in the end I couldn't see myself doing that, not at all appealing.*

4. He may see his misfortune as a blessing in disguise, feeling enriched by it, a better person, and passing on to others what he thinks his suffering can teach them. *I could hardly imagine seeing *IT* as a blessing. I disliked what I saw in the mirror and although I had acquired a few insights from my year as a stigmatised person, it seemed highly unlikely that I would find much meaning to pass on. But maybe someday...*

5. He can find it very therapeutic to reassess the attributes of 'normals' and discover that what he assumed to be their strengths are actually only superficial and that he has a much stronger satisfaction with life. *No way. I was hopelessly jealous of what everyone, especially my fellow students, took for granted: their good looks. I felt bereft of them – and therefore weak in every social encounter, and deeply envious of my peers who could approach every meeting, especially with women, without fear. My only vague hope was that any friendships I did manage to make might be more profound. No superficial one-night stands for me. Sadly!*

DISCOVERING STIGMA

Was Goffman right? Were these five the only options available? Surely not.

As I sat in my tiny room that first evening, I trembled at just how insightful those forty pages were about what I was going through with *IT*. But I also trembled at how painfully thin my options seemed to be.

I was moved that Goffman had written so cogently about what I was going through, but despite all his brilliant analysis, his words told me directly, without exaggeration or platitude, the mountain of the challenge that faced me.

He said that I was starting on a new 'moral career', but where were the 'career guides'? Nowhere in sight. It felt like I was back in kindergarten, a kindergarten without teachers.

The only role models I had been encouraged to look at – or up to – were the Guinea Pigs, the Battle of Britain flyers who had been operated on by a man called Archie McIndoe at a hospital in East Grinstead. Some had written books, one of which I'd read – *I Burned My Fingers*[12] – but their experiences in the 1940s and 1950s were very different to mine, and the tone of their books was heroic, brave and upbeat. They were heroes losing their face in the wartime service of others. I'd lost mine in a stupid accident of my own making.

The Guinea Pig Club was closed to me anyway, being restricted to those who had been operated on by Mr McIndoe. No chance of career guidance from them.

So, was there *any* way out? My reaction to Goffman's analysis was bleak.

But over the next few days and weeks, I kept going back to one of his key paragraphs – and focusing on one tiny phrase (in italics).

> The central feature of a stigmatised individual's situation in life… is a question of what is often, if vaguely, called 'acceptance'. Those who have dealings with him fail to accord him the respect and regard which the un-contaminated aspects of his

social identity have led them to anticipate extending, and have led him to anticipate receiving; *he echoes this denial by finding that some of his attributes do not warrant it [respect and regard].*

This was the crux for me. What if I didn't do that?

WHAT IF I did *not* echo this lack of respect and regard; might I also be able to dissuade others from doing so?

WHAT IF I could figure out a way *to fully respect and highly regard myself* and accept *IT* and myself; might I then be able to persuade others to do so too?

I had absolutely no idea on that bleak night during my first term at Oxford how I could possibly do those things. But I did know one thing deep down. I *hated* the idea of resigning myself to my situation, and of accepting my inferiority in the eyes and minds of others — and in my own eyes too.

I loathed that thought and the feeling it gave me. I loathed it deep in my guts.

And although when I looked at *IT* in the mirror, I could not envisage ever liking what I saw, let alone others doing so, I did chuckle to myself just occasionally… and think, 'Let's prove them all wrong.'

I loathed the idea of resigning myself to a life on the margins. I also loathed the labels 'one of the stigmatised' or 'a disfigured person'. I could feel my hackles rising every time Goffman used those phrases to describe my — our — predicament.

I rejected the labelling with every ounce of my being, and yet I knew that it was a 99.99 per cent futile objection.

I had virtually no chance of changing it. Nobody else had, as far as I knew. I had no clue how to do it either.

But if I could tackle those big, big WHAT IFs, I might just find a way of beating the stigma or, if not beating it, rendering it harmless to my prospects.

10.
RESTARTING LIFE

The autumn days in 1971 after the discovery of *Stigma* were bleak. I was reminded daily of the total lack of guidance from Goffman or anyone about how I could deal with the stigma that I now knew I was being subjected to — and was subjecting myself to. Hope for the future seemed again like a mirage — seemingly so real but actually a fantasy.

But the good thing was that I had forced myself to live with *IT* in the social setting of a university and in the unique college system of Oxford for more than a month. I was also learning, and not just academically. I had no choice but to attend two or three weekly one-to-one tutorials for which I had to produce essays or other pieces of work based on hours of study in libraries — and read them out loud too. Or I'd be sent down in disgrace.

HIDING IN PUBLIC

So, there was no hiding in my academic life. And although in my everyday life, it would have been so much easier not to have left my room, I hadn't taken that line.

I was learning how to live with the certainty that a high percentage of the people I met in my everyday student life and most of the strangers I walked past or stood next to or was observed by looked at *IT* with sympathy. They might applaud my bravery, but more than likely also labelled me as damaged goods and imagined my sadness and shame.

These are instinctive public reactions over which I had little control. And although I was fearful of those reactions and completely unskilled in how to handle them, I lived less and less in a survival, lonely mode, beginning a trial and error existence instead.

Although it was only in the privacy behind my student room door that I could ease up my daily struggle, I didn't stay there. Instead I chose to hide my scars and conceal my shame. I became an expert in disguise. Big flat-brimmed hats in the Clint Eastwood Spaghetti Western styles of the era were a favourite. And high-neck shirts and sweaters, long trousers, never shorts, gloves, hands in pockets to hide my distorted fingers, long overcoats and, above all, dark glasses; big ones.

I became a bit of a celebrity in Oxford – 'There goes that man with the scarred face' or words to that effect. My hat and dark glasses increased the mystery but also told of my vulnerability – as two people I met then have told me since:

> *A:* On one occasion… I was in the college lodge, turned round to leave and someone asked me directions to a room. This was a man wearing a large-brimmed hat but it only took a moment to realise that the face underneath it had been badly burned and scarred. It took a fraction of a second for me to realise how much we rely on the appearance of the other person in conversation.
>
> I may well have reacted typically – glancing at you, then glancing away thinking that it was rude to look for too long, then looking back because looking away is no way to hold a conversation. You've probably seen it a million times.
>
> This chance meeting really brought home to me that I want to, need to and will try to see the person behind the surface layer. You made me aware of a very important aspect of being human.

> **B:** *I was a contemporary of yours at Oxford, studying the same subject, and a number of times found myself reacting to you in a visceral way that made me embarrassed and ashamed. I recall several times looking up from my books in the library as you walked by and literally gasping. You must have experienced this kind of thing constantly, and I sincerely apologise for my part in it. At the time I did not have the maturity or social skills to speak to you directly. I am sorry for the hurt or harm I caused you, and for my inability to reach out to you.*

The internal argument I was going through was hard to resolve: one side kept telling me not to hide ('It looks like you're ashamed'), but its case was not very strong or convincing; the other side won out frequently ('Just let me get used to *IT* and how people react to it first – maybe I'll stop hiding later'). It was an ongoing argument which was far more important to me than the Oxford Union debates about workers' strikes or oil prices.

Ironically, of course, many of my hiding tricks did the reverse to what I intended: they actually drew attention to my scars instead of helping me to hide in the shadows. I stood out – like a sore thumb, you could say. And I had one of those too... painful.

ESCAPING THE PAIN

So how did I try to escape this pain?

The early seventies was an era of permissiveness. Students played loud rock 'n' roll music; clothes were loud too, hair was allowed to grow to unheard-of lengths and patterns, and all manner of aromas pleased the senses. And in this atmosphere, I found a freedom of my own.

Drinking definitely allowed me to forget. After a few beers, quite a few, with blokes, yes, usually only blokes, in a pub, I would drift away from my shame, almost forget about *IT* and find a little glimpse of freedom. But then waking up the next morning was an even more ghastly reality. Not only did I have the sore head that they all had, but I also had the stark reality of my scarred, weak, puny legs and my scarred, distorted visage, my *IT*.

Get another drink? Very tempting. The easy way out. And I often took it.

Soft drugs, too, were a superb way to find unfettered freedom for a short time. Illegal, of course, but they offered me a glimpse of a life without the daily angst. Have another joint? I very often did.

Addiction was around the corner, I knew, and not just to tobacco, on which I was already hooked. But — and this was a very strong force for me — I knew that many people had invested hours and hours to bring me back from the brink, had backed me totally. I was determined not to let them down.

But another joint freeing me up from my inhibitions was so tempting. I fought a daily inner battle: the drugs and drink liberated me from my self-doubt, but I could feel myself falling into dependency... and failing those who'd committed so much to rescuing me.

It was inch by inch stuff, moment by moment, day by day. I wrestled with myself. Sometimes, I would be down for days, weeks even, drinking too much to drive away the demons and give me Dutch courage and then waking up to the ghastly reality, unmotivated, hungover, depressed... looking at *IT* in the mirror.

My belief in my likely likeability with *IT* was very low. I could not imagine making new friends (or winning them, because that's how it felt). I knew that I wouldn't have become a friend of someone with an *IT*.

But making new friends is what I did. Sharing pints and joints had an incredibly profound effect on my self-worth. A new friend, Hugh, remembers:

The memories and images that I have of those 'distant' days at Oxford seem to start at the King's Arms (KA) which is where, I think, we first met. I recall some of the protagonists dimly but not their names. You distinguished yourself with the black hat, scarf and long coat – a protective ensemble?!

In those early days of finding our niche and circle of friends – often in the beer and smoke-filled atmosphere of the KA and elsewhere – we were all caught up in the new experience that was Oxford, and although I must have been astonished by your story, meeting someone with whom I would get on so well so quickly probably took the sting out of the situation.

I can remember certain moments in the early days of feeling protective towards you when we encountered hostility and a lack of understanding. The best course was always to move on and leave the ignorant to their ignorance. The handicap was theirs!

I have been attempting to recall just to what extent we understood or appreciated the fact that you had decided not to put things on hold for a year and to come up to Oxford when you did, and the incredible challenge that that represented. I guess that as the rest of your life unfolded, and we got to know you better, it showed that your fundamental inner drive was never going to allow you to do anything else but take the bull by the horns and make the best of an extremely difficult situation.

It would be easy to say that we provided you with the support you needed, but friendship can never be a one-way relationship, and you also provided us with an equal measure of support; in fact, there were times when you were the driving force in the relationship!

The winning of new friends – and very different ones to those I'd ever had before – was vital in my rebuilding. They did sometimes serve to protect me, but most of all, they gave me new confidence – and especially when they introduced me to friends of theirs and I could make my own impact... make another friend...

I had discovered by accident and without being able to articulate what, in my first book, I called 'being proactive' in my social encounters. Friendships followed naturally.

Instead of waiting for others to react to *IT*, I took the initiative – I was proactive, some might say extravagantly so. Speaking first, starting the conversation, offering to shake hands, making good eye contact, making small talk expertly… I was clumsy at it at first, of course, but I got better and better as I practised. See more on this in chapter 14 (pages 141–146).

I discovered that it had the desired effect: I was meeting people with all my damagedness – with voice, eyes, hands, gestures, *IT* and all – and they were not given even a microsecond to be put off by *IT* or to be negative. I took the wind from their judgements instantly.

Which isn't to say I was not still terribly vulnerable. Nor that being proactive was easy and not fraught with risk of rejection. But I was starting to get an inkling of a modus operandi that would allow me to shed my disguises.

IF NOT INTIMATE, THEN PLATONIC

Young women were around me too, but never with me. I was still bereft of intimacy, an oft-dreamed-of experience, but one that seemed far, far beyond reach.

But I did experience a very unexpected consequence of my position which was not just shame-shedding but brought me a step closer to the intimacy that I craved. I became a confidant to other students, men and women. I was sought out and confided in, it seemed, by some who were feeling inadequate, anxious and unsure about how their lives were evolving. Extraordinarily, my experience of spending a gap year in and around a burns and plastic surgery ward had opened up my understanding of pain, unhappiness and emotional turmoil. This now became something that my peers wanted to know about – and in the process, I think I helped some of them to tackle their inner demons, or at least see them in a new perspective.

I could see and hear from others' mouths some of my pre-accident anxieties in these conversations. People – especially young women – confided in me and sought my advice about how to manage new relationships, particularly ones that were clearly lust-led. I had no clue, of course! But I listened and played back what I heard. And enjoyed them coming back with the next instalment.

Men asked different questions: how was I so successful in making friends, especially with women, or how could they dissociate themselves from their past lives? I was astounded by the idea that I had anything to offer, but flattered too.

I developed a listening ear, and my room was sought out. One friend gave me the nickname of the 'trick-cyclist', a malapropism for psychiatrist. It stuck, and of course I was ridiculed mercilessly for it – but inside I treasured it. And, probably because I presented no threat to them, I developed lots of lovely platonic relationships with beautiful young women.

DEVELOPING MY TALENTS – AND PHYSICALITY

Before *IT*, I had enjoyed playing sport and had reasonably skilled hand-eye coordination. There was a squash court in the college and I knew that I needed to see if I could still play. I stole myself into the court one afternoon in the autumn of 1971, with my still-bandaged legs covered by a tracksuit, and barely able to run. I discovered that I could still hit the ball reasonably well and although I was very unfit, here was something that I might be able to do well – quite well, anyway.

I started practising and found a partner who was kind and supportive – and I even considered taking off the tracksuit. But not yet.

Over the course of that first term, I got myself on the fringes of the college team. In the vacation, I challenged the junior plastic surgeon who'd admitted me to the burns unit a year before (who I assumed would thrash me) and he arranged for us to play at his very smart squash club. I dressed myself up and took *IT* through the front doors to the reception, where he greeted me. Much to his amazement, I won! The drink in the bar afterwards – with the looks from fellow players washing over me – was a huge boost. A small victory, but proof that with application, I could possibly live with *IT* and my hidden scars. Tracksuit still on.

The next term I made it into the college team, which involved matches against other colleges, a much more daunting prospect because my opponents had no idea what they were letting themselves in for.

Did *IT* actually give me an advantage? I certainly didn't think so, imagining them thinking that I'd be a walkover 'looking like that'. But I was no walkover. I was competitive (until my lack of fitness and smoking caught up with me). And I started to revel in, even love, the surprise *IT* engendered!

I even started to enjoy the attention of the watching eyes from the gallery. The beers afterwards were all the sweeter – and next morning the scars didn't seem quite so loathsome or shameful.

Hugh again:

Memories of the squash court at Univ come back too: an example of your sporting and most competitive streak; did I feel like your whipping boy, coming back for another beating time after time? Was this part of the rehabilitation in giving you the opportunity to prove your superiority?

I say this with tongue in cheek, but at an elemental level I think that there may well have been some truth in it; at any rate it was a good excuse to make room for the beer! Certainly, it served to prove that you would not allow your perceived disabilities to be a handicap.

And the squash also had another unexpected benefit. As I got fitter and more competitive, I had to throw off my tracksuit – it was too hot to keep it on. I had no choice but to reveal my legs and arms, scarring all over, jagged and distorted, some still with scabs on, skin grafts, all still red and livid. Surely impossible. No, it wasn't. I did it. Somehow.

I can recall walking back from a game at another college in a late afternoon, after a few beers admittedly. All the way down the High Street in shorts. I was half-daring people to look, but watching for their reactions too.

I took up jogging again and that rebuilt muscle into depleted limbs and gave me the endorphin rush that is so uplifting. I was rediscovering my physicality and with it, throwing off a bit more of my shame.

My self-belief and most importantly, my self-respect, were starting to rise. By the summer of 1972, I was ready to sunbathe and spend whole days in shorts. The scars on my legs, hands and body were becoming part of a new 'me' – even if *IT* was not. I was willing to show them to the world. And I found the world was respecting me, too.

LOSS AND GAIN

The first anniversary of my accident, 5 December 1971, was an emotional one. I decided to spend part of it with new friends and then in the evening meet up with old ones and my family. It was a day when people kept remarking on my strengths, but it was also a day when I was reflecting on my loss. All the near-perfect certainties I'd had were gone, the eighteen years of preparing so carefully for my successful future a distant memory. Now, after just one year with *IT*, I yearned for any tiny indication that life might be worth living, that I would succeed in any way.

Instead of cruising through life, my overriding feeling was of crawling blindly along – and I had started to appreciate what the college chaplain had said to me some weeks earlier, almost as a throwaway remark. As if he thought I already knew it: 'I guess you are likely to go through a sort of bereavement, like people do when they lose someone close to them.'

I knew nothing of grief and how to navigate it. And nobody helped me with it. But bereavement was certainly with me, not perhaps felt daily, but regularly. A sudden and unpredictable welling up of intense sadness, uncontrollable crying and emotional torment. I recall one occasion when I went to a funeral of an old family friend and felt myself suddenly awash with what I described to myself as self-pity, and struggled to get to grips with it in that circumstance, blubbing quietly to myself: 'Not what you should be showing.' Nonsense!

Actually, it wasn't self-pity so much as my psyche being stirred by the emotions of the funeral, entirely understandably.

But the other thing I remember about that first anniversary of the accident, as I sat late into the evening with my parents, probably drinking Scotch, was hearing myself saying something like, 'You know, now and again I have the sense that I might be gaining from this experience... much as I have lost and am struggling to master, I am starting to see that I am gaining, too.' I couldn't quite believe my ears – and nor could my parents, I suspect. But there was a glimmer of truth in it, a glimmer of hope.

ON MY OWN?

Before my accident I had never known anyone who looked like I did now. In fact, the closest I'd come to meeting someone with an *IT*, a burned face, had been at the cinema.

The 1969 film *Battle of Britain* had won much acclaim with a huge all-star cast including Laurence Olivier, John Gielgud, Christopher Plummer, Trevor Howard, Kenneth More and Susannah York retelling the 1940 story, underpinned by William Walton's superbly triumphal music.

I had enjoyed the film in a cinema shortly after it came out. But I now remembered one scene in it: Susannah York is introduced to a man with severe burns. She hesitates and shudders. I recalled catching my breath at the shocking sight – the whole cinema did. She turned away and got back to her duties.

Little did I imagine that, within a year, I would be incarcerated in a burns unit being treated by surgeons and nurses whose training had been shaped by treating pilots and tank crew burned in war. If Susannah York shivered when meeting that man (Bill Foxley), albeit in a film, what chance had I of any intimacy with anyone, let alone a Susannah?! On my own for ever? Yes, I had to assume… no doubt whatsoever, I would be. The curtains would remain closed on my future in that respect.

Douglas Bader's example – wartime hero and now a married man – resonated with me a little more because it was his stupid mistake which saw him lose his legs; and get artificial ones fitted, in fact, down the corridor from the burns unit at Roehampton. I watched him in the film *Reach for the Sky* (played by Kenneth More) flirting outrageously, and reflected ruefully that at least he had a good-looking face.

But that was before I met a man who inspired me more than anyone else.

One of my father's business friends wrote to me about him just weeks after my accident, said he could introduce me. John (not his real name) had been injured in a plane crash like Bader, but he'd been severely burned. I think it might have been his fault. The letter said, 'He's now married a beautiful woman and they have two little daughters.' Hard to believe.

I wrote to him out of the blue late in that first year at Oxford and, without hesitation, he invited me to their home for a lovely summery Sunday lunch. I arrived very nervously and he proudly introduced me to his wife and two little girls, both under four years old. The children were completely unfazed by his looks – and, delightfully, by mine, too. Of course.

I observed his entirely normal and loving interactions with his wife with amazement. She seemed to see him with the scars and through the scars. In fact, I wondered if she saw the scars at all. They both seemed very strong characters, and she said several times during our conversations over lunch, when I was encouraged to ask any questions I had, 'I really don't see what the problem is.' She might not see the problem, but it was very clear in my mind!

What I gleaned from that lunch and from a number of other conversations with John, however, was that he had also been through great bouts of doubt and darkness. But he had battled them and won through. His accident was ten years before mine and he said it had taken a good five years before his self-belief returned in a robust way, no longer liable to be knocked back by some small incident. He had a large family and they had helped to get him back to work and supported him when he was 'down in the dumps'. And he had found love!

That Sunday gave me another small injection of hope. I saw for the first time that living with *IT* completely confidently was not an impossibility, even if not a likely possibility.

But there were absolutely no other role models in the media or in my line of sight in those days. I was entirely on my own, I thought. At the hospital where I was treated, one of the nurses attempted to create a support group. I went to one meeting – there were maybe ten people there, all battling with lost looks. I came away disillusioned and angry. It all seemed like wallowing, everyone hoping to get the miracle surgery that we all knew was not possible. A ghetto of lost souls. I never went again.

ALL OPTIMISM GONE?

The inner self-belief of my first eighteen years in the 1950s and 1960s had been strongly underpinned by the idea that my good looks were very important to my prospects and would stand me in good stead – indeed, would give me an advantage. Along with my education and

RESTARTING LIFE

talents, they were my passport to success. I had foolishly lost all of that and instead 'gained' *IT*.

I met some people in hospital who had never had such an advantage. One young man in the plastic surgery ward told me of his life with a cleft lip and palate, almost bereft of self-belief. Another woman with a large and complex birthmark over her eye and cheek told me of her painful school days, scarred by bullying. They had never had good-looking faces, nor had those with craniofacial conditions and early childhood accidents, like the seven-year-old girl with severe burns who came in for regular operations. I winced inside at their stories and the idea that they felt excluded from much that I had taken for granted for eighteen years.

My life with *IT* seemed to be destined to be like that of those patients. Like them, I had no passport to the future – mine had been destroyed in the flames of my accident. We were all stranded and without hope. Pessimism swirled around me.

And yet I had an inkling deep inside that I could make something out of the ruins. Optimism is not an absolute, in my view, but a 'tendency', partly innate and partly nurtured in early life by parental, educational and spiritual influences. By the time I was eighteen, my tendency was certainly towards optimism – and after the accident, I was beset by people telling me to 'Look on the bright side' and that 'There's a silver lining to every dark cloud' and similar clichés. Easy to say, but not at all easy to believe.

So how did my optimism return? It's a complex story because I was exposed to many influences and events. But the word 'inkling' touches something about my inner journey. I had an inkling that I was not done for. There was a tiny ember still alight deep inside me of my hopes and dreams about my future that my accident had not extinguished. Although you might find my use of the fire metaphor here awkward, I find it a good analogy.

My pre-accident optimism had been radiant, like a camp fire sparking with life. The accident in the heavy drizzle of Usk had drenched the fire, just like a huge rain storm would, rendering it cold, lifeless and dark. But a skilled firelighter (and I became one of those later on) knows that, even after a major storm, there may still be life in a doused fire. If you can very carefully unearth that tiny ember, it may hold just enough heat to spark a little bit of paper, and then some dry kindling wood, and if carefully nurtured with enough oxygen – but not too much – the whole fire can be reignited into a new blaze.

My inkling was like that tiny little ember. So how did it survive? And what oxygen did I use?

My earliest realisation of the ember's existence came during what was one of the first and most difficult operations, which involved my badly burned eyelids. Getting skin grafts to take in those indented areas without contracting is very problematic – today just as in the seventies. Eyelids also have the finest skin on the human body, with nerve ends very much on the surface, so operations are exceedingly painful and removing stitches excruciating.

The first operation I had on my eyelids was in the burns unit in January 1971, two months after my accident. My eyes were stitched shut for a whole week in an attempt to achieve the best result. It was terrifying to start with to live in darkness, totally dependent on others for help and cut off from an active life.

And yet, having my eyes forcibly closed gave me access to new insights – in-sights. As the week went on, that darkness became a source of peace and calm.

I found myself reaching into my depths. I'd grown up in a Christian tradition but was far from a convinced believer. And my accident shook all that to the very core. I screamed inwardly, 'Why, God? Why me? What's the point? Why didn't you protect me?' With eyes stitched closed, I waited for answers. And, although none came, I sensed in the darkness that an answer might just emerge.

My anger was held at bay by discovering a tiny, tiny inkling of hope. Maybe not everything was lost. Maybe I would find some meaning eventually. My mother certainly believed I would. Whether that was a religious moment or not, I have long wondered. But there is no doubt that sensing that ember sustained me.

Another moment when the ember was nurtured was eighteen months later. I went to a party in Bristol and was returning to London by train. I got into a fairly empty carriage and found myself a seat with a table on which to pretend to do some academic reading. It had been a long night and reading a newspaper had more appeal. Just before the train left the station, a man came and sat opposite, got out a book and started to read.

Just before Swindon, the train stopped. For a long time, as it turned out. And we got into conversation. And he showed me the book he was reading. It had just been published. *True Resurrection* by Harry Williams.[1] I'd never heard of him. But the title hit a nerve. He asked what had happened to me and, before I knew it, we were in what I still recall as a transformational conversation. He gave me the book.

This man was Canon Sydney Evans, Dean of King's College London, a very holy man as I came to find out. He was oxygen, a mentor, and I kept in touch with him for a few years. And Harry Williams' book was to become a constant companion, though one which, like *Stigma*, I kept hidden, clutching it close so that it lost none of its magic.

In *True Resurrection* Williams asserts 'The miracle (of resurrection) is to be found… within the ordinary round and daily routine of our lives. Resurrection occurs to us as we are, and its coming is generally quiet and unobtrusive and we may hardly be aware of its creative power.'[2] Sydney Evans was convinced of that transformation – and he suggested I could experience it too.

But I wasn't a believer, just a doubting searcher. He said, 'You don't have to be 100 per cent sure, but as you find ways out of the wilderness, I think you will come to be more sure.' And then he cited one of the great verses of the Old Testament that I had taken to heart from my early school days (again all alone, this time at a boarding school): 'Be strong and of good courage and be not afraid, for the Lord your God is with you whithersoever thou goest.'

So another force was caring for my ember too? Yes, he asserted firmly.

All these spiritual awakenings and experiences gave oxygen to the tiny ember of hope I had found back in January 1971. But although, just occasionally, the ember glowed into a little flame, it didn't take much to extinguish it again. Nevertheless, as the second anniversary of my accident approached (December 1972), I was definitely restarting my life with my new-found university friends giving me great encouragement.

11.
RECONSTRUCTING *IT*

GIVING MY CONSENT
TO MORE (PLASTIC) SURGERY

I am not going to elaborate on all the fifty-plus reconstructive surgery operations that I had in the years from 1971 to 1975, some being small local anaesthetic procedures but mostly major operations.

I am not going to describe the agonising procedures I endured to get good skin grafts on to my eyelids, for example, but I have all my hospital notes available – they smell of hospital still! – if I really want to cause myself pain again.

But what I can relive is the fact that I returned to hospital for treatment to *IT* after every single term at university. Having started to become a regular student, I became a patient again for a month, dreading the pre-med hallucinations and all the grottiness of post-op recovery. Then there were the dressings, the infections and the graft failures – a far cry from studying or partying!

Why did I put myself through it? I wondered this every single time I was asked to sign a consent form. On every occasion I had to persuade myself that the next operation would improve *IT* or the functionality of my hands. That meant making a decision.

In the early days, my giving of consent was very uninformed. I trusted my consultant. I did not know enough about wounds and surgery to make any judgement. I just signed the form.

But, after a year or so, it became more and more difficult to just sign. I was giving up my student life for a month. Was it worth it? I knew more now, but were the promised changes actually being achieved? 'Yes' seemed to be the answer, because slowly, very slowly, *IT* did start to change, and look a bit less shocking. I couldn't say 'better'.

The biggest decision I made during the years 1971–75 was to refashion my chin, and it illustrates well the difficulties inherent in all medical decision-making.

My chin had been extremely severely burned in my accident. The roll-neck nylon jumper I was wearing had caught light and completely devastated it, most of the fat layer as well as the outer skin.

Superficial skin grafts were harvested from my one good leg, buttocks and anywhere with clear skin to cover all these wounds – yes, 'harvested' is the word used in medical parlance because the expectation is that once a donor site has healed after yielding up its skin, it can be harvested again – and again and again; you should see my left calf!

Tiresomely, however, my body's healing mechanisms (like many young people's) caused all the superficial skin grafts to contract and tighten, thereby pulling my lower lip down and out. I effectively lost my chin.

You can see in the photo taken six weeks after the accident (on page 89) that my chin and mouth still look relatively normal – but then look back at the next one (page 29), taken two months later on my Face Day.

Zoom in your gaze on my mouth and chin and you can see the scars, swollen and raised ('hypertrophic') and how the chin has disappeared.

Over the next two years, during every university vacation I endured much surgery on the rest of my face – little by little, the surgeons created relative symmetry around my eyes and gave me back a top lip.

But despite a number of efforts to insert skin grafts into my chin, it remained a mess, contracted, less swollen but very unsightly.

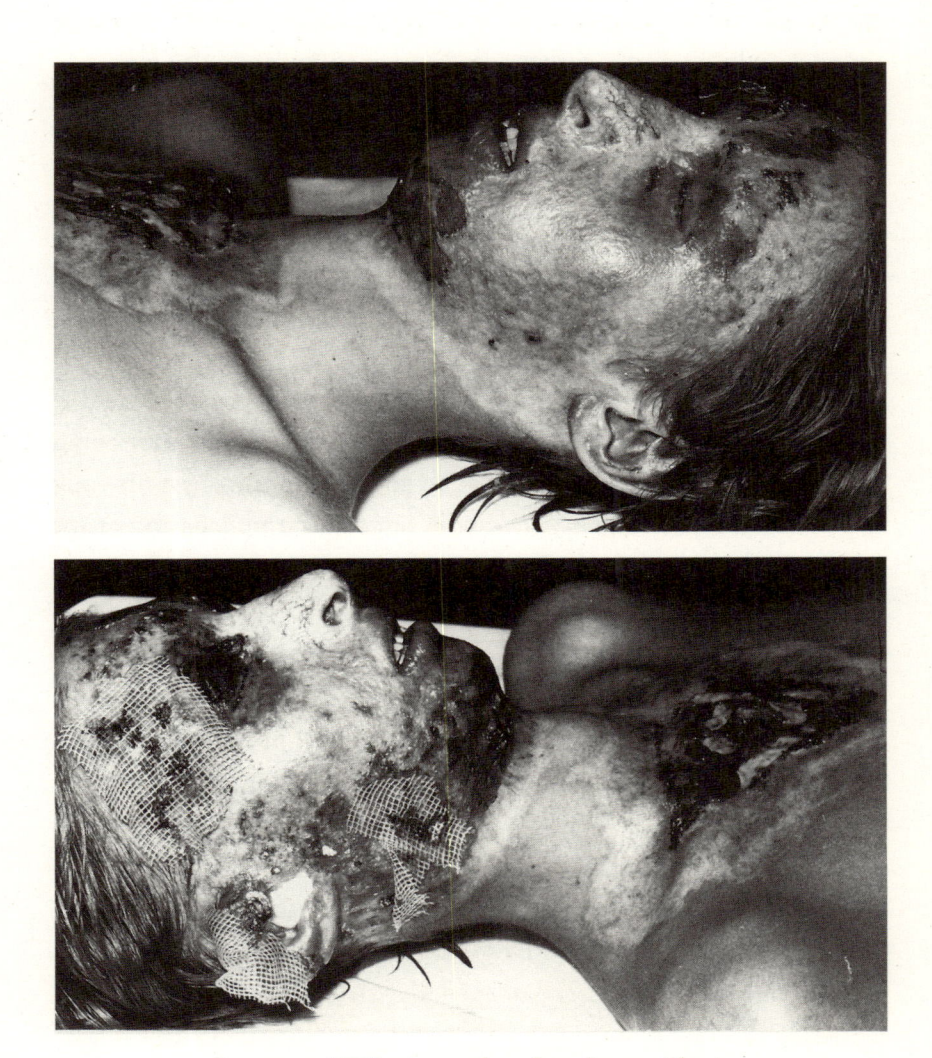

January 1971, six weeks after the accident.

The worst thing about my chin was that it effectively pulled down the rest of the skin of my face towards my chest – as you can see in the stretching in my neck in the lower photo opposite, two years on from the earlier one. (Try to ignore the 1973 hairstyle!) My chin was thus seriously inhibiting my surgeons' attempts to improve the look and function of my eyes especially. I heard it called 'an intractable problem'. My medical team seemed to have no answer. I was starting to lose faith.

After more than two years of plastic surgery, I confronted my consultant. Much of the work he had done was being compromised by the mess and continued tightness of my chin. My eyes remained skewed even after much very painful surgery. What to do? He had no obvious plan. I left feeling disappointed.

I was at that time (spring 1973) recovering from a painful operation on my left hand, nose and right ear, and, frustrated at not being allowed to leave hospital, I arranged to go and visit the physiotherapy department, to exercise my still-weak but recovering legs and arms. I got talking to the guy on the neighbouring clinical bed, as we both lifted weights, and asked him about his reason for being there – 'I'm having a "cross-leg flap" done,' he said.

'A what?'

'A cross-leg flap, to tackle an ulcer that won't heal up.'

It was a light-bulb moment! Over the next hour, I quizzed him, getting the physios involved too... and suddenly I was an active patient, no longer in the dark.

I went straight from the physios to the surgeons' room and literally accosted my consultant. Here's the conversation:

'Thank you for seeing me so speedily, Mr Evans; I need to ask you a question.'

'No problem, please sit down.'

'I have seen a cross-leg flap this afternoon. Could a flap be the answer for my chin?'

'That's an interesting idea; your chin is certainly a problem. How do you think it could work?'

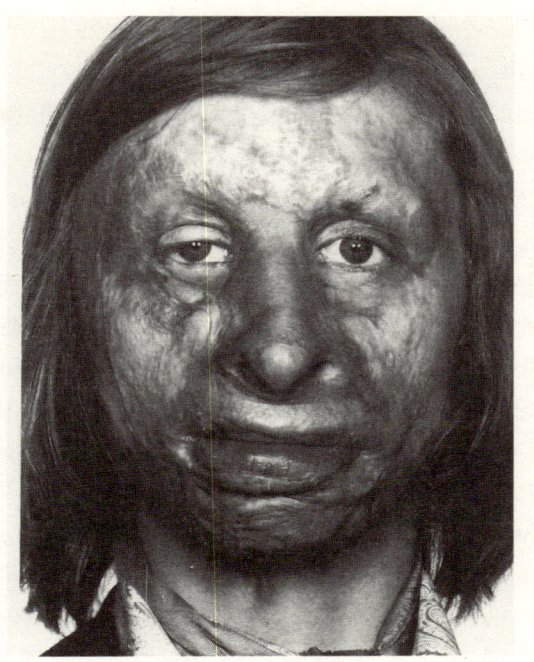

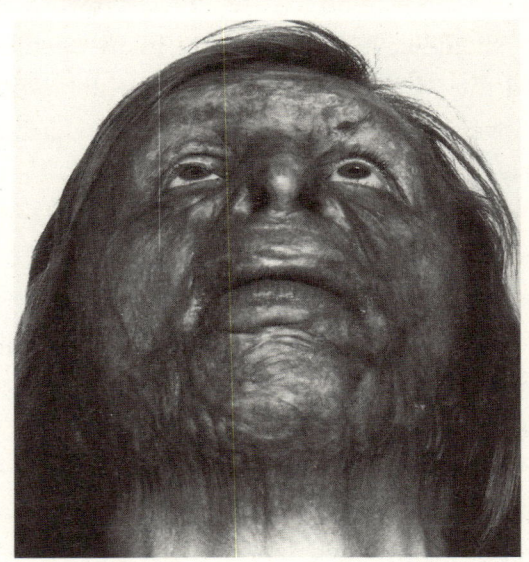

*March 1973: 'An intractable problem.'
Despite several skin grafts, my chin was
still contracted and dragged my face
down towards my chest.*

'Well, you could raise a flap from my stomach, perhaps, and put it on my arm and then transfer it to my chin.'

'Mmmm. I need to give you some facts about flaps – pedicles, as we call them. They are *extremely* risky operations because the blood supply in the tube has to be achieved every time it is moved – very difficult – and the more times we move it, the more risky it becomes. Pedicles also have to be long enough to cover the entire wounded area. The one you saw to cover a big leg ulcer was probably six inches long. To do your chin we would need at least twelve inches, *very* long, probably needing a two-stage development – more risk. And I don't think you'd have enough clear skin on your stomach given the burns on your right side.'

'Ah. Not so simple then. Could you raise one on my back?'

'Technically it's possible, but the risks are even greater and the chances of success are even smaller because I won't be able to use your arm to transfer it. We'd have to attach it to your chest and twist it over your shoulder. It would involve many operations – maybe fifteen… and the whole process couldn't be done quickly, because after each move, we have to leave the flap to establish itself.'

'So I'd have to be a patient for how long?'

'Maybe nine months. I'd have to do much more detailed planning, but that's a rough idea.'

'Oh, gosh.'

'Why don't we fix up to have a more detailed talk in a week's time, by which time I'll have got my team to do some more thinking?'

'Well, OK… but it's not sounding a very good idea after all.'

A week later:

'Come on in… and firstly, let me thank you for coming up with such an interesting idea.'

'That's OK, but I really don't think I would want to get involved with such a risky process, especially as I could spend nine months in hospital and then it could all go wrong at the last step – right?'

RECONSTRUCTING *IT*

'Yes, it is true that at any stage in the process, the flap could literally die because the blood supply fails.'

'What does that look like?'

'The flap goes gradually black – and it can happen quite quickly.'

'No, I don't like the sound of it at all.'

'I appreciate that, but we have been doing some thinking too, and we think a pedicle could produce a really good result. Your chin would look much better and all the contraction that it presently causes to the rest of your face would be significantly reduced.'

'Yes, I appreciate that, but the risks seem huge to me – and anyway, where could you raise the tube if not on my stomach?'

'Well, we think we could use your back.'

'Gosh – how would that work? Twist my arm around my side?'

'No, we'd attach it to your chest over the shoulder, so your hands and arms would not be affected.'

'Would I have to stay in hospital? And what would my back look like afterwards?'

'No, you'd have to come in for spells but we think there would be some time away too – but it might take up to nine months in all… And yes, you would have a large area on your back that would be grafted with skin from your legs – and without the fat layer, so no sweating on that area of your back (just like your grafted legs)… This is a lot to think about, isn't it? And I'm sure you'll want to go away and consider.'

'Yes… I suppose there's no way of telling what the end result would look like, is there?'

'I have done quite a few big flaps like this, although not one to someone's chin from their back. But we might be able to find another surgeon's patient to let you see the sort of result we can hope for.'

'Thanks, that would be good. It's difficult to weigh up all these different factors and I'm going to need to work out how I feel. I suppose I could try to take a year off from university, but that would be quite a wrench and there are such risks… I'm not sure. I think I'll need a few weeks – can we meet again then, please?'

Three weeks later:

'Hello again – how's your thinking going?'

'Well, I'm getting close to saying yes – and it's been good to talk to Mr G and Mr C [junior surgeons] and Mr H [an ex-patient]. I'm now thinking that I want to know more about three things: first, about the risk that the tube will fail after each transfer. There are three big moves: over my shoulder, up to my chin and across my chin. How will you manage the risk?'

'We have to use surgical skill, and once the operation is done, we will have to ensure all blood clots are manually rolled out, hourly at the start... and we will have to manage any infection very aggressively. But we cannot rule out failure.'

'OK, so the next question: what is Plan B? If the graft fails, especially in the last stage when you open the flap and spread it out across my chin?'

'Yes, this is a serious challenge, but our experience is that flaps with a good blood supply do settle in very well – and again, we'll be rolling out blood clots for perhaps up to two weeks after the operation. If, after all our efforts, the graft or some of it fails, we'd have to go back to split skin grafts from your legs – and the result would be much the same as you have today.'

'Hmmm – and third question, what will the chin feel like? Will I have full movement and feeling in it?'

'Oh yes, it will hopefully give you back a proper bottom lip and full movement – but you might not have that much feeling on the surface of the chin because the nerve ends may not grow.'

'But there won't be any long-term problems associated with the chin? It won't need constant attention or special treatment?'

'That's right, but of course you'll need to be careful not to cut it badly in the early days – and you know no shaving will be required!'

'Yes... OK, so this is a close judgement, isn't it? Not obvious or easy... But I think after many conversations with my parents, friends, my tutors and some of the staff here, I'm getting ready to say yes. How long can I have to make the decision?'

RECONSTRUCTING *IT*

'Good – you can have another month or even more if you want, but we need to be starting in September [1973]. We also need to do one or two other tests on you.'

'OK, meet again in a month. Unless I decide no!'

'No, even if you are thinking like that, I'd like to meet you – OK?'

A month later:

'I'm glad to say the tests were fine – you are not resistant to the drugs we'll need to use to manage the common infections and your haematology status is good. What's your thinking?'

'Well, it feels rather a big decision, because I know I could go with my chin as it is with a few much smaller ops to make it look a bit better. But those would not make the really big difference to my whole face, which the pedicle might – and the expressiveness in my face in social encounters should be considerably improved. I've been agonising but, on balance, I have decided to go ahead with the pedicle. My tutors have agreed that I can rejoin the course a year on. Which will be a bit weird but should be OK. So, what happens next?'

'Good – and we will do all we can to make it go well, I can assure you.'

I went into hospital in early September 1973 after a summer travelling and spent the next ten months in and out of it, bound to the clinical team by the umbilical cord that was my pedicle. It was a very long process, fraught with risk and pain. In stark terms this is what happened. They had to:

- Stage 1: raise a six-inch pedicle tube, like a suitcase handle, on the right shoulder bone, covering the donor site with skin grafts from my legs; ensure that the tube had an excellent blood supply over the next four weeks.
- Stage 2: lengthen the tube down my back by a further six inches with further background skin grafting, again ensuring an excellent blood supply.

This is what the pedicle looked like.

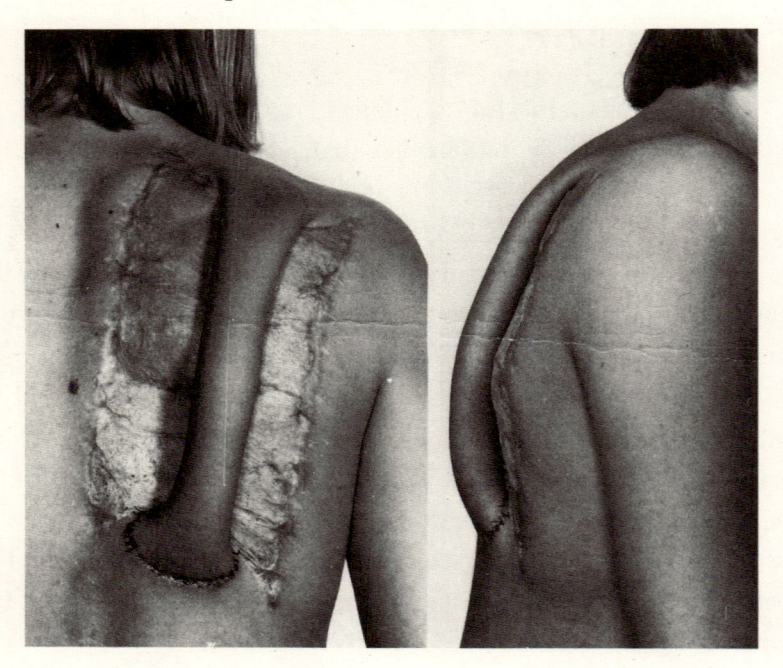

- Stage 3: after a month's delay, detach the lower end of the tube and move it over the right shoulder and attach it to my chest, again ensuring blood circulation was achieved – the first of the very risky manoeuvres.

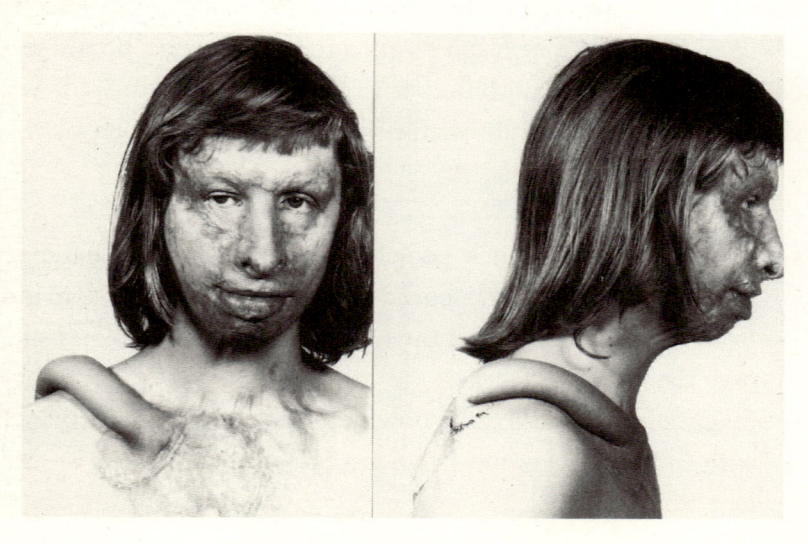

RECONSTRUCTING *IT*

- Stage 4: six weeks later, detach the top of the pedicle from the shoulder and attach it to my chin, close to the right ear – another very critical move as I now had a tube running parallel to my neck.

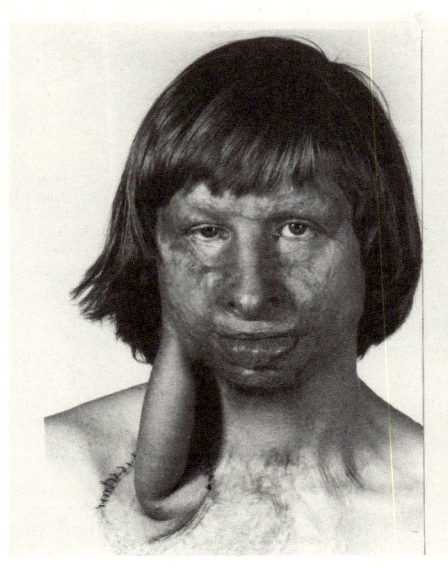

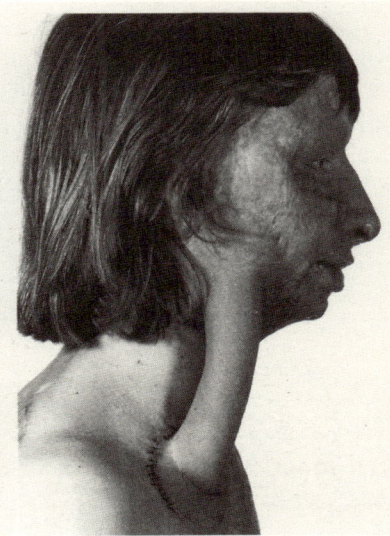

- Stage 5: detach the tube from my chest and attach it as far across my chin as possible – regaining the blood supply somehow.

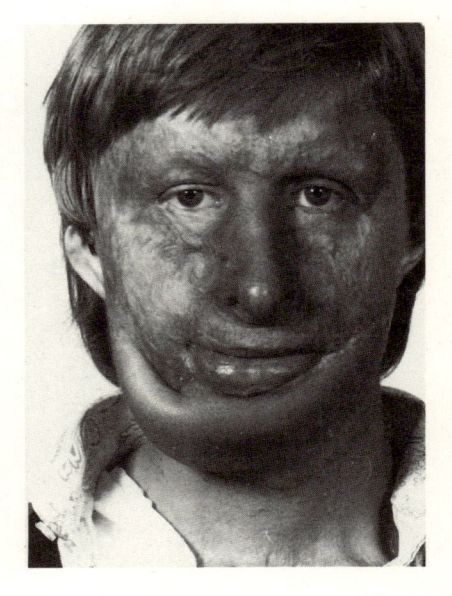

- Stage 6: spread the whole pedicle across the scarred chin, removing all scars in the process – and stand back and admire!

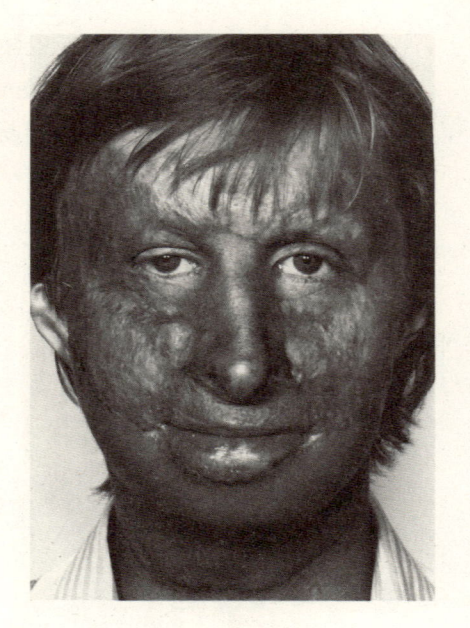

Ten months full of days of discomfort, many operations, dressing changes, meticulous nursing care and the final result was incredibly satisfying for everyone involved.

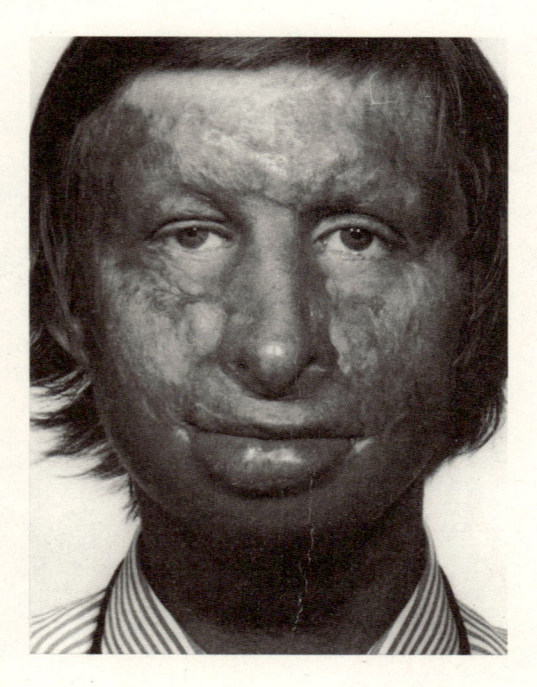

RECONSTRUCTING *IT*

In the process, I became an expert patient, completely informed about every nuance of my treatment and its complications, of which there were many along the way. The surgical, anaesthetic, nursing and paramedical staff became friends and allies.

At the end, my parents brought in some wine and we celebrated what had been a brilliant team effort. I treasure a green operating theatre cap I was given as a memento. It is used for our Scrabble pieces still!

And, crucially, I was pleased with the result. I now had a protruding bottom lip and a slightly chubby chin in place of scars. Amazingly, an area of skin and fatty tissue that had been on my back for my first twenty-one years of life had given *IT* a new look – it was far from perfect, but gone were the pulls and distortions that my previous constricted chin had caused. The surgery had been worth doing.

12.
BUILDING A NEW ME

That year out of Oxford (after my second year) to have surgery on my chin proved to be a watershed year in many ways – intellectually, spiritually and emotionally. Whilst the surgery carried with it pain and uncertainty and required serious endurance to stay the course, the year gave me a chance – which perhaps nobody appreciated at the time – to work further on building a new identity in a safe atmosphere. A new Me started to emerge.

The year away in hospital – not quite like an indulgent gap year! – from September 1973 onwards could have been an isolating year, but it wasn't. The timing was good because I had acquired by then a strong circle of friends – and they and my family were amazingly supportive throughout the ten long months of surgery. I was allowed out for brief episodes as a citizen, even managing with a cleverly designed backpack protecting the tube to sit and drive around.

But the key thing was that my university friends did not desert me – and in the days before emails and texts, that was a serious risk. Instead letters and cards kept coming. And they would come down to visit me in hospital with suitcases of books. We lounged on the hospital lawns with bottles of wine and lots of goodies to eat – such a strange experience for all of us, and I remain eternally grateful to them. They kept me sane.

INTELLECTUAL CHANGE

My entire pre-eighteen education had been dominated by maths and science subjects, and my reading was very limited as a result. Before *IT*, I was destined to be a geek.

Now in the long months of surgery, I read and read and read as I had never had the chance or inclination to do before. I worked my way voraciously through vast tracts of English literature and colossal Russian novels too. *The Brothers Karamazov* consumed me in its brilliance. And I read *Lord of the Rings* in two days.

I was particularly drawn to what is characterised as 'outsider' literature, and Colin Wilson's seminal overviews were really helpful in guiding me to the key tomes and how to interpret the different authors' perceptions.

Instinctively, I related to being an outsider. I loved Colin Wilson's first lines from *The Outsider*: 'At first sight, the Outsider is a social problem. He is the hole-in-corner man.' But if you read Camus' *L'Etranger*, Kafka's *The Trial* and Hesse's *Steppenwolf*, there is a sense that the outsider believes he is the only sane man in a sick society. The outsider is a strange, surreal character, often challenged by physical deprivation or incapacity, who feels left out and unaccepted by society and without any hope of changing that reality. Sometimes they find some kind of salvation – in T.E. Lawrence's case, through physical hardship and self-denial/discipline – but, for most, their pessimism is all-consuming.

IT had exposed me to stigma and exclusion, and so I knew what it felt like to be an outsider, alienated and unaccepted. But my search for an optimistic outcome was gaining momentum, and these outsider views gave me a curious uplift. Perhaps I was not as outside as all that.

Politically, too, I was changing. In place of the cast-iron certainties of the dominant British and male culture that I had grown up with, I was now experiencing the stark realities of burn care and the views of the staff and fellow patients. My assumptions about the world were all turned upside down. I was no longer one of the elite, guaranteed to succeed by virtue of birth and education. I had become a doubter and a questioner of much that I had previously held inviolable, albeit guiltily so.

It was a time of cultural change, of course. The early years of the 1970s were fascinating to live through and observe in an academic sense. Britain was being assailed by a mix of drug- and music-driven permissiveness, a breakdown of social deference, a massive quadrupling in the price of oil, for so long assumed to be cheap and unlimited, and a union-led defence of workers' rights in the face of spiralling inflation.

I revelled in these years, and I'm sure the freedom of thought and action (epitomised by my very long hair) helped me – and those around me – to accept *IT*. As a student, I could observe the political and economic maelstrom with detachment – and then engage in forthright arguments with my father, who was caught up in the reality of it.

I was also very lucky to be able to witness at close hand and engage in the emergence of new thinking on three absolute certainties of my first eighteen years: meat-eating, oil/energy and alternative technology. *IT* had opened me up to new perspectives on life.

One of my university teachers was Peter Singer, the moral philosopher who was (literally) cooking up his seminal book *Animal Liberation* in his North Oxford home – and as his young students, we were invited to come and sample his vegetarian recipes. I became a vegetarian for five years, and even a macrobiotic devotee for one of those years, in a student house that became famous for its home baking and fresh produce.

On energy, the Club of Rome's 1974 report on the limited resources of Planet Earth was a stark reminder of the profligacy of our Western lifestyles, and I started to look seriously at the way that food was produced. Western society was so wasteful – the affluent and effluent society. It seemed unacceptable to participate thoughtlessly. Back in Oxford, I took to cycling everywhere. And we got an allotment, cleared it of bracken and weeds, made it organically productive and revelled in its harvests.

Later on, organic farming started to attract me too, and a good friend from the old days invited me to help him on his family farm, which he was converting to organics. Exciting days with much reading about self-sufficiency and living frugally. All so different to my views in my first eighteen years.

E.F. Schumacher's *Small is Beautiful* was a delight and David Dickson's *Alternative Technology* threw wonderful new thinking into my brain that reinforced a sense of finding a new view of my world. I started to debate what the planet's future was going to look like – which had nothing to do with what *IT* looked like. I was being fired up by other things.

Dickson's 'alternative technology' (challenging the relentless search for economies of scale that epitomised modern economies by advocating what he called 'design for a small planet') and Schumacher's 'appropriate technology' (appropriate to the scale of the economy and the state of its development) seemed to me very significant new ideas, and I strongly disagreed with the gainsayers who tried to portray them as tantamount to arguing for economic stagnation.

My growing interest in these ideas drove me to work, after university ended in 1975, for a summer at the pioneering British National Centre for the Development of Alternative Technology (known as NCAT) in Machynlleth in mid-Wales, with its wind power experiments and early solar panels – both scoffed at by its detractors. NCAT still stands and thrives. And years later, this strand of my new outlook was the force behind a decision to try to create an organic farm business in Guernsey.

CHANGING NAMES

Throughout my school days, I'd acquired the nickname of Dick. Dick because of partridge, a 'dicky bird' as suggested in a school play and latched on to by a clown at my primary school. It stuck with me all through secondary schooling – and on admission to the burns unit I was Dick Partridge. All my hospital notes have it. And I went to university owning it too.

But Dick was not how my family knew me. To them, I was James.

During the year of surgery and away from Oxford, I spent much time in close family contact and began to use James more and more. Eventually, I climbed right into being James, a new character, leaving the old Dick behind with all his aspirations and foibles.

Years later, I read the classic account of the Dax case, about a US veteran of Vietnam, Don Cowart, who was so badly injured in an oil fire on his ranch in Texas – coincidentally in July 1973 – that he insisted that no attempt should be made to save his life. The case went all the way to the Supreme Court – and he lost. In the years that followed, he became a lawyer. And he changed his name to Dax.

Some of my close friends found my new name hard for a short while, and even today I occasionally meet old school and early university friends who still refer to me as Dick.

Changing my name was a smart move. In my mind's eye, even my own self-image shifted. In place of my image of Dick as that handsome, appealing young man with a successful business career and happy life ahead, I was now creating a picture in my mind of a James, a different man with very different values and aspirations, a man much less certain of his future but one with a degree (already) of determination to make something of it.

SPIRITUAL SEARCHING

Religion isn't everyone's cup of tea, but I'd been exposed to a low-church form of Anglicanism from a young age, so it was natural to me to ask religious questions – although *IT* had rendered me virtually faithless in the early days. But my first two years in Oxford saw me exploring many faith traditions – not just Christianity but

Buddhism, Hinduism, Sufism and even a new sect, Divine Light, led by a young Indian, Guru Maharaj Ji, one of the many gurus so popular in those days.

My bookshelves filled up with the *Bhagavad Gita*, Zoroastrian stories and tomes on Buddhist tea ceremony rituals. During all this spiritual questing, how to live in *IT* was always my focal point – selfishly, as I now realise. A few sketchy answers emerged, and closing my eyes (praying for help?) and stilling my mind were definitely healing. I adopted a slogan – 'Face Damaged, Mind Untouched' – from a rather obscure spiritual tome by Alan Watts called *Cloud-Hidden, Whereabouts Unknown*, which recommended a spiritual path.

But not all paths were productive. My dalliance with Divine Light led me to believe that I could literally forget *IT* by immersing myself in the Indian cult as a follower. I went all the way to Hardwar on the Ganges in search of this enlightenment, to the cult's premier ashram. I imagined that I would find my elusive breakthrough there but left just forty-eight hours later, bitterly disappointed. Asceticism was their way. I knew it wasn't for me.

Instead I found myself in a tea shop close to the bus station in this North Indian city so full of life, poverty, spiritualism and also lots of disfigurement and disability that nobody seemed to mention or even see, pouring my heart out to a total stranger, an old man with a friendly face and an aura of serenity. As I left him, unburdened, he gave me wise words: 'You have far to go, my friend, and much to learn...' – how prophetic. It would indeed take me years to reconcile myself with *IT*.

Probably the most telling advice I found was from the recently deceased and much lamented Ram Dass, one of Timothy Leary's friends, who went to India to become a yogi and would then write a seminal book, *Remember, Be Here Now*.

Be Here Now seemed so apt because it instructed me to leave the past and all my old hopes behind and to try not to second-guess the future. Instead, I should focus on living in the present, seeing

BUILDING A NEW ME

the love of my family and friends and all the opportunities around me. And that was important because it helped me to see the beauty and even the little daily blessings happening to me.

Years later, one of my first allies in Changing Faces, Kathy Lacy, a woman who had battled with neurofibromatosis all her life, told me how she had always secretly treasured a short set of phrases from her childhood: 'The clock is running. Make the most of today. Yesterday is history. Tomorrow is a mystery. Today is a gift. That's why we call it the present.'

Be Here Now also fitted in with another big message that came from my accident: that having got so close to losing my life, I had been given another chance – and I needed to use it to the absolute maximum. Which was best expressed, it seemed to me, in the lines from Kipling's 'If—': 'If you can fill the unforgiving minute/ With sixty seconds worth of distance run,/ Yours is the earth and everything that's in it.'

Crucially, I was supported in all my searching for meaning and hope by my rather bemused family. My parents were both Christian people, my mother strongly so, my father much more unsure. And my half-brother David was a parish priest – 'a great pastor', people called him, because of his wonderful support for people in need. He placed absolutely nothing in my way in my searching – instead he joined me 'on the road', as he would describe it. He encouraged me and I passed on to him my fascination with Hermann Hesse especially. Hesse's books, like *Steppenwolf, Siddhartha, Narcissus and Goldmund* and *The Glass Bead Game*, were all incredibly important to me because they all in their different ways, explored how people searched for authenticity, self-knowledge and spirituality. David read them, too, and we discussed them avidly. And that mattered greatly.

In 1974, he and I also drove in my little Mini to the French community of Taizé with Bob Dylan's 'Blowin' in the Wind' and many other tracks enlightening our journey through the car's less-than-brilliant speakers. That year was Taizé's Festival of Youth, a huge international celebration of peace and love but without any hippie trappings. The high points (and I mean spiritually high) were sitting in the beautiful monastery for evening prayers and hearing the monks chanting out the office.

None of these searchings resulted in a very definite sense of what my belief, if I had one, was or consisted of, but what they did was give me space to explore, meditate and, above all, listen to others in their seeking. Like David, I became convinced that an ecumenical plurality of faiths was healthy – all had answers of a kind, and it depended what triggered hope, healing and community-giving in each individual.

CARRY ON OPERATING?

Back at university in the autumn of 1974, I arranged to have a further planning discussion with my consultant just before Christmas. He was pleased with his handiwork. My whole face had been released by the successful pedicle transfer. I now had a chin as smooth as a baby's bottom and that had helped skin grafts in other areas, especially around my eyes, to 'settle down', as he put it – shorthand for 'soften and bed into place'.

But *IT* was still not perfect.

'So what's next?' It was he who asked the question, not me. I let him go on. 'We could now turn our attention to your mouth, the cheeks, more on the eyes…' He tailed off, as if he could sense I was distracted.

'Yes,' I said, 'we could go on… But I think the time has now come, thanks in large part to your team's brilliant work, which has taken away the shock factor in my face, for me to try to become a citizen again, and no longer a patient.'

It came out fluently because I had been preparing and practising that sentence for weeks and months. I saw him take a deep breath and exhale slowly as he realised what I was saying. He didn't flinch.

'OK, that's fine. I could explain what we could do, if that would be useful.'

BUILDING A NEW ME

'No, I think I have a very good idea of what you could do. And I know it would be superb. Thank you.'

'OK, that's fine. If ever you want to have more done, you know where to find us. And if you discover how to be a citizen, do write it down, because we surgeons can't do that.'

He smiled a big smile, a rarity, and came out from behind his desk, still the 'big white chief' but now an emotional human being whom I hugely respected. He shook my hand warmly and wished me well. I said that I was immensely grateful for what he and his fellow surgeons had done and promised to stay in touch.

And that brought to a close my relationship with plastic surgery, which had lasted almost exactly four years. It had started not by my choice, but I had ended it. It felt the right thing to do – and I have never been back for more surgery.

I am often asked how on earth I could have reached the conclusion that I would not have more surgery. Over the years since, I have met a few people who have urged me strongly to have 'more done'. I haven't ever done so, but that in no way diminishes my unwavering and very high respect for what plastic, reconstructive surgeons can do.

I haven't done so because I had started to discover in those four years, and it was confirmed in the next few, that I could indeed learn to live confidently. Not easily, because I was still vulnerable to stigma, low expectations and exclusion. But if and as long as I learned, practised and persisted, I found I could break free of the chains of my conditioning and society's prejudices that trapped me. And even come to like my face, no longer *IT*.

One other unexpected consequence of the surgery was that my face became very youthful – and so it has remained! Yes, even forty-five years on! Not a wrinkle in sight… and there never will be, because my face is still very tight. So I look much younger than my sixty-seven years!

LIPS AND LOVE

Even before I could look at *IT* in that mirror, such as on January 1971, when the picture on page 89 was taken, I knew at a deep-down-inside level that my intimate life was never going to be the same again. My visitors did not come up and kiss me; they just came in and sat down awkwardly – and probably tried not to look. I detected that very early on. My hands were all bandaged, so touching was out too. I lay virtually naked. Very lonely indeed. People shuddered.

My lips were not very experienced at kissing anyway, but I craved it. A lovely girl I'd met in Spain the previous summer and rather treasured lived near the hospital I was taken to in London. She came to see me once and then wrote a letter. I could not read it because my eyes were so sore, so my mother did – out loud. The letter said she was going travelling on her gap year and wished me well… It was expected. I groaned inside. My mother moved on to another letter without comment.

Many letters and cards came in the early weeks after my accident. They were my lifeline to the outside world. I've still got them all, treasured for their words of empathy and encouragement. Do please send cards to anyone in hospital. The act of sending will mean something special even if you write, hesitatingly, only a few lines.

Intimate human contact was made even more remote because, to avoid me catching any infection, everyone who came into my room – whether visitors, nurses, doctors, cleaners or anyone else – had to wear a face mask. So my communication with them was severely impeded – or so I thought. Not being able to see their facial gestures was tiresome, but I accepted it as necessary; I'd already seen how infections could delay healing and make me feel very ill very quickly with a high temperature.

I could not tell what any nurse's or doctor's face looked like and could only see their eyes and forehead and listen to their voice. But there was a delicious irony in what I experienced.

BUILDING A NEW ME

I lay there with *IT*, communicating with people with no visible faces about my likes and dislikes – simple ones: NO to beetroot, YES to pink blancmange, NO to more Complan (a body-building drink that surely cannot still be on the market, so revolting did it taste, but I discover it still is!), NOT THAT NURSE to remove dressings (please!)…

But I was also able to communicate much more complex feelings. 'Please come back and talk to me more' was one I recall strongly about a masked-up and therefore faceless student nurse. I could see her humour and feel the gentleness in her touch. And I loved it. She knew I could and did too. We flirted outrageously whenever she could get time to see me or do my dressings (very slowly, please)… she from behind her mask, me with *IT* but really with my eyes, my laughter and my words. And then she was transferred to another ward. Gone. Agony. I think I only saw her face once!

That such a thing could still happen, though, was a tiny positive. But it seemed very, very remote. And I was so young, and had little idea how these things happened.

And then another woman was brought into the burns ward a few weeks later who attracted my attention in a way that I would never have imagined possible.

H was a young pretty American woman who'd come to London for a Christmas break from Los Angeles and had been horribly injured when a gas fire caught her nightdress. She was in the intensive care ward and I didn't meet her for weeks, but just heard little snippets of news. She was severely ill, but gradually she stabilised and the massive skin grafting effort to cover the 50+ per cent of her body that was burned began.

When I was eventually allowed to meet her, I discovered that her face had been largely untouched, but not so her neck, chest, back or upper legs. We compared notes and I felt an instant warmth, a compassion towards her, our shared experiences pulling us together. I went in to see her every day and started to feel strong emotions for her…

Which were, of course, absurd. She was a mid-twenties divorcee and had a daughter. She was going back to the States as soon as she could travel. I was going to Oxford. My lips and *IT* were hardly attractive, but I knew inside that my unspoken feelings were shared. I think I completely missed the deeper point until much later – that I had fallen for a woman whose looks were very far from perfect, and so it might just happen to me, too.

Two years later, I visited her in Los Angeles after we had exchanged a string of letters. I was travelling with a friend around the States on the Greyhound and by good chance (or so I thought), the company lost our luggage between San Francisco and LA – so we were 'forced' to spend over a week at her parents' house. Which could have been delightful but was actually agonisingly painful, as we failed to find any intimate moments together.

It became quickly apparent that, despite our written words, our love was just for a few moments in a hospital thousands of miles away. I travelled back to the UK deeply hurt but did not show anything to my friend. My lips were sealed, top lip stiff beyond belief.

There was one other woman in those days who brought me hope. She was the girlfriend of a school friend, lived near the hospital and was training as a nurse, and I was amazed that she made visits to me two or three times a week. She was petite and vivacious, and I loved to laugh with her. I was head over heels for her but I knew I did not have a chance. But the intimacy that she allowed me was so warming to my cold and fearful innards.

I had a few relationships in Oxford but they were not long-lasting, much as I might have wanted them to be. One broke up because I sensed she was mothering me, another because I wanted more commitment than it was fair to ask for, I suppose. And in London, too, another unsatisfactory fling had left me wondering if ever…

GETTING WORK

Getting a job with my face was always going to be a major challenge, and I'd ducked it for years – every vacation during university I was sucked back into hospital for another operation or two. My only 'jobs' were voluntary and didn't count for anything, and I knew it. It was an unspoken horror still to be faced. And the fact that I could live at home and be supported financially was a massive advantage. I procrastinated.

My final year at Oxford, from October 1974, was, somewhat surprisingly after my very lazy second-year performance, a hard-working one because I had returned after my year away to get my chin reconstructed in a much more determined frame of mind. I lived in a house where macrobiotic cooking, yoga, bread-baking and a disciplined approach to doing eight solid hours of academic work every day became the norm. I really wanted a good degree, and now had the right mindset to get one.

But what was completely off my mental radar was how I was going to answer the question: 'What are you going to do next?' My pre-accident aspirations – assumptions – did not seem at all relevant. I now gave accountancy not a moment's thought; it was just not for me.

But there were no alternatives – and no career guidance on offer. My parents tried in vain to get me to focus but, of course, what we all knew I was running from was the rejection that I was liable to face. Eventually, after much pressure, I agreed to see someone in the academic world about doing more studying. More procrastination.

But this was actually a blessing in disguise because, with hindsight, one of the very best decisions I made was to try to get a Master's degree after university. My first degree was in politics, philosophy and economics; I majored in the first and last and got a good 2.1 – and that felt good. It was enough to get me a place on a taught MSc in medical demography at the London School of Hygiene and Tropical Medicine.

It was such a stimulating course too – epidemiology, statistics, demographic modelling, third-world health, human fertility and mortality studies, the history of the demographic transition in Britain, the role of population growth in perpetuating poverty and much more. I realised that I could combine my interests in economics and health studies with the new emerging discipline of health economics. And in the era before computers (BC) and the web, I found out that a new Health Economists Study Group (HESG) was meeting, and joined up.

I determined that I had to get a job in health economics. Not easy because there were very few jobs around, it being still in its infancy. But then I spotted an advert in the *Times Educational Supplement* for a research assistant in health economics at St Thomas' Hospital's Community Medicine Department in the University of London. I filled in the form and waited nervously. To my surprise, I was invited to an interview.

It was June 1976, with Britain in the throes of an economic crisis and history being made as the IMF was called in to bail the country out. But just across the Thames from the Houses of Parliament, my own tiny bit of history was being made. I arrived at the august wood-panelled halls and offices of St Thomas' with my heart beating so strongly it was bulging out of my ill-fitting suit. I waited nervously as two other candidates were shown in and emerged confidently half an hour later. And then I heard, 'Do come in, Mr Partridge.'

I was asked to sit in front of a long desk with five people behind it. I had no time before I sat down to say hello to each. And then the man in charge, a senior academic, ran off their names incomprehensively, so I was none the wiser except that they all seemed terribly impressive. The questions started with technical ones about economics, which I think I handled well enough, then a few about the NHS, which did not seem difficult either, and then the gargantuan out-of-the-blue stinger: 'I see you've had quite a lot of plastic surgery, Mr Partridge; do you think you'll be needing some more?'

BUILDING A NEW ME

I was completely thrown by such a very personal question; I am sure the other candidates would not have been asked anything similar. I could feel my hackles rising, but realised this was no time for assertiveness. Rather, I had to keep calm, and so explained in a few sentences that I had not had any surgery for two years and that my surgeon saw no need to do more – unless I wanted or needed it. That felt like a good answer. But like an idiot, I didn't stop there. Unable to control myself, I threw the question back to the rather austere academic who'd asked it: 'Do you think I need some more?'

It was a mistake, I knew, as soon as the words had left my lips – and I could see the whole panel blanch, if not recoil. She tried her best to put a brave face on her answer and I could sense that everyone wanted to end the interview as soon as possible. I certainly did!

'Thank you very much for coming, Mr Partridge. We'll be in touch.' No chance. Blown it.

Imagine my surprise two days later when I got back to my flat, after a day in the library working on my 20,000-word thesis, to find a letter offering me the job. It was like manna from heaven because I could now spend the summer writing the thesis and prepare for proper work in the autumn. Best of all, I had done it without grovelling. My rather acerbic reaction to the question in the interview had not counted against me. Perhaps it had even marked me out.

And so it proved because, when I joined the team at St Thomas', that interview team stood with me – and the doctor who had asked the stinging question became a firm ally.

Ironically, too, I started that job when facial burns were much in the news because Niki Lauda, the F1 driver, had been severely injured in a race three weeks after I was offered the job – as I described in a blog post when *Rush*, the film of that crash and its aftermath, came out. Here's a bit of that post:

1st August 1976. A date to remember. Niki Lauda crashes – the world stops.

It stopped me in my tracks, too, and forced me to think back. I had handed in my MSc thesis the day before after much toil and was set on a month's holiday before starting a first highly unexpected job. Instead, it was four tough weeks reliving my accident and its aftermath through the news of Niki Lauda.

I sat with my parents that evening and we went back over the night when I had been in a car fire too – not going at anything like the speed of Niki Lauda, but, like him, failing to get around a corner.

Would Lauda pull through? Surely his motor-racing days would be over? Would his meaningful life be over with a ruined face? I desperately hoped not, because he could become a new international role model who would tell the world that facial burns and disfigurement do not spell the end of meaningful life.

Over the next month I watched with increasing admiration as Niki fought a very public battle to get himself healed and fit enough to compete again – and I loved the reports that he was doing so against his doctors' orders!

And I also shared in what must have been his immense frustration that he had to withdraw from the crucial Japanese Grand Prix because of the pouring rain. His badly burned eyes and lost tear ducts prevented him getting enough clear vision. I knew what he was going through – my eyesight had been damaged in exactly the same way.

But it did not matter that he didn't win the Championship that year. He had proved beyond all doubt to a massive worldwide audience that, if you survive, facial burns are not a barrier to living life to the full. I rejoiced! He gave me a tiny inkling that I, too, could make something of my life.

I was often asked in those days – and have been many times since – about the horrendous pain that Niki (and I) must

BUILDING A NEW ME

have gone through. How on earth did we bear it? What my five years of pain and surgery taught me was that resilience was not innate. It had to be learned. The pain that flattened me in the first days and weeks after my accident became something that I soon discovered I had to mentally stand up to, not because it felt 'good' to do so but because the alternative was to be avoided. I would be consigned to deep sedation and powerlessness – which I hated.

I became what I can only describe as bloodyminded. 'Focused', as the modern idiom has it! Which doesn't mean that I did not flinch at the pain of the wounds, the operations and the dressing changes. But I told myself to bloody well hold fast. And the more I did so, the stronger I felt.

Niki Lauda epitomised bloodymindedness. I met him fifteen years ago and he still did.[1]

Back to 1976. The job was a great opportunity, which I grabbed with both hands. But the project on which I was employed sadly fell apart and I had to find another job – again with success in the first interview.

I went on to work in the Unit for the Study of Health Policy at Guy's Hospital, founded by the inspirational Dr Peter Draper, a modern-day public health doctor, which argued strongly for the NHS to become a health, not an illness, service.

It was an extraordinarily stimulating atmosphere in which to work – although our funding was always shaky and dependent on Peter's charm and connections. My chief project was to work on 'The NHS in the next 30 years: A new perspective on the health of the British',[2] which we published in mid-1978 to mark the first thirty years of the National Health Service. It set a radical agenda, some of which is still highly relevant today – like taxing sugar content in sweets and drinks, putting health warnings on tobacco products, chlorine in water and controls on fatty food advertising.

DISCOVERING FEMINISM

One of the most unexpected influences on me in those years, 1976–78, years of rising self-confidence and self-acceptance, was to come from finding accommodation in a house in Highgate, close to the famous cemetery where Karl Marx is buried.

My landlords were a Marxist couple, the Versluysens, who introduced me to some very indigestible political treatises by the likes of Heidegger and Gramsci – which I can now confess not to have read in full!

But Margaret Versluysen engaged my interest in something far too unfamiliar, feminism, a movement that my sister was starting to espouse strongly. I needed to understand and know more.

And, quite unexpectedly, this was perhaps the final piece of the jigsaw in my finding new hope and meaning – and accepting *IT*.

Through conversations with Margaret, who was doing a PhD on the roles of women in health care under Ann Cartwright, and by reading seminal books by the likes of Kate Millett (*Sexual Politics*), Germaine Greer (*The Female Eunuch*) and Virginia Woolf (*A Room of One's Own*), I started to liken my struggle with *IT* to that of women in their struggle with a male-dominated world. It dawned on me as never before that my deep-seated conditioning about the dominance of 'good looks' and the power that was wielded against those of us who were deemed inferior had me trapped, chained by my own beliefs.

That led me to start reading Doris Lessing… and what a find she was! And so it was that in August 1977, with Doris Lessing's huge tome, *The Golden Notebook*, in my bag on Margaret Versluysen's recommendation, this happened:

TAKING THE RISK

I set off in my little Mini for Pembrokeshire to spend ten days with my brother David and his two young sons, for whom camping on the cliffs was to be a wonderful escapade – as it was for us all, with superb sunsets, long walks, camp fires, rolling surf and wonderful sandy beaches and, for me, *The Golden Notebook*.

The book tells the story of writer Anna Wulf through four different notebooks in which she records elements of her life. It was the blue notebook in this amazing novel that really got to me – this was Anna's personal journal, where she records her memories, dreams and emotional life. The other three notebooks engaged me too: the black one, where she tries to make sense of her South African past; the yellow, about the ending of her long-standing love affair (not very relevant to me but nonetheless an eye-opener) and the red, about her political journey (I could see parallels in my journey 'leftwards'). But the blue one touched me to the core.

Why was the book so unputdownable? I am sure there were many other books that spoke such truths and radiated such honesty, but they had not come my way. I had read so many outsider novels and political liberation diatribes, but there were no emotional hooks for me in any of them.

The blue notebook of *The Golden Notebook* came at just the right moment – it allowed me to glimpse the inner emotional world of a woman who was trying to free herself from so much of her past, her lineage, her conditioning, her anger, her emotional numbness… and her terror at being hurt again by taking risks. But she came to realise that she could take risks again – and that it would be worth it.

Through her story, I began to see a future in which I might be able to reframe my relationships, risking the rejection that I felt would be inevitable – and had been so far. I just might be able to free myself from the astonishingly powerful chains – the tyranny – of my assumptions about *IT*: that its ugliness would always reduce me (and all like me) to a life in the shadows, third rate.

Even though my lovely friends reminded me powerfully (though rarely in words) that I was worthy of love, I did not really believe it… until I read the blue notebook charting Anna's emotional journey.

The dawning of her self-belief helped me to realise that the risks I saw as absolutely terrifying were not so – they were just small hurdles to get over. And like Anna, if I could take them, I would be liberated in a way that belied all my expectations.

So, on those Pembrokeshire cliffs, and later in a little café near Clifton Down station (only 400 yards from where as a schoolboy, I had learned the absolute reverse), I began to break free of the tyranny of the beauty trap and embrace – yes, embrace – me, face and all. I can feel the shivers down my spine as I write this, just as I did when I was reading the book.

Strangely – happily, ecstatically – I went from that café, having finished the book, to see an old friend, and within thirty minutes, was meeting a woman to whom I felt an instant attraction. Was this the moment (too soon?) to take a risk? I took it... forty-two years later, I'm still with her!

But this homage is not just to celebrate and thank Doris Lessing. It is more than that.

Because I truly believe that had I not found that book, I would not have done any of the things I have done over the past forty-two years. She gave me courage in a way that no political diatribe or self-help book could have done. The courage to take the risk, to break out of the chains that constricted me, to believe that not-perfect-face and all, I was worthy of love – and could give it fully, too.

13.

LOOKING BACK AND MOVING FORWARD

By that Christmas of 1977, seven years after my accident, I had left *IT* behind. I was now living fully in 'my face' with a woman I loved and in a good job. I had built a new strong resilient me. I now fully accepted my face and had incorporated it into a new identity.

Revisiting my reading of Goffman in November 1971, here was the crux for me:

> The central feature of a stigmatised individual's situation in life… is a question of what is often, if vaguely, called 'acceptance'. Those who have dealings with him fail to accord him the respect and regard which the un-contaminated aspects of his social identity have led them to anticipate extending, and have led him to anticipate receiving; he echoes this denial by finding that some of his attributes warrant it [respect and regard].[1]

What if I did not echo this lack of respect and regard for myself because of *IT*; might I be able to dissuade others from doing so?

I now had very high self-respect and I believe everyone I met could see it very clearly.

What if I could figure out a way to fully respect myself and accept *IT*; might I then be able to persuade others to do so too?

I was now able to transform others' thinking every single minute of every single day.

The stigma that others might impose on me had not changed, but *the stigma could not touch me.* Within seconds of meeting me, people realised they'd got it wrong! And that was because I had invented very proactive communication skills and a potent mental armour-plating to manage other people's reactions in hundreds of different settings.

I had developed my interests and talents and had become completely immersed in life. Wherever I went, I had zero self-consciousness. Living in my second face became second nature. I simply managed every social situation expertly as it came along. I had acquired, practised and perfected 'disfigurement life skills'.

In the terms of the cycle of learning, I went from being 'unconsciously incompetent' before my Face Day in March 1971 to 'consciously incompetent' for months in the aftermath, through to the autumn of 1971 when, after reading Goffman, I lived awkwardly with 'conscious competence' for years. But now I was the master of my face – and my fate. By the winter of 1977–78, I was unconsciously and unself-consciously living life to the full. I was whole – not whole 'again', but in a new way.

The changes brought about by surgeons had made *IT* far less shocking to behold, but my face still attracted stigma. Yet by 1977, surprisingly, I had come to accept and like my face's features – scars, skin grafts, asymmetry and all. And I mean like it aesthetically. It was no longer alien or odd. I owned my face physically. Despite its tightness, my face fitted; it fitted the new 'me', even if it was not in line with prevailing perfect-face norms.

To sum up this aesthetic and physical ownership, I often say with deliberate irony that 'I'm very attached to my face,' stroking my chin as I do so. I love saying it and I mean it in a gentle, non-arrogant way to challenge people's assumptions: *How is it possible for a man with a face like that to have children? Have a job? Appear to have such high self-esteem... etc., etc...?*

My very first reading of Goffman's *Stigma: Notes on the Management of Spoiled Identity* in November 1971 undoubtedly gave me valuable eye-opening insights about my plight as one of 'the stigmatised'. The question for me as an individual was could I – would I – ever get to the point where I was not just managing my 'spoiled identity', but no longer saw it as spoiled? The answer was that I could – and had.

Goffman was right, I had had to set out on a new moral career. And I had to do it without any career guidance or counselling, without any route maps or guides or even many fellow travellers. I feared my life and career would be a third-rate existence on the margins, that I would be labelled forever as a stigmatised person because of *IT*.

Those seven years, 1970–77, were ones of trial and error as I wrestled to find a purpose and a way of life. Far too much trial and too many errors. And they were years of diminished and confused ambition, too, because all that I had previously hoped for seemed unachievable and irrelevant. Acquiring *IT* had changed me, and my identity *was* spoiled.

There were many highs and lows along the way, but somehow I found my new mojo, as a good friend described it.

In retrospect, here are the ten key 'transformations' that I made:

1. Discovering that concealing my face, although it allowed me some anonymity, did not gain me the acceptance I craved.
2. Becoming proactive in my approach and my communication skills in every single social encounter... a massive effort at the beginning but with huge dividends later.
3. Building on my talents and capabilities to the utmost yielded the best results possible, because I was then judged on them and not by people's views of my face.

4. Finding one or two people with a face like mine who could inspire me meaningfully (not superficially) was a big bonus, probably a prerequisite.
5. Reigniting the tiny ember of hope inside me took years, but the critical thing was never letting it die, despite my despair.
6. Finding out about reconstructive surgery options and taking a calculated risk to improve my facial appearance – but realising that there was no magic bullet.
7. Creating and purposefully cultivating an intellectual and philosophical identity that was congruent with my face and the insights I was gaining through it.
8. Taking the plunge into the job market well prepared to show my ability in answering technical questions and unafraid to be firm if asked personal ones.
9. Not allowing myself to get too depressed by failed relationships and eventually opening myself to love and loving.
10. Dealing with my loss not by denying it but by confronting it and revisiting 'the corner' – definitely critical in enabling me not to heap all the blame for the accident on myself.

I could not have got to this point without the help of hundreds of people far too numerous to name, but I particularly thank my close family and friends. Some are named in this book, but there were lots of people I met only once who had a profound and lasting impact on my journey.

MEZZANINE

Living full-on – and finding my voice

The woman I met that night in 1977 was Caroline Schofield, from Guernsey. She is a very remarkable person, has an exceptionally testing past and a zest for life that I loved the very minute I met her. She came into my life like a hurricane, blowing away so much doubt and giving me a level of reinforcement that was irresistible. She was to make my future – in fact, we created our own future in ways neither of us could possibly have imagined. We bonded over the washing-up, after a party at the house of a mutual friend, and many years on are still doing that, using our combined resources carefully, focusing on what has to be done, devoted to our children and their children.

We married in 1978 and, against everyone's expectations, moved to Guernsey the next year, leaving behind my job in health economics and hers in publishing. Instead, in the era of John Seymour's self-sufficiency and *The Good Life*, we bought a derelict farm and aimed to live life with ecological values uppermost. I was proudly (but hopefully not arrogantly) demonstrating that it is perfectly possible to live a very useful life as a fully active citizen with a less-than-perfect face.

That might have been the end of my story, but it wasn't. Here's what happened...

We arrived in Guernsey to start the new chapter two days after Mrs Thatcher was elected prime minister in May 1979, and I threw myself into farming and integrating myself into the island. I was just twenty-seven years old and had energy in abundance. I gave my face hardly a thought because I was loving life so much. There were very occasional moments of doubt when I felt exposed or was in the presence of people who didn't know how to cope with my face, but they were few and far between and I cruised through them totally unfazed.

And so it was for years. Our children arrived in amongst all the busyness of our lives — Simon in June 1981, Charlotte in November the following year and Harriet just as silage-making was starting in May 1986. We adapted and changed as they grew up – and they had to take whatever the 24/7 life we were living threw at them.

There were many crazy moments – piglets running amok during one of their christenings, or heifers getting out on the beach in the middle of the night – but we grew in strength and resilience to cope. Friends from our London days who came to stay marvelled at the non-stop pace, and it was relentless and constantly demanding financially.

Guernsey was a very different community then to what it is now. Dairy farming was still a business that could be done on a small scale – there were over fifty farmers then, compared to just sixteen today. We started growing organic vegetables but soon realised we were ahead of the game; there was no premium price for such crops in the island's markets. So, from one house cow, Fleur, a lovely old girl (an eleven-year-old, which is rare today) which Carrie bought at an auction and hand-milked twice a day, we grew a herd of Guernsey cows.

Over the next ten years, by buying a motley herd from Sark and heifers from other farms across the island, we gradually expanded our herd to about seventy head, invested in new buildings and a milking parlour, embraced modern methods and, with the aid of a great young stockman, our business started to become viable. Slowly.

But it was not enough to earn us a living. Then, out of the blue, in 1985, I saw an advert for a part-time A level economics teacher at the local girls' school. I got the job after an interview with the headmistress and the head of history, during which I needed to use all my

*Summer 1991, with our herd of
Guernsey cows and Petunia, our lovely pig.*

social interaction skills to the maximum. They understandably had to be convinced that I could do the job. I wasn't at all sure myself. I explained my face without prompting.

It turned out to be the ideal job because I could fit it into my farming schedule – I'd milk the cows early, shower and be in school for the first economics lesson by 8.30 a.m.... and then back for lunch. But it wasn't just that it worked logistically. I loved the classroom and my students seemed to thrive too. I suspect I was somewhat unconventional – I may have smelled of cattle occasionally and even turned up by tractor on snowy winter days – but I knew my economics and found innovative ways of passing it on.

There were many newsworthy and important economic events through those years, of course – like the hurricane that swept through Britain one Thursday in mid-October 1987 (we lost thirteen huge trees that night, but remarkably no cows were injured across the whole island), which was followed immediately by Black Monday, when stock markets around the world collapsed 20–45 per cent in the space of a few days. What juicy topics for A level economics students!

And it was during one of these forays into the real world and away from the textbook that I accidentally found something which would propel me out of my absorption in my students' and my family's affairs. During the spring of 1988, I was preparing my final-year students for their A level exams and casting around for ways to illustrate how price indexes can be used to correct money income for the effects of inflation – creating so-called 'real income' tables.

The dairy industry in Guernsey had recently been the subject of an external consultant's report to inform the States of Guernsey about how its future well-being could be best promoted – and how the price of milk should be determined, it being in the hands of politicians, because there was a monopoly of supply on the island and no milk imports.

What a perfect source of price inflation figures! I got hold of a copy and late one Sunday evening set about preparing the next week's work for the girls. Much to my amazement, I came across some heinous errors in the ways in which the price indexes had been used, errors which, to my mind, completely undermined the consultants' conclusions. They had used the milk price index rather than the Retail Price Index (RPI) to correct farmers' money income for inflation. Which meant that, according to their calculations, farmers' real incomes had gone up steadily over the previous five years; actually, when correctly calculated, they had deteriorated badly.

What to do? Obviously, get my numbers checked… and who better to do that than twelve eager young brains? The next morning, without declaring my suspicions, I asked them to do the calculations. They reached exactly the same numbers as I had.

That afternoon, I called up the president of the Guernsey Farmers' Association, Peter Hocart, and we spent several hours in his kitchen explaining my findings and discussing what to do next.

What followed were transformational weeks in my life: suddenly, I was a voice with a distinctive, not-easily-forgotten face and was engaging on a bigger platform, albeit a tiny local Guernsey one. My findings hit the local media, and, almost without knowing what was happening, I was drawn into representing people – dairy farmers – to fight for fairness and public recognition of their crucial role.

A year later, I joined the Agricultural and Milk Marketing Board as one of two non-States representatives. And from this came other opportunities and openings, such as being invited to join the States of Guernsey's Health Ethics Committee.

I became, almost overnight, someone who was respected for his intelligence, views and soundness of mind. It was a turning point – I discovered that I had a voice and, totally unexpectedly, could use my face to great advantage.

A local BBC Radio Guernsey presenter, Jim Delbridge, suggested that we might do some radio shows together. A slot called *Down on the Farm With Jim and James* was born – and what fun we had… We unearthed some superb stories. Two of my favourites were about the rescue of Alderney cows before the Occupation and how Sark farmers managed on their tiny island.

It was during one of those shows, too, that Jim came up with the epic line, 'You have a very good face for radio, James.' I groaned, but was secretly thrilled. I did have exactly that, but had hardly given *IT* a thought for years.

The only time I really concentrated on my face and its impact on my life was during the first week of each new school year, when I would give the girls I was taking on for A levels lots of time to quiz me. I was totally upfront about what had happened, and they were pretty direct with their questions, too! I am fairly sure my information-giving filtered around the school – all to the good.

I also had reason to think briefly and occasionally during those years about what impact my accident had had on me whenever Simon Weston (a burns survivor of the Falklands War in 1982) or *The Boy David Story* (David Lopez, filmed by Desmond Wilcox) were on the TV – or when there was news of a big fire, and there were several.

The Bradford City stadium fire in 1985, which killed fifty-six and injured 265, got under my skin significantly because the lead surgeon was David Sharpe, who'd learned his plastic surgery under Jim Evans' guidance and had therefore treated me. I called him to wish him and his team well, and his patients too. But that was it. Back to the fields.

Piper Alpha in July 1988 was another ghastly disaster, when 167 men died. I prayed for the fifty-nine survivors. But then back to haymaking. The King's Cross Underground fire in November 1987 was the same – thirty-one killed and over a hundred injured. I watched with horror and heard the cries of the survivors. But could do nothing.

And then in early 1988, I received a letter from a woman called Paddy Downie. I'd not heard from her since the early 1980s. Back then, ten years on from my accident and having chuckled hard over David Lodge's *Changing Places*, I'd cobbled together a synopsis for the book I wanted to write on the lessons I'd learned and titled it

LOOKING BACK AND MOVING FORWARD

Changing Faces. Through a good friend in publishing, we got it to Faber and Faber, who very nearly commissioned it.

But those were recessionary years in publishing and it didn't get the final vote. However, Paddy, an editor there, invited me to write a chapter in a textbook for physiotherapists which she was editing – *Cash's Textbook of General Medical and Surgical Conditions for Physiotherapists*.[1] I was pleased with the chapter and Paddy kindly referenced it strongly in her foreword. My first piece of writing, dated 1983. I got a small fee for it too, which paid for a new front door!

Now in January 1988, she wrote to me again asking me to update the chapter for the next edition of the textbook… and in handwriting at the end of her letter, she wrote: 'Perhaps after the King's Cross and other fires, your book might get a better reception. Would you like me to approach Penguin about it?'

It turned out that Paddy no longer worked for Faber and Faber and had some strong links with Penguin. Within a few weeks, I was presenting myself to the Penguin editorial team in London… and my life was to take another unexpected turn.

I negotiated a deal which would see me deliver a manuscript by March 1989 for a book to be published a year later… long lead-in times, but all very deliberate. I signed on the dotted line and we invested in our first computer – an Amstrad with a dot-matrix printer – and we enrolled in evening classes to learn how to use them!

So, out of the blue, I had the chance to write the guidebook I had craved and which my surgeon had asked me to write – how to be a confident citizen with a distinctive face.[2]

WRITING CHANGING FACES: THE CHALLENGE OF FACIAL DISFIGUREMENT

To be commissioned by Penguin to reflect on what I'd learned from my eighteen years with my disfigurement was a massive affirmation. But could I really transform a short synopsis into something meaningful?

Penguin had required not just a synopsis but a sample chapter, which I concocted somehow. They gave me some tough but supportive comments – and a year to complete the manuscript: deadline 31st March 1989. I set time aside to write, but months went by and nothing got written. Too many other things were happening that demanded my attention. Eventually, in July, I made a start by writing to about seventy friends to ask them for their reflections on what I should say. They were people whom I'd met at various stages after my accident – in hospital, at university, in work and as friends – and quite a few from before it; certainly not a representative sample. They gave me a crucial resource of memories and ideas which shaped my thinking.

But none referenced other relevant books on the subject. So I made a strenuous effort to scour bookshops and public libraries in Guernsey and, on a hasty trip, in London. And I didn't come up with many; some heroic stories of Battle of Britain pilots, which were good reads but not particularly relevant to today – although Richard Hillary's *The Last Enemy* struck many chords because of his obvious angst about his changed face. I related to him not just because of his English public-school background but because he clearly traded on his good looks before he lost them. His determination to return to flying had however, a slightly bitter ring to it, as Sebastian Faulks so sharply explored later in 1997 in *The Fatal Englishman*.

With so little material to draw on beyond my seventy friends' suggestions, I found myself writing in the dark when I eventually got started in September, and I adopted a pseudo-sociological objective mode using the impersonal pronoun, 'one', and trying to tease out the key experiences that I believed anyone with a disfigurement went through: 'One is likely to...'

By November, after months of struggling to find the motivation and time to write, I sent off about sixty pages to Pam Dix, my editor at Penguin. And waited for her response with trepidation.

When it came it was ruthless and very painful. Not by email but by letter, with the entire manuscript covered with critical red ink. It was a complete failure in her eyes. Not at all what they wanted. And I knew she was right. But I didn't have a clue how to do anything differently.

Just before Christmas, at her suggestion, I made a day trip to London to meet Pam and hear her suggestions face to face. She was kind, took me out to lunch just off High Street Kensington and was as constructive and supportive as she could be. But, as she said, I had to do the work. Only three months left. I went back to Guernsey hoping for enlightenment.

It came in a tragic way, because Pam's brother was killed in the Lockerbie plane crash. When I spoke to her a few days later, she said: 'I'm now looking for the sort of book that you are going to write.'

And I cannot thank her enough. It was from that simple statement that I found my voice. This was my 'note to self' to guide my pen (actually pencil):

> If disfigurement happens to *you* for any reason, here are some ideas that might help *you* deal with it, adapt to it, live fully with it... even come to embrace it. The journey of 'changing faces' is one that *you* and your family need to travel... learning to live life to the full with *your* unusual looks... and that applies just as much if *you* have been born with a congenital condition or a birthmark... and 'changing faces' is also a process that many people *you* meet need to go through, a process that *you* can encourage and facilitate.

These six introductory lines, using the personal pronoun 'you', gave me a great surge of writing creativity that I didn't think I had in me.

For three months, January to March 1989, I became totally absorbed, and even with three young children running around me, a farm business ticking over thanks to Andrew, our stockman, and my teaching and other responsibilities rumbling on, I wrote every evening – with black coffee, BBC Radio 3 and in pencil. Carrie would somehow find time in her days or nights to type my pages into our new computer, editing as she went along… quite heavily at times!

The pages flew out of me, and I managed three iterations of the whole manuscript in three months. Remarkably, I was able to stand back and be reflective at the same time as being specific, which is what Penguin were seeking. What emerged was a short, concise and cogent thesis. I was pleased with it.

I delivered the manuscript on time at the end of March 1989, went for a short holiday in Europe and came back to find Pam's very positive review – 'hardly anything to change'. A huge relief – all I had to do now was get on with life and wait for the book to appear.

I was exhausted but exhilarated by the writing. It wasn't so much cathartic as creative. Catharsis is what authors own up to when writing about a major life event – and certainly there was an element of that. My book had snippets of my story in it, but I'd written about it before. No, it was the creativity that so excited me, because as I sat and reflected on the twenty years since my accident, I really felt I had identified and explained the physical and psychosocial challenges as well as I could in the time available.

The key points? Essentially three – which I think are still valid today:

First, that the emotional impact of any face-affecting condition like burns, being born with a cleft lip and palate, a Bell's palsy or facial cancer treatment, is massive and is not given sufficient attention by clinicians. Over and above the well-recognised effects of the event or diagnosis itself, the psychological and social impact of revealing your

LOOKING BACK AND MOVING FORWARD

less-than-perfect face in today's looks-obsessed, face-perfect society can be devastating. From the moment of looking at my face for the first time onwards, I needed much more help than had been available or was still available as far as I could judge – and I suggested a role for psychologically trained professionals.

Second, that adjusting to looking 'different' required me to bolster my self-esteem and find new self-confidence – and I had to do this entirely by trial and error. I proposed steps to rebuilding self-worth and gave advice to help 'you', if you acquire a disfigurement from any cause, to deal with the common reactions you are likely to face: the SCARED Syndrome, as I coined it. That advice centred on being proactive in all social encounters, taking the initiative so as to quash any negativity in the first seconds of an engagement.

Third, that the prevailing stereotyping of people with disfigurements did nothing to help public attitudes to be anything other than uncertain and prejudicial. This had to change. However, this argument, although understood as vital by Penguin, was limited to one chapter because the book was meant to be a self-help guide. But I could at least observe that you had to avoid imposing those perceptions on yourself and grow a very thick skin to prevent them poisoning your life.

Eventually, in April 1990, the day came for the book to be published.

We managed to get away from the farm for a few days and friends arranged a couple of parties in London, and I did some publicity arranged by Penguin.

The greatest thrill was to walk unannounced into bookshops and see my book on the shelves – and yes, I probably went to five shops just to get the buzz!

People were very flattering about it, too. Little reviews appeared, the *Observer Magazine* did a feature on me and, back on the farm, I was interviewed for Channel TV in our garden with the cows in the background by a young reporter called Sarah Montague, now highly acclaimed at the BBC.

And I got some great letters via Penguin from people I'd never met, thanking me for the advice. Some said they wished they'd had the advice earlier. Clinicians wrote too, saying they'd be sure to make copies available for their patients.

I was pleased. I'd done what I wanted to do: pass on the lessons I'd learned about how to be a citizen, distinctive face and all.

Life could now get back to normal. Or so I thought.

PART 2

The Professional

14.

INVENTING CHANGING FACES

MEETING NICHOLA RUMSEY

A month on from the publication of *Changing Faces*, I was invited to go on Gloria Hunniford's BBC breakfast chat show. She was arranging to get a psychologist to review my book. I said OK a little nervously. Because Gloria had not done one of these programmes before, the first show would be a pilot and not broadcast, but it was almost certain to go ahead as a full-scale series in the *Kilroy* chat show slot at 9 a.m. in the morning.

So I arrived in the BBC studios in Shepherd's Bush after a complimentary night at a five-star hotel to be taken to the green room to meet 'the psychologist', a young woman called Dr Nichola Rumsey. How come she was doing this, I wondered? She introduced herself and reached into her bag – 'Have you seen this?' she said, revealing a large academic tome with the imposing title of *The Social Psychology of Facial Appearance* by Ray Bull and herself.[1] 'Never heard of it.'

She signed the copy for me. Thanks, I said... and offered to sign a copy of mine, which she had read. But inside, I could feel panic welling up immediately. Hold on, shouldn't I have read this? I flicked through it and saw that there were thirty-plus pages of references –

and I recognised absolutely none of them. What was meant to be an exciting interview was turning into a nightmare. We were called into the studio.

There is no evidence of that first interview, thank goodness. I recall being dumbstruck and awkward, terrified of what Nichola would say. Gloria asked gently about my experience and why I had written what I had – and what I'd learned. I said that the physical and surgical challenge posed by my severe burns had been dwarfed by the psychological and social challenge of facial disfigurement. And I explained how my adjustment, my 'changing faces', had required a complete rebuilding of my self-esteem and self-confidence – and that central to that transition had been my somehow figuring out how to proactively manage other people's reactions to me.

'What do you think, Dr Rumsey?'

I shivered as she started, but she did not even point out my very poor literature review. Quite the contrary; she was very complimentary and even concluded: 'We have reached very similar conclusions from totally different directions' – she from her PhD studies, me from personal experience and insights. AMAZING!

In particular, she said that she and a few other researchers in the field had started to identify the potential for what she called 'social skills training' in helping people with facial disfigurements of all kinds to cope successfully in today's appearance-oriented society, saying words to the effect of, 'Mr Partridge's book is very helpful in that regard, because the second half of it reads like a social interaction skills training manual.'

Afterwards, with me in a cold sweat, she warmly reiterated her kind words and started to reveal her research findings. Over the next few weeks and months, I devoured her PhD and many of the references in her book – and was amazed (and hugely reassured too) to find that she was right. By the time the 'live show' went ahead, I was prepared – and to judge from the tape of that show, Nichola could hardly get a word in!

INVENTING CHANGING FACES

That second interview also gave me a chance to quiz her more afterwards. She gave me articles to read and introduced me to the seminal work of Frances Cooke Macgregor, an American social anthropologist who had followed Korean War veterans back into society:

> In their attempts to go about their daily affairs, [people with facial disfigurements] are subjected to visual and verbal assaults, and a level of familiarity from strangers not otherwise dared: naked stares, startled reactions, 'double-takes', whispering, remarks, furtive looks, curiosity, personal questions, advice, manifestations of pity or aversion, laughter, ridicule and outright avoidance.[2]

This was such a concise summary… and as I read further, I realised that Macgregor had captured so much that I had experienced:

> For the majority of people their days involve face-to-face encounters which… involve certain rituals, behaviours, and rules of social conduct, that are both learned and patterned and which people normally observe automatically and without thinking. For example, in salutations or when addressing another, proper eye conduct (in our culture) requires looking at the face of the speaker with eye contact that is neither a fixed gaze nor fleeting. With strangers or new acquaintances there are rules about keeping one's distance, asking personal questions, and avoiding topics that might be embarrassing or inappropriate.
>
> It is during such encounters that those with deviant faces experience flagrant disregard for the rituals and rules governing social behaviour. Not all forms of behaviour experienced by the disfigured are as overt or blatantly intrusive as staring or asking personal questions. Nevertheless, they can be equally discomforting and stressful. These are the

subtle and complex 'small behaviours' that occur in everyday face-to-face interaction that seem to mean nothing but, as students of human behaviour such as Goffman [and others] have clearly demonstrated, do indeed mean something. In fact, they frequently provide more information than verbal exchange. These small behaviours are known as micro-levels of communication or the 'silent language' by which people unconsciously and sometimes consciously, send messages to one another without the use of words. Usually perceived on a subliminal level, they nevertheless have positive and negative effects on interaction.

Macgregor observed that some of the veterans coped better than others – and they were those who appeared to have – or had developed – more effective communication skills. Hence, she had posited that there might be a role for social interaction skills training for someone with a disfigurement. Nichola's PhD research took this further.

First, having interviewed a number of patients with facial disfigurements in a plastic surgeon's clinic, she tested their observation that they believed they were avoided by others. She had herself made up with a birthmark on one side of her face and proved categorically on the Circle Line of the London Underground that people did avoid sitting next to her on the birthmark side.

She achieved this finding by having an observer count the numbers of people sitting down next to her over the course of a long day. But during one of the few breaks, she ate a sandwich and read a newspaper – and later, the observer remarked that during that short period, the avoidance effect seemed to have gone away.

This was an absolutely key observation because it led her to consider whether the behaviour of someone with a disfigurement might influence others' behaviour. This was when she started to look at Macgregor's recommendation that social skills training could be helpful.

INVENTING CHANGING FACES

Nichola wanted to test the hypothesis that if a person with a facial disfigurement had effective social skills, they would receive a better reception than if they had low social skills.

Her seminal experiment – and the one that clinched the thesis in her mind – cleverly recreated a classic social psychology experiment[3] in which she played a market researcher in a shopping mall in four different scenarios: two in which she was made up with a facial disfigurement, and two with her usual face. In both circumstances she would also demonstrate either high or low social skills. Again, she had an observer watching how many people stopped to answer her questions and for how long, and how many passed by. And she could measure people's reaction to her by the number of questions they answered.

Much to her amazement, the best result was when she had a disfigurement.

	No disfigurement	With a disfigurement
High social skills	✔	✔ ✔
Low social skills	✘	✘ ✘

Shopping mall research — From Rumsey (1986–88)

She was *very* surprised by this result. But I wasn't. Not only did it demonstrate that, with high communication skills, a person with a facial disfigurement could achieve a better interaction – as she had hypothesised – but also, very unexpectedly, that the quality and length of those exchanges far exceeded those of someone with a 'normal appearance'.

The result was precisely what I had found out by trial and error. But nobody had told me how critical social skills development was. Once I started to evolve effective ways to communicate with others, I found exactly what her research had unearthed: that people were surprisingly willing to be with me – and my self-respect rose, as did my capacity to rebuff stigma.

It was as if I had released people I met from their anxiety and fear of saying the wrong thing or looking in the wrong place, saved them from embarrassment and, almost without knowing it, they warmed to me. Nichola's shopping mall experiment also proved that market research companies would be well advised to hire people with facial disfigurements and high social interaction skills. I loved the irony!

I asked her what further research she had done after she'd completed her PhD. Not much, she said. She finished her thesis – and passed – and, she feared, it was placed on the shelves of North East London Polytechnic to gather dust and be read by a few students at best. She'd got a bit of media coverage, which I'd missed because it was in the psychology press. And then she'd had to find work, and thought little more about the subject until the idea of combining her thesis with Ray Bull's was mooted, which came to fruition in 1988. For the last two years, she had been teaching psychology in Bristol to nursing students.

So no social interaction skills training programme had been developed, as she had recommended in the last chapters, as the next step? No, sadly no money for such a project. Disappointing.

'What,' she asked, 'are you going to do next?'

'I've got to get back to milk the cows.'

CREATING A CHARITY

Meeting Nichola Rumsey in April and May 1990 was a watershed. It was comforting, a relief, to know that the ideas in my book were not just ramblings from one man based on his experiences and a few people he'd met along the way.

But the meeting was more meaningful than that. I could not stop myself thinking that Nichola's academic and my personal recommendations needed to be translated into real services and campaigns. I felt it wasn't good enough to say that I hoped people would find my book to help them, or perhaps light upon her research on a dusty shelf.

That summer of 1990 Nichola introduced me to a small group of like-minded academics and clinicians who had formed an informal 'interest group' (later to become the Disfigurement Interest Group). I met them at an Oxford retreat and they confirmed that virtually nothing was going on to translate Nichola's research (or anyone else's, come to that) into new ways of helping. How frustrating.

I was feeling a profound urge, an obligation, to do something – which was starting to become very complicated, as my first priority was and *had* to be my family, the farm business and my teaching. I – we – had to earn our bread and butter every single day.

Then in the autumn, I got a call from a man I'd mentioned in my book, the first British Professor of Plastic Surgery, Gus McGrouther. He said he'd like to come and see me to talk about the Phoenix Appeal, which was aiming to fund that post in perpetuity at University College London (UCL), an appeal set up by another plastic surgeon, Michael Brough, after the King's Cross fire. Of course, he'd be welcome...

Within a week, Gus was sitting on my rough lawn with the cows behind, telling me about the ambitious plans recommended by a 'strategy consultant' (Buzzacott's). They suggested the Phoenix should become a national charity. Would I like to join it? We could construct a charity. Like a Phoenix, it would have two wings – one focused on pioneering biomedical scientific research and clinical change, the other on pioneering psychological, social and cultural research and change. His idea was that he would lead the first, me the second. Very exciting.

Over the next nine months, during which the first Gulf War erupted, I manipulated an already contorted life so that I could join the Phoenix's efforts. I got my first taste of charity work by travelling regularly into London and strategising with Michael and Gus on how their plan could be implemented and discovering for the first time how charity fundraising supposedly 'worked'.

But, for a variety of reasons, that Phoenix dream didn't pan out the way I'd hoped – and assumed – it would. Had I misunderstood the intentions of the founders? Was I misled? I have asked myself that many times. But it didn't work primarily because, I still believe, the host institution, UCL, did not wish to let the Phoenix develop two wings until it had raised the monies to endow a Chair in Plastic Surgery in perpetuity. As I gradually discovered this sad reality, I came to realise the stark implication for me. Rather than lead and develop new research and programmes, their idea was that I should become a fundraiser in the small existing Phoenix team alongside a new head of fundraising and an administrator. I liked the people, but this was not my cup of tea. Not what I'd expected at all.

By August 1991, I was utterly bereft. Very, very sad indeed. Not just for all the people who could have been helped and empowered by the Phoenix and for whom I was prepared to work very hard; mostly, I was bereft for me and my family, because we had by then taken a massive plunge into the future we'd hoped for. We'd sold our lovely herd of Guernseys in April. A disastrous decision.

It seemed I had no option but to fundraise for the Phoenix.

I was distraught. Farming life gone. Dream of building new disfigurement programmes totally shattered. I lived that August in a haze of disbelief. They were deeply unhappy days, especially for my wife, who had agreed that I should pursue this new direction. How could I have been so stupid?

It was during that month, August 1991, that I was invited to play tennis with a local friend and two friends of his, one of whom was from the UK. 'What do you do?' I asked.

'I photograph computers.'

'You do what? How come?'

His explanation was life-changing. He said he'd always loved and been fascinated by computers from the get-go, but had decided to study a second love, photography. He'd gone to college, got a good job, started his own business, which had thrived, but as the company grew, he needed to develop its USP (unique selling point). He put all his strengths in the mixer and out came 'photograph computers'! So simple.

I drove home after the tennis with my head buzzing with the germ of an idea: to set up a charity (not a business, because it felt right to make it not-for-profit) that would combine my USPs/strengths to achieve social goals. Personal experience, business skills, teaching experience, media nous and health studies... Within days, the germ was on paper and I was ready to try to find supporters. We could not afford to wait long to find them.

The idea was highly, crazily, ambitious. It was to invent a charity, to be called Changing Faces, that would innovate and promote new forms of psychosocial help for people with disfigurements and their families, and eventually seek to challenge public attitudes towards them. I believed that, working in partnership with people with disfigurements and condition-specific support groups, researchers, clinicians and many fellow travellers, it might just succeed.

The first step I specified for Changing Faces was to pioneer and provide a new package of psychosocial help – and its effectiveness would be evaluated objectively by an independent research project managed by Nichola Rumsey. If that first step proved possible, we would then start to advocate for the widespread adoption of the new help. And, eventually, I hoped we would try to start a movement to raise public awareness and challenge attitudes to people with disfigurements.

But 'nice idea, dream on' – I could hear the doubters in my ears. As my wife and I celebrated our wedding anniversary in early September, I knew that I had to convince her above all others that there would be a living for us in this crazy idea. Because it *was* crazy. My wife definitely thought it was. But she agreed we should have a go. Just. 'You have six months.'

Where to start? Money had to come first, the testing of the pioneering ideas a close second. I was already familiar enough with charity fundraising to know that start-ups had a chance of getting support from philanthropists and some charitable trusts whose remits allowed them to back potential new projects. So, without any compunction, I started applying. I had to assess whether this was a runner well before seeking Charity Commission registration.

In fact, I could have no scruples in asking anyone – and to do that, I produced a three-page summary of my aims and what monies I needed to make them a reality. It added up to a first-year budget of about £60,000, which included the aspiration for a properly funded research project costing £15,000. I scoured Luke FitzHerbert's *A Guide to the Major Trusts* from the Directory of Social Change[4] and made many bids – begging letters, some might call them, but for me, they were no different to making the case to my local bank manager for investment in our dairy farm business, now defunct. I came to know that trusty fundraising bible by heart. Luke was a great servant to start-ups. I met him years later and told him so.

The same was true of my approaches to wealthy people I knew – or knew of. And it was one of the latter who really sparked the whole project into life.

Greville Mitchell is a very well-respected local philanthropist in Guernsey – he'd put up the initial funding for the island's hospice. I didn't know him, but managed to get an introduction and met him in his garden one afternoon in early October 1991. I explained what I was thinking of doing and asked him if he would advise me on whether he thought it a viable and worthwhile idea. He agreed to review my 'business plan' (I shuddered at its three-page paucity) and said he would come back.

A few days later, I had just finished spreading slurry on a local field, fully clad in protective oilskins, and stopped at the end of our driveway to rescue the post from the mailbox. I climbed back into the tractor cab and opened one of the letters, the writing on which I didn't recognise. It was from Greville: 'Thank you for your book and your plan... I think it is a very good and exciting idea and needs doing... and here's £5,000 to get it going... and I'll go on supporting you if you do get it up and running.' Wow.

And so Greville became our very first donor – and was as good as his word. Every single year, he gave.

His donation was a huge fillip. I could write to other prospective donors and say, 'I have already received substantial support' – and £5,000 was a very large sum in those days (the equivalent today would be about £10,000). But it was not enough on its own.

PIONEERING WORKSHOPS AND FINDING SUPPORTERS

Greville's donation also allowed me to start working with Nichola on inventing social skills workshops. To do so, I spoke to many people, such as experts who ran courses for those who were very shy or who stammered, and for enabling senior business people to face the media. And I watched the videos from John Cleese and his company, Video Arts, which was developing ingenious courses for managers to prevent them behaving like Basil Fawlty.

But the most valuable advice I received came from a unique company called Jo Ouston & Co, a specialist career development company which Jo had set up in 1990. I went on several of her courses, and they were excellent, enlightening and reassuring. I witnessed how she and her trainers were able to transform the confidence of people from many backgrounds by instilling some new communication skills, and to develop presence and charisma in a way they had never imagined they could. Many of those who were on the courses I attended had their careers transformed.

And so it was that in early November 1991, I placed adverts in the *Nursing Times* and one or two other London publications for 'workshops' to be held at Regent's College in central London in early December. And people started to get in touch, wanting to know more.

I conceived the first workshops with Nichola Rumsey and one of Jo's trainers. Eight complete strangers enrolled, seven with facial disfigurements from different causes and one parent. It was exceedingly testing – experimental, of course – but, in the end, a great success. The workshop ran over two days, with the first day broadly about 'the problems', emotionally and socially, that all of us with unusual faces had to endure in our daily lives. The first afternoon then started to explore what could be done, and everyone was sent away to test out an idea and report back. The second day – and everyone came back for more – expanded into a social interaction skills training course.

On the strength of that workshop and two trial others run before the end of January 1991, I was able to arrange a 'launch meeting' at our lawyers' offices, bringing together people I hoped would support the new charity.

My bid-making was also paying off. Gradually, charitable trusts came on board, making pledges based on Changing Faces gaining charitable status. I was invited by Kathleen Duncan, the Director General of the TSB Foundations of England and Wales, well known for supporting innovative start-ups, to put in a major bid, which came good. And Nichola and I were invited to present our ideas for a proper objective evaluation of the workshops to Dr Michael Ashley-Miller, Director of the Nuffield Trust. And he too gained the support of his trustees. And then the King's Fund pledged support.

But – and this fact was horribly obvious as I approached people – Britain was in the grip of a deep economic recession. Was I mad? I tried to convince myself I wasn't.

INVENTING CHANGING FACES

There was one critical piece of the jigsaw missing: assembling a group of people willing to act as trustees. Much of my time in London during those months was spent lodging with my good old friend, Andrew Jarvis, then owner of a small publishing company, Two-Can – I think he was the first to agree to be a trustee, a little uncertainly, probably!

I knew I needed a range of voices and that none of them should be uninformed. A plastic surgeon seemed essential: Mr John Clarke, one of my surgeons back in the 1970s and by then leading the team at Queen Mary's Hospital, Roehampton, came on board – with the warning that he might not agree with everything I did or said. Absolutely. Exactly what I wanted.

My sister, Alison Partridge, a very experienced social worker, and Juliet Campbell, recently retired HM Ambassador to Luxembourg (a cousin of my wife's) made up the initial group. But who to be Chair? I needed a well-known name.

The first I tried was a family friend: Sir Campbell Adamson, once Director General of the CBI and now Chairman of Abbey National. I psyched myself up to call his office and managed to get a thirty-minute slot in his hectic schedule.

I need not have been nervous, because Campbell was charming, listened carefully and asked a series of pertinent questions. Chief amongst them was who else I'd approached to be trustees. I reeled off the names and gave them all a strong write-up. He leaned back and looked at me quizzically – a look I came to know as presaging some wisdom or a challenging query.

'Are they all "Yes, James" people?' he asked. 'I don't want to have to be the only one to challenge you – because I suspect, if I hold the reins, I'll have to do much more reining in than urging you on!'

Such a good question. And I could answer honestly: 'No, they are not all "Yes, James" people. They are all "Yes, James, but…" people.'

And so it proved. From day one, indeed even at the launch event, I was challenged by Campbell and all the trustees. And rightly so.

Campbell agreed to be the first Chair and said that he'd try to bring the lessons he'd learned in helping Marjorie Wallace to launch SANE a few years earlier. He chaired the first meeting in April 1992 and, in his inimitable way, invited Andrew Jarvis to be treasurer: 'Andrew, you look to have all the right credentials to keep the money under control – how about being the treasurer, OK?' Andrew, very surprised, said yes, unable to challenge a man of such gravitas – and served an outstanding sixteen years in that role.

The launch event in February went well. It allowed me to apply for Charity Commission registration, and to plan a public launch in mid-May 1992. And for this, I sought out a small specialist health sector PR company, Joan Scott PR, run by its CEO, a woman called Claire Marley. She, Jane Landon and her team created a superb media launch at the King's Fund Centre in Camden on Tuesday 26th May, the day after the May bank holiday — and a day, luckily, of very little competitive news. Claire later became my hugely valued PA.

The charity's launch was covered on BBC TV news throughout the day and on ITV, and a short film of one of the workshops in action created by another friend, Martin Lucas, was shown on the ITV's two evening news shows. Newspapers the next day carried photos and text and much more.

Changing Faces was up and running. And the phone started ringing loudly and often.

THE FIRST WORKSHOPS 'FOR REAL'

Were there people 'out there' who might want – and benefit from – the sort of help I envisaged Changing Faces would offer? Or who would support my dream of challenging public attitudes? I could not be sure. But I need not have worried.

From the first day, the phone rang and rang, people enrolled on our workshops and letters came in. After a month, I could be in no doubt. I was definitely *not* alone – and had not been alone all those years – in finding it very hard to live with *IT*.

People and parents started telling me their stories, recounting their journeys through social anxiety, isolation, exclusion and insult. They told me of their medical and surgical treatments, most of which improved their appearance somewhat but almost none removing their disfigurement. Despite their hopes.

Facial stigma bore down on them incessantly as soon as they left their homes. Many were very far from being adjusted to living in our society. They were just forlorn. And angry. And impotent to change anything about their situation. And although some had very supportive families – sometimes too supportive – the families couldn't change anything either.

I was deliberately upbeat from the start. Yes, you could have more control. You could change your life if you were prepared to reconsider your knowledge, your mindset and your behaviours.

I shared my story as empathically as I could and focused on the things that had helped me. And gradually I gained other stories too. People wrote to me who had also been through the slough of despond but had figured out a way to live with confidence, often without any formal help whatsoever – something I was determined to change. And their journeys had very similar lessons to mine.

I conveyed my belief that gaining that control, which is what Changing Faces offered to help people do, meant 'changing the way you faced the world' – and, I assured them, Changing Faces would also eventually try to 'change the way the world faced you'.

But I tried hard not to suggest that changing the way you faced the world was easy. It wasn't. It took persistence, determination and courage. And it was not a fix for the attitudes and behaviours we have to witness every day.

What I was advocating was that you had to become very well prepared for those slings and arrows, but also that you needed to find your own way to let yourself shine in every encounter. You had to give yourself an aura of strength, even if you didn't quite believe it initially.

People doubted me, of course. Because they came with what seemed intractable problems. Like the woman with facial burns scarring who'd become phobic of many public places and had tried every kind of make-up to conceal what she knew were unconcealable scars.

Like the twenty-three-year-old woman who said that she'd never been to a hair and beauty salon because of her facial birthmark. She hated mirrors and said she knew that she would be judged by others in the salon as sad and as someone for whom love and intimacy would never happen, a woman who would live an inferior life far removed from the glitz of beauty salons.

Or the man whose facial palsy, acquired unexpectedly and inexplicably in his teenage years, had plagued him, turning him into a recluse, 'always hiding in the shadows'. He was a very talented pianist but never risked developing a career, working instead in a packing factory.

The workshops and one-to-one sessions we (because I soon had to employ someone to work with me, Kathy Lacy) created gave people a safe place to divulge and share their pain. One of the strongest exercises was where people shared moments when they were happy and carefree (always with family and close friends) and compared them with times when they felt exposed, always in the presence of strangers or acquaintances.

The behaviours they had to endure formed a long list:

- Uncontrolled staring
- Intrusive questions
- Name-calling
- Harassment
- Physical bullying
- Ridicule
- Pointed jokes
- Patronisation ('so brave')

INVENTING CHANGING FACES

- Avoidance of social interaction, and especially of eye contact
- Ostracism and not being invited
- Discounting – 'people like you can't...'
- Half-hearted support/lip service
- Low expectations in schools
- Rejection in work
- Underemployment
- Poor customer service

And many variations on those themes – and much more.

They griped at and seemed resigned to what were seemingly 'the ways of the world'. Like the use of words such as deformity and abnormality in medicine and surgery – and in the media. And the use of facial scarring as a lazy shorthand for 'evil/baddies' in films. And the tedious media stories about the 'victims' of scars and the 'sufferers' of facial paralysis or skin conditions. And the loaded job descriptions, like 'good-looking person sought', which meant they couldn't apply.

That was 1992 and 1993, but this is still the way that facial stigma is experienced. The prejudice and discrimination comes in many forms – and I fear these small words don't do justice to the serious impact they can and do have on people's psyches and chances in life.

And worst of all, the oppression is not going away quickly. For most workshop participants, all they could do was keep their expectations low and live as best they could in this society. And many who contacted us were doing so resignedly.

My argument was that there is a better way. There were things that all of us can do, in our thinking and behaviour, to minimise the impact of the culture. Above all, we have to find and perfect ways to take the initiative in every single social encounter. If you can do that, others cannot touch you. You are in control.

I use the word 'argument' quite deliberately here, because I/we did have to argue at some length with quite a few of the participants to convince them that not only was this a valid approach, but you really could learn how to manage things differently. We argued that they should try it as conscientiously as they could. And we gave them the reasons why, so that they could repeat these arguments to themselves whenever doubts crept in. As they inevitably would. We heard people say, 'But why should I have to do anything differently? It's other people's problem!' And of course, in some ways that's right: it *is* other people who should change their thinking and behaviour.

But – and it's a very big BUT – there are several problems with that approach. It may take ages before they change; in the meantime, you may go on in anger and isolation. And they are highly unlikely to do so without some persuasion or reason to do so, which you could provide if you were so minded. My/our view was – and is – that if the person with the disfigurement takes the initiative, they can effect the change they want.

Sometimes that means being very assertive in the face of ridicule or rudeness. But, for the most part, it is about recognising other people's (mostly) understandable hesitation and ignorance when faced with someone with an unusual face, and then providing them with the chance to break out of it.

So the purpose of what came to be known as the 'foundation workshops' was twofold: first, to provide an analysis of what happened in social interactions if you have a disfigurement – the SCARED Syndrome, as I'd called it in my book: you were often scared of others and they were scared of you.

People do often **S**tare at you, often ask **C**urious questions, often express **A**nguish, often **R**ecoil and avoid looking, often feel **E**mbarrassed and often **D**read meeting you. And when any of these things happen, you feel lousy, angry and impotent.

These are the everyday reactions that you will face if you have any kind of disfigurement to your face – and it doesn't have to be a full-facial difference. You'll get the same if you have a cleft lip and palate, or a birthmark, or psoriasis, or a Bell's palsy.

This is par for the course. It happens and will go on happening whether you like it or not – and I'm sure you don't. You need to be prepared to deal with it.

But the problem is that you may well be trapped in SCARED-ness yourself: you may feel **S**elf-conscious, behave **C**lumsily, become **A**ngry or **R**etreat out of harm's way, **E**mbarrassed and **D**efeated. And when two parties – you and others – meet, both bothered by SCARED-ness, the chance of a good outcome is slight. Like trying to connect the negative poles of two magnets. It can't happen. You are left out.

Once they had the analysis, we then introduced participants to new proactive social skills, using another acronym, REACH OUT which offered ways of taking control of social interactions of all kinds, to make them go far better. And then we practised and practised them. I describe REACH OUT and other aspects of this 'social interaction skills training' in the next section.

Vitally, however, we didn't just run the workshops; we also had them evaluated by a third party: an independent researcher, Emma Robinson, supervised by Nichola Rumsey.

And they worked! Yes! The research project followed up the first hundred clients and was reported in an acclaimed peer-reviewed journal.[5] How proud we were!

But it wasn't just the research results that were pleasing. The woman who had never been to a hair salon wrote a couple of months later to say she had now been to one and had come out with five sets of highlights 'just for the hell of it'. The woman with facial burns started to socialise again, and the factory worker decided to join an orchestra. And many others reported significant changes.

Improving their self-confidence in social situations had enabled them to get positive vibes/feedback from those they met – and that, in turn, boosted their self-esteem.

Facial stigma was kept at bay, even sent into retreat. They didn't impose it upon themselves and instead showed their self-respect in the milliseconds of first meetings. They became resilient to the belittling that had previously dominated their lives – it could no longer touch them.

We then developed other workshops – and in time, self-help guides – to enable people to delve more deeply into particular concerns they had: being assertive, making friends, getting work, handling staring, speaking in public, developing intimate relationships and related subjects. And then we evolved workshops for children and young people.[6]

But increasingly and in many ways, even more important than those developments was the evolution of our one-to-one counselling. This became our daily bread… on the phone, by letter and later by email and, best of all, face to face. Kathy and I struggled to keep pace with the demand for this. She was the most brilliant 'listening ear', never, ever discounting what a client said, always imparting warm, calm words of encouragement, and quite quickly we were swamped.

Equally crucial for the lives of these clients, it was clear that their families and friends also needed support. We knew – and they often did too – that quality social support was of great benefit. But how to provide it? This too became a focus, and our self-help guides for parents gave some positive ideas.

There was no doubt at all: people with facial disfigurements of all kinds found life tricky – the psychological and social impact was often extremely distressing. And they had not been able to find effective help. Until now. I had to find the resources, especially the money, to make a difference. Full-time, full-on. Which is what I did for the next twenty-five years.

15.

FACES: THE PRINCIPLES OF EFFECTIVE PSYCHOSOCIAL CARE

The lessons of those first and many subsequent workshops and the thousands of one-to-one sessions were refined and developed over the next twenty-five years by my team at Changing Faces. We had much support from Nichola Rumsey and the academics at what became the Centre for Appearance Research. What emerged became known as 'the FACES package of help' – and in this chapter, I explain the package in some detail.

The FACES package is, in psychology terms, effectively 'a disfigurement-specific Cognitive Behavioural Therapy (CBT)' package, which I have tried to write in lay language so that it is accessible to everyone.

Changing Faces identified five principles encapsulated in FACES that have proven to be effective in enabling people with less-than-perfect faces or bodies – and their families too – to develop the life skills needed to live with confidence in our perfect-face world. Some people, perhaps a third, acquire them without formal help – and research continues to identify why this is so. But almost everyone would admit to valuing some help.

Changing Faces also developed the FACES training programme, through which suitable professionals would be trained up to join our team and/or work in the NHS to deliver the FACES package. They could then take on the role of 'Changing Faces Practitioner' (CFPs), working safely and confidentially with each client to assess what would be best for them and then helping them in a sensitive and empowering way.

Let me look first at the five principles of FACES and then give some examples of what they might have meant in my own adjustment.

F – FINDING OUT

Finding out is about taking control of your situation – in the jargon, the locus of control needs to be with you, not the clinical team. Medical jargon, uncertainty about prognosis and sudden hospitalisation in connection with any condition that affects your face – or that of your child – can all be overwhelming. You and your family need to work out the questions you want to ask your team on an almost daily basis – and how to ask them, not passively but assertively. You may also want to search for robust answers on the internet, but you need to avoid dodgy answers too, which is far from easy.

Taking control of your medical condition and its treatment is not only good for you but enables you to explain your situation to others in an informed way – without ducking its seriousness or using euphemisms.

> In my case, as well as my desperate search for a surgical fix (as described in earlier chapters), the time when I most needed to 'find out' was right at the beginning:
>
> **1. What damage do burns do?**
> Burns can cause major damage to all the layers of your skin. Some burns, like scalds, are 'superficial', affecting only the top

layer, the epidermis. They can be extremely painful whilst raw, because the nerve ends are exposed in the lower layer. Healing of superficial burns takes two to three weeks and is usually only prevented by infection. Usually, there is no sign of the scald on the skin afterwards, although the area can look slightly paler.

Deeper burns that go into the dermis and the hypodermis (the underlying fat layer) are less painful, involve major fluid loss and, because they will not heal quickly, are unlikely to heal properly unless they are covered by skin grafts from other parts of the body.

Burns and very major wounds heal in a way that is still not fully understood in scientific terms – or, more accurately, is more or less understood as a process, but not yet with enough knowledge of how to intervene successfully, how to speed the healing and prevent scar formation.

In a normal healing process, an open wound gradually granulises from the edge inwards, helped possibly by a skin graft; a scab forms as the body creates a new cover for the injured area, and eventually, ten to fourteen days on, the scab comes off, usually leaving a red and slightly raised scar below.

The healed area on which the scar has formed can become very itchy, and because of the complexity of microfibroblasts in the new structure, can become lumpy too. These are called 'hypertrophic scars' or, in their extreme, overgrown form, 'keloid scars'. They can be very unsightly and because of the contractures they cause on the neighbouring skin areas, can distort and tighten your face. Most such scars, left to their own devices, will very slowly lose colour, flatten out and come to what is called 'full maturity' after two to three years.

Avoiding hypertrophy is a primary goal of today's surgeons and their surgery choices for full-thickness burns now often involve using skin flaps to prevent scarring forming and taking hold around split-skin grafts. They also prescribe the use of silicon masks and pressure garments (not available in my day) to try to hold back the physiological momentum that causes scarring and leaves huge swollen scarred lumps.

2. Will my face be permanently changed?

Clinical teams play a crucial role in enabling patients to acquire realistic expectations about the aesthetic impact of the treatment that their face (or body) is likely to receive – and that role starts on day one. In my case, I was denied such information for months – or 'protected from getting depressed', depending on your viewpoint. This is what I would have liked to have been told:

'Your face has been severely injured. We are not sure how deeply the burns have gone but it is likely that a large part of your face has third-degree burns – that is, the heat has burned through the top layers of your skin. These burns and some of the lesser second-degree burns will not heal up of their own accord, but the more superficial burns that you got from singeing will heal within a couple of weeks.

'Luckily, we have now developed a range of plastic surgery operations so we will be able to cover those difficult wounds by moving skin from other parts of your body to your face. This will take quite a long time, probably several months, and the end result will not look much like your previous face. We cannot predict exactly what your appearance will be but you should prepare yourself to have to carry facial scars for the rest of your life – and we will help you in every way we can to do so.

'Frustratingly, plastic surgery has not evolved enough yet to be able to recreate your lost looks. That will take many decades to bring about, if it is ever achievable.'

FACES: THE PRINCIPLES OF EFFECTIVE PSYCHOSOCIAL CARE

> And in an ideal world, I'd have liked them to add (if it were true): 'However, we have evolved ways to help you live a very full and happy life through a mixture of surgery and empowerment, so please do not worry.'

But isn't the internet the answer to 'finding out'? Not so, sadly. Although there are some websites that now provide excellent and expert information for patients and families (such as that provided by the British Association of Plastic, Reconstructive and Aesthetic Surgeons – www.bapras.org.uk) – and it is well worth looking at those – the internet is also full of 'magicians' peddling their skills and using airbrushed photos to show off their results.

It is vital that you are not seduced. My best advice is to speak to your consultant to find out the best source of information, in their opinion. What you need is the chance to discuss your treatment options with an informed expert who has only your interests in mind – not commercial gain.

Whatever your condition, you should learn more about it, its likely prognosis and discuss all the treatment options. And keep doing so over time – be persistent! Your clinical team should provide that information, but make sure that it is realistic information, relevant to you. Don't be afraid to question or ask for more clarification. (I loved it when clinicians contacted me and said, almost complainingly, that they had a patient who had been in touch with Changing Faces and 'was asking all sorts of difficult questions'!)

The surgical techniques available to my clinical team in the early seventies were much less sophisticated than they are now – and indeed the way in which my burns were initially treated, very conservatively, would not have been followed today. Instead, all the wounds would have been 'excised' very soon after the accident. In other words, the scabs would have been removed before they could harden or harbour infection, and microsurgery would be used to lift skin flaps to cover the wounded area. That would have greatly reduced the number of reconstructive operations required.

But what has not changed is that it is still incredibly difficult for non-expert patients like me, and you too, probably, to make informed decisions in consenting to our treatments.

For someone like me with major facial burns, one of the greatest research developments in reconstructive surgery over the last forty years has been face transplantation. The idea was hatched in the 1990s, when British surgeons suggested it would technically be possible to remove the face of someone who has died to replace the severely damaged face of a living person. This started a major international debate which brought clinical science into the public glare as ethicists, psychologists and the media wrestled to have their views heard.

The breakthrough came in late 2005 when a French woman, Isabelle Dinoire, chose to have a face transplant to replace a section of her face which had been scoured by her dog. Since then, over forty patients worldwide have also take a similar 'leap into the dark', as the Royal College of Surgeons of England's Working Party described it.[1] (I address this in more detail in Part 3.)

I am sure that if this had been happening in the years when I was going through reconstructive surgery, I would have wanted to know much more. Would it have been for me? Would I have put myself forward for a face transplant? I decided to get a clinical viewpoint on this from Gus McGrouther, Britain's first Professor of Plastic Surgery. He made three key points:

First, I would be best advised to take a lot of time to find out and weigh up the risks of having a face transplant, such as whether the aesthetic improvement would be significant or relatively small; whether I might lose some facial movement; whether I would be dependent for the rest of my life on immunosuppression (to prevent my body rejecting the foreign tissues of a donor's face) and what its side effects would be.

I should set those risks against the potential benefits of a much less scarred and even possibly smooth facial complexion that might give me (more) social anonymity and make me feel better about myself. He discouraged me from consenting to the procedure until I had pondered the pros and cons for a long time.

Second, he said that although the actual procedure of doing a face transplant was relatively well practised now and was technically not that difficult, there was one serious issue that I should explore: what was the surgical team's Plan B if the transplant failed?

Thirdly, he was unsure about the emotional impact on me and my family. I might be resilient enough to tolerate the surgery, but how would we feel about me acquiring someone else's face? Was I really in such distress about my own? And if I was in distress, had I sought out the very best psychological counselling?

The parallel between the reconstruction of my chin in the 1970s (as described in Chapter 11) and face transplantation in the twenty-first century may seem tenuous, but there are considerable similarities. I now realise that I had (inexpertly and without guidance) gone through exactly the same steps, and that these can be summarised in the following advice:

- Get very well-informed and take time to make the decision (if you have time).
- Check out the risks of the procedure in great detail and look for alternatives.
- Assess the emotional impact on you and your family and look for counselling too.

Amazingly, I am occasionally asked today whether I am thinking about having a face transplant! My negative response then requires explanation, which I attempt to give in as concise a way as possible.

In conclusion, the F of the FACES principles points to the importance of finding out as much about your medical and surgical options as you can. This means doing your own research, not being swayed by hype from any one source, and asking questions persistently and patiently of your clinical team. You can then make informed decisions for yourself or your child. You will feel better about those decisions than if you make them under pressure or in a state of ignorance. And you will be able to explain what you are going through to others, too – which will help you to 'own' what's happening to you.

Above all, you will be in control, not a passive recipient. The locus of control is with you! Not your clinical team.

One implication of finding out is, of course, that you may discover and decide that your best option is *not* going on and on with operations or forever searching for the medical fix that will magic your face to the perfection that you might hope for; or even believe is vital for a successful life.

For most of us, medicine and surgery are only a partial answer. And that can be a stark and painful realisation. The other four principles of FACES are all about helping you to come to terms with and manage that reality.

A – ATTITUDE-BUILDING

Getting 'attitude' – being robust and positive – about your (or your child's) distinctive face is neither easy nor quick for most people. There are two aspects to this process: (i) debunking the negative thoughts you are likely to have, and (ii) cultivating the positive ideas that will promote 'attitude'.

'Attitude' is hard to attain for yourself or your child when you will almost certainly have grown up with three unspoken and almost unquestioned assumptions about what life is going to be like for someone like you or your child. They are 'the stigmas of disfigurement' – and we are all liable to impose them on ourselves unthinkingly, which can make you very depressed and pessimistic.

FACES: THE PRINCIPLES OF EFFECTIVE PSYCHOSOCIAL CARE

A major task in adjusting to having a not-perfect face (or body) is to debunk these prejudices and refuse to let them affect, let alone dominate, your thinking and life. You need to understand them intimately, be able to identify and challenge them whenever they crop up and thereby banish them from your thinking processes.

I give this subject much more detailed treatment in Part 3 but in summary, the three key facial stigmas are:

1. People with not-perfect faces have sad and second-rate lives.
2. People with not-perfect faces have moral failings and undesirable personalities.
3. Not-perfect faces aren't necessary and can be fixed.

First, the stigma of the sad and second-rate: the view that success and happiness, especially in relationships and at work, are highly unlikely – and although one or two people with unusual faces do appear to do 'quite well', they are exceptions. On the strength of this belief/stereotype/prejudice, you – and your family too – can expect to receive sympathy, patronisation and low expectations from people around you: professionals, teachers, even your friends.

This prejudice is deeply embedded in twenty-first century culture, conditioning and consciousness. Everyone's daily visual diet of advertising billboards, magazines, social and traditional media and almost all aspects of popular culture promotes the idea that being 'perfect-looking' is the sure way to being happy and successful. TV programmes with titles like *The Undateables* sustain this mythology, but probably the strongest reinforcement is celebrity culture. The most beautiful women and men in the world with blemish-free faces obviously lead very happy lives – Hollywood divorce rates notwithstanding, of course!

This visual diet amounts to a cult of perfectionism and is incredibly unhealthy for everyone because it is liable to promote self-inspection, vanity and narcissistic thinking. I cannot stress too strongly: the prejudice is a complete fallacy. Debunk it at every turn!

Happiness and success do not come from what you look like. They emerge from the quality of your relationships with other people and your capacity to make the most of your talents, skills and personality. And, critically, neither of those factors depend on what you look like either – although you have to learn how to manage social encounters effectively (see more on this under 'S' of FACES, which stands for social interaction skills).

Another favourite ruse is the 'don't judge a book by its cover' argument, which gets translated as, 'Don't worry, James, it's what's inside you that counts'. This is perhaps the clearest statement about our society's aesthetics: your facial scars are certainly rather displeasing to the eye but your beautiful personality and soul are what matters. Whenever I come across this view, I instantly challenge it! It is not just what's inside me that matters. My outside matters a great deal. I want people to respect my scars and distinctive face.

Second, the assumption of of moral failings and undesirable personalities: in a nasty flip side to the cult of perfectionism, people with scarred or unusually shaped faces are portrayed in popular culture as likely to be 'different', misfits, odd, inferior and immoral.

The worst form of this prejudice is the lazy use by Hollywood and other film-makers of facial scarring or disfigurement to portray 'baddies'. Examples are numerous: Bond films are notorious (*Dr. No*, the character of Blofeld, etc.) but many thrillers, dramas and horror movies use such devices. The horror genre takes it to a higher level with *Dracula*, *A Nightmare on Elm Street*, the dead reincarnated and many other ghouls.

This prejudice is so widely promulgated, but it is outdated and totally unacceptable – and it needs to be consigned to the dustbin of history. Don't let it touch you – and develop a strong assertiveness streak to do so (see the 'S' of FACES below).

Third, the myth of a medical/surgical fix: that people with not-perfect faces should make use of the sophistication of modern surgery and medicine now available – it's up to them to get it 'fixed'.

FACES: THE PRINCIPLES OF EFFECTIVE PSYCHOSOCIAL CARE

Of course, this doesn't just apply to people with 'imperfect' faces. Wrinkles, irregularities and sticking-out features can and should be erased or corrected... it's so easy to 'have work done'... and if you don't, you really are falling behind. I strongly commend philosopher Heather Widdows' book *Perfect Me* on this subject.

The reality is very different indeed. Plastic and reconstructive surgery is still very far from the miracle science that is popularly imagined. You need to explore what is possible for you (see 'finding out', above) and then come to terms with the aesthetic limits and risks of modern plastic and cosmetic surgery. And you are well advised to take every opportunity to explain to your friends and others those limits so that unrealistic expectations are discouraged.

It's all very well, I can hear you say, to talk about not letting these prejudices affect your life, but that's easier said than done. Yes, I agree. Debunking – getting rid of your unhelpful thoughts and negative beliefs about your less-than-perfect face – means rescripting your internal dialogue and is excruciatingly difficult, but vital.

The process can seem very noisy, too. I worried that my internal monologue could be heard as I walked along or entered social groups. I was constantly battling inside to stop my old thinking patterns from reasserting themselves, taking me back into pessimism. It worked in the end.

Psychology has developed one form of therapy which I think can be particularly useful: Cognitive Behavioural Therapy (CBT)'s central message is that you *can* reason yourself out of negativity – and that this is worth doing, because how you feel about the world around you stems from how you think about it, your cognitive processes. If these are irrational or unhelpful, you can be constantly down or depressed. But, by restructuring them, better outcomes can be achieved.

For example, my reasoning that the stories of the Guinea Pigs from the Battle of Britain were irrelevant to me took me backwards. It would have been much better to have argued inside that '*in their era*, their stiff upper lips were the accepted means of coping, as was their camaraderie.' It may have felt alien and artificial to me in the 1970s, but the important thing was that it worked for them. As it was, I had to reason with myself using different arguments. 'If you really concentrate on that exam, you will demonstrate your skills and worth' and 'It's not helpful to interpret that person's seeming disinterest as antipathy – it could just be awkwardness.'

Some of the typical patterns of thought that CBT suggests people are very liable to demonstrate are as follows (and the examples are all mine):

- All-or-nothing thinking: 'People will always see me as a sad sufferer.'
- Over-generalisation: 'Everybody I meet with burns scars is depressed.'
- Focusing on the negative and discounting the positive: '*He* might have come through, but there's no chance for me because I'm not an extrovert, nor do I have fortitude.'
- Mind-reading and forecasting the future: 'I know as soon as I enter the shop that I'm going to get bad service.'
- Asserting that you are responsible for things that go wrong: 'Parties are never fun, nor do they go well when I'm around.'

So, it may be worth considering seeking out such therapy. It would encourage continual self-awareness and cognitive correction over a sustained period, until positive thinking becomes ingrained.

The other side of the coin in gaining 'attitude' is to cultivate the positive ideas that will promote it. This is something that all your friends and family can – and indeed, should – do too.

A key to this is to find your own 'heroes/heroines', people who you consider role models. They may have your condition, but not necessarily. And, thankfully, this is made considerably easier these days because, with social media now so global, you can locate people you admire in wider society. You can read about them, even gain some connection with them perhaps. They can demonstrate that

FACES: THE PRINCIPLES OF EFFECTIVE PSYCHOSOCIAL CARE

finding happiness, love, intrigue, excitement and success in life are not the preserve of society's aesthetic elite.

Similarly, you probably need to rewrite your ambitions and expectations as a person with scarring or an unusual face. Which *doesn't* – shouldn't – mean downplaying them, but reshaping them. Some of your previous goals may not be achievable, but others will come into view and become just as important, probably more so.

Identify and work on your talents and skills – and take pleasure in them; like Marcus Powell, who has a serious facial condition and (not but) has become a UK national trampoline champion!

Lastly, it might be tempting to imagine that 'attitude' is all you need – or that you'll never get it. Neither is true. Attitude alone is probably not enough. But you can nurture and develop it. And if you need help, it's worth looking for a psychologist or counsellor who has been trained across the whole FACES package.

C – COPING WITH FEELINGS

Being born and growing up with a condition that affects your face or, at some age, having an accident, surgery, a paralysis or a skin condition that changes it can be very distressing indeed for the individual affected and their family.

Everyone is liable to have feelings of grief, shame, anger, loneliness and isolation, and loss of self-regard, anxiety and depression are common as a result. In fact, you need to realise that these are normal reactions, not emotions that you should feel are odd or unacceptable. They go with the territory. Your face is a very precious commodity, central to your identity and self-image, the canvas on which you paint and others observe your moods and personality. So, don't beat yourself up if you feel down. It's normal.

The reason why C is for coping with feelings is that, in Changing Faces' experience, people very rarely eliminate these feelings completely, however well they eventually adjust to their unusual face. Instead, they learn how to cope, using methods that can be employed in everyday life and even years later when some incident triggers the old emotions. Importantly, there are ways in which you can be helped to do that coping.

The key trait that you need to develop is resilience. Contrary to popular mythology, resilience is not innate, but can be learned over time. It's the ability to adapt well in the face of trauma or adversity and so cope with difficult situations for the rest of your life.

There are now many books on this subject, but one of the best is *The Road to Resilience* published by the American Psychological Association in 2008.[2] It identifies several key factors that are associated with resilience:

- Having strong supportive relationships within your family and with friends.
- Having the ability to make realistic plans and carry them out.
- Having a positive view of yourself and confidence in your strengths and abilities.
- Having good skills in communication and problem-solving.
- Having the capacity to manage strong feelings and impulses.

Few people with a not-perfect face are likely to have all these strengths naturally – we all have to work at them.

Interestingly, in the UK, a major study known as the Appearance Research Collaboration study in 2008[3] highlighted a further set of indicators that can affect how well someone copes with imperfect appearance:

- Whether or not the person is optimistic or pessimistic.
- Whether or not the person fears negative evaluation by others.
- Whether or not the person is satisfied with their social support network.
- How much value the person places on their physical appearance.
- How the person perceives their appearance, how they would like to look and how they feel they should look.

FACES: THE PRINCIPLES OF EFFECTIVE PSYCHOSOCIAL CARE

So, there's a lot to explore if you want to develop resilience, but a crucial element, as the APA indicates, is having the capacity to manage strong feelings and impulses. Some of the most complex are those related to reliving the events of an accident or incident. Post-traumatic stress disorder is a serious condition which needs proper diagnosis and prompt treatment – please seek appropriate help if you are having flashbacks, nightmares or other unexplainable symptoms.

In my own case, the thirty minutes of my accident remain etched into my mind, especially the terror of being in the fire and sitting in the back of the car, shocked to the core. The speed at which everything happened has now been slowed by my memory. But every time I hear of or see live or on TV a disaster, a car accident or a terrorist attack, I am taken back to my own trauma. I am at peace with it now, but was not for many years. And it was so impossibly difficult to explain it to anyone else; which is why the appropriate type of and timing for psychological support is so hard to specify for anyone who goes through such events. But it must be there, available, when it's needed.

One of the other strongest emotions is that of grief – for the loss of your highly valued face or the face of the child you were meant to have. I have often wished that I'd been pointed early to an analysis of grief – in fact, **Kübler-Ross'** famous *On Death and Dying*, which outlines the five stages of grief, was published in 1969, the year before my accident.[4] But it was many years before I studied it, and I had to grapple with my grief without its insights.

Here is a graphic description of the process Kübler-Ross mapped out, which she suggested accompanies the aftermath of any traumatic or sad event. The horizontal axis is time since the event and the vertical axis measures morale, how you feel about the situation and competence, how well you are coping with it, which is closely related to your feelings.

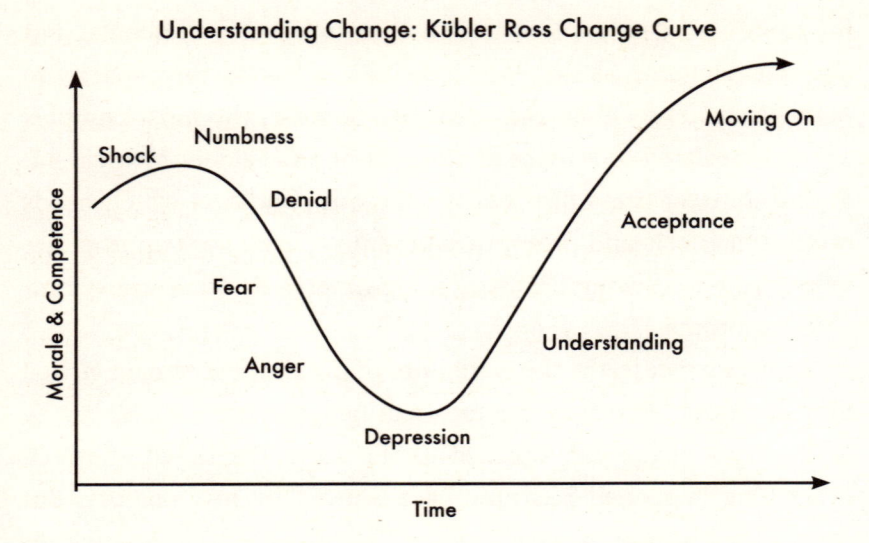

Understanding Change: Kübler Ross Change Curve

[Graph showing a curve plotting Morale & Competence against Time, with labeled stages: Shock, Numbness, Denial, Fear, Anger, Depression, Understanding, Acceptance, Moving On]

The Kübler-Ross analysis has been argued about and contested ever since she first described it – but for my purpose, there are three things of note in her admittedly oversimplified description:

First, there are no points marking the months or years after an event. How long grief or change takes is entirely unpredictable and individual. Therapists will tell you that they see people decades after a loss still trying to come to terms with it. The passage of time is by no means an automatic healer.

Which means that there is no such thing as a 'grieve-by date', a moment when you are over it. The last words on the graph, 'moving on', suggest that you can forget and leave the event behind. I don't believe this is the way grief happens. Grief never completely disappears; it just becomes less immediate. And you learn how to navigate it, to go round it, whenever it surfaces.

Second, what looks like a smooth 'change curve' does not conform to reality – it's illustrative only, as Kübler-Ross was at pains to stress. The process of bereavement is very far from smooth – you can seem to be passing from one 'stage' to the next, especially towards 'acceptance', when something can happen and take you all the way back

FACES: THE PRINCIPLES OF EFFECTIVE PSYCHOSOCIAL CARE

to 'anger'. Grieving is forward-and-back, jerky, hopefully two steps forward and one step back.

Third, the 'stages' of bereavement are worth explaining a little:

- Shock: the early rising curve indicates how a shocking event can provoke in you relief that you survived... and people close to you will gather round to help you feel strong.
- Numbness: it's hard to believe what has happened; reality hasn't hit yet... and maybe you are undergoing medical treatment that sedates you.
- Denial: your early reaction may be that 'it's not as bad as people are making out' or 'there will be a medical or surgical solution'.
- Fear: as other people's concern wanes, you start to feel alone and fearful about the future, and may not be able to express this to anyone.
- Anger: you begin to realise what has befallen you and feel surges of anger at the unfairness of it all: 'Why me?'... which can emerge in painful outbursts to those you love.
- Depression: things cease to be doable; everything is difficult; nobody understands; easier to stay at home, say nothing, suffer in silence and isolation.
- Understanding: a dawning of truth about your situation can happen out of the blue but often requires someone else to trigger it, a friend or a professional.
- Acceptance: a simple ten-letter word expressing a discovery that your life can be made whole again, but an immensely difficult and long-drawn-out stage for many people because you can easily lurch back into anger and sadness.
- Moving on: the sense that you can leave behind the worst pain of the event and may even have been strengthened by it – note the curve is higher than at the start.

The idea that you can 'grow' as a result of your experience of having a distinctive face was probably first postulated in 2002 by Ron Strauss in his delightful address to an American parent conference on cleft and craniofacial care, called 'Blessings in Disguise: A New Paradigm for Thinking About Children with Craniofacial Conditions' – it is worth reading in full.[5]

Since then and with many other research papers to support it, the concept of Post-Traumatic Growth Syndrome (paralleling PTSD) has evolved to try to capture what some people experience in terms of higher levels of self-esteem and personal strength post-adversity.[6]

Which is not to recommend having a severe accident or major face-changing experience. But there are some unintended and beneficial consequences of such events. Some people say, 'I'm a better person now' years later. But achieving this is not straightforward – certainly not automatic or guaranteed after a certain length of time. Studies of resilience (how to bounce back after adversity) and strong mindedness (how to be strong in the face of difficulty) need to be encouraged.

To conclude on 'coping with feelings', however you acquire a less-than-perfect face, you and your whole family and friends may well find it very distressing. You may experience intense and long-lasting feelings of loss, grief, anger, sadness, blame, isolation, shame and lost identity – and physical pain too – and that is entirely normal.

There are many things that can contribute to how you cope with these feelings. Social support from your friends and family can be vital, but lots of people find it difficult to tell their family or close friends how they feel. So, you may find that contacting a Changing Faces Practitioner (CFP) or a local counsellor allows you to confide how you feel about what you are going through. Contacting a local or online support group may help too; but remember, most do not have psychologically trained staff.

FACES: THE PRINCIPLES OF EFFECTIVE PSYCHOSOCIAL CARE

E – EXCHANGING

It is well recognised that many people going through a difficult time find it very useful to meet others who are going through – or have been through – a similar experience. This can enable them to exchange notes, share feelings and gain mutual support – and above all, to find out that they are not alone in their feelings and isolation. But it is worth realising that finding someone wearing the same T-shirt is not for everyone, nor is it an automatic fix. Some find it rather depressing or dread such meetings.

Today there are a huge number of chatrooms and social media channels through which to communicate, especially through private Facebook pages and, with the caveat that these need to be very secure and carefully monitored, I'd encourage anyone who is seeking to find others with the same condition or going through the same 'stuff' to make contact – or at least observe the interactions.

In my case, I would definitely have looked at those online portals for burn survivors like the Phoenix Society for Burn Survivors (www.phoenix-society.org) and maybe tried to go to the biggest 'bash' for burn survivors, their annual World Burn Congress. And in the UK, I'd have looked up Dan's Fund for Burns (www.dansfundforburns.org/) and the Katie Piper Foundation (www.katiepiperfoundation.org.uk). Whether I would have been a regular on their chatrooms and peer support activities is, I think, more doubtful, because I am essentially a private person. Which is not to take away the value that I know I would have derived from seeing and being inspired by successful role models like Katie Piper herself.

For people with other facial conditions, I recommend the following in the UK:

- Alopecia UK
- Bells Palsy Association
- Birthmarks Support Group

- British Acoustic Neuroma Association
- Cleft Lip and Palate Association (CLAPA), UK
- DEBRA
- Facial Palsy UK
- Goldenhar Family Support Group
- Headlines Craniofacial Support Group
- Ichthyosis Support Group
- Microtia UK
- National Eczema Society
- Nerve Tumours UK
- Psoriasis Association
- Scleroderma & Raynaud's UK (SRUK)
- Vitiligo Support UK

For support groups and organisations in other countries, please consult the website of Face Equality International.

S – SOCIAL INTERACTION/ COMMUNICATION SKILLS

Many times throughout this book so far I have mentioned the importance of 'communication skills', social interaction skills or, even shorter, 'social skills'. So here is a more detailed account of what I've been talking about – from the point of view of 'you', a person with the lived experience of facial disfigurement.

Any and every time you leave the sanctuary of your own home or even your room, you have to deal with social encounters. As social anthropologist Frances Cooke Macgregor said, 'people with facial disfigurements experience 'a loss – or lack – of civil inattention… which everyone else takes for granted'.[7]

First-time meetings with strangers (or perhaps with old friends) are challenging – for you and them. And dealing with the unpredictable mix of staring, shock, avoidance, ridicule and sympathy from

FACES: THE PRINCIPLES OF EFFECTIVE PSYCHOSOCIAL CARE

people you meet is par for the course – they all come with having a face that stands out in the crowd.

The playground, walking down the street, going on public transport and being in public places in general all pose particular difficulties – and dealing with bullying and ridicule is complicated, as is harassment at work. It's understandable that if you aren't managing such negative reactions, you may retreat and avoid social situations. Social anxiety, depression, other mental health concerns and behavioural issues can arise in response to these experiences – and their impact on school engagement and employment (critical factors in quality of life and well-being) can be extremely detrimental.

That's the problem – without confidence, all those social interactions can be agony. But confidence doesn't grow on trees, nor can it be sprinkled on you by somebody else. You have to work to develop and practise your communication skills, and as you do that, your confidence will grow.

In psychological terms, the problem can be illustrated using 'feedback loops'.

The first feedback loop is a negative one. If you enter a social situation expecting it to go badly, your behaviour may well produce precisely the negative reactions you predicted… which will then make it more likely that you anticipate negative reactions in the next encounter. A vicious circle that throttles your self-esteem and confidence.

Negative Feedback Loop

Anticipation of negative reactions
↓
Typical behaviours
Shy   Evasive   Aggressive
↓
Negative reactions from other people

It doesn't have to be like this. Communication skills training can help.

In *About Face*, neurophysiologist Jonathan Cole explores the biological evolution of the human face and how by facial displays (or sometimes a lack thereof), most children initially bond with their mothers and then grow up to be able to read others' faces – though not always correctly![8] Some children, for example those with autism, without sight or with Moebius Syndrome (where they have no facial expression) have much more complicated development processes.

But for all of us, the human face is what distinguishes each of us – and it is the primary place where other people look for signs of your mood, character and intentions. Crucially, the key part of your face which they look at is your face's 'communications triangle', the area between the edge of your eyes and the point of your chin. In that triangle are your eyes and mouth, two critical tools for communicating with those you meet. In that area, you make – or can make – incredibly subtle and tiny movements, the little inflections and nuances that make up your unique facial expressions.

My communications triangle is most definitely not what it was. It evokes a myriad reactions in those I meet, cues that I need to read correctly. And I need to use all my facial expressions very well indeed, especially what I do with my mouth, smile, eyes (although I don't have any eyebrows after so many skin grafts, I can come up with the equivalent of 'raising an eyebrow' when required), because my signalling box is no longer 'usual'.

Facial expressions are, of course, only a part of how we communicate. Becoming a great communicator calls for a whole range of verbal and non-verbal skills: what you say and how you say it (quietly, loudly, hesitatingly, firmly…), how you stand and move, what hand and other gestures you make, how you dress and look, how close you stand to others… all can be modified to make a positive impact – or not.

If you are not conversant with communication skills, it is worth starting to observe those of people around you and maybe reading

BILL COOPER

I was born with a large red birthmark, a port-wine stain, covering most of the left side of my face. I remember being called names like 'beetroot-face' at primary school, but I always had a good group of friends who didn't seem to be worried by my face, so those early taunts didn't bother me too much. At secondary school, what gave me confidence was sport. When you win a race, score a try or take a wicket no one cares what you look like. I have never experienced any facial discrimination at the athletics track. And in my career in financial services I have sometimes been able to turn my unusual face to my advantage – no one ever forgets me!

More complex are personal relationships. I have a wariness of intimacy, which I fight to this day. I am happier in a group than in one-on-one situations. Making a speech to 500 people can be easier than having a conversation with one person. I have been married for over twenty-five years and have three more-or-less grown-up children. This has been fantastic, especially as I wondered whether I would ever get a girlfriend because of my looks.

These days I find it amusing that I get stared at in the street, and that people tend not to sit opposite me on the train. I guess I am just hardened to it. But in thirty years of business life I have never been in a meeting with someone who looks unusual like me. Surely I should have come across a few? So there is implicit prejudice out there, for sure.

MARC CRANK

Living with a very visible manifestation of neurofibromatosis, which caused tumours to grow over the right-hand side of my face and head, was never going to make life easy. Doing so in a society obsessed with perfection and good looks made it a lot harder.

I was helped by a teenage discovery of the most alienating factor: fear of the unknown. It is always easier to build a rapport once the 'elephant in the room' is dealt with and people know the cause of my disfigurement. However, it never completely dispels exclusion from the adulated group: those with perfect looks…

CARLY FINDLAY

I have ichthyosis. It causes my face and body to be red, and my skin to be itchy, painful and prone to infection. I didn't see myself in beauty magazines when I was young. I still don't. I didn't think there was a place for me – because people with facial differences, scaly scalps and dry skin are framed as ugly and unworthy. Little Carly was too embarrassed to have her photo taken – because that would mean her perceived ugliness and unworthiness was there for everyone to see.

But now there's social media, and anyone with a smartphone can allow themselves to be seen, which means everyone can see there's diversity in appearances. We aren't just limited to finding beauty in beauty magazines. I put photos of myself on social media at least twice a week now. I appear on TV. I wanted my face to be on the cover of my book – unaltered – so that young people with ichthyosis can see what's possible for them. And so that other people can stop being afraid.

A friend told me that her six-year-old daughter had seen me on TV, and wanted to know how I made my face so pink and glittery (because she liked it). It was such a lovely thing to hear – a child seeing my difference as a positive, associated with beauty, rather than something to be feared... Well, it's simple, I told her. Paraffin ointment. Ichthyosis. And a level of confidence that I wish Little Carly had had.

I am not afraid to show my face anymore – in fact, I make a point of it. That's how we will achieve face equality. When everyone is seen.

MATTHEW JOFFE

At seven, I said to my mom that most people's faces were works of art (pause), but my face was Op Art. We laughed hysterically. THAT was the first time I acknowledged I was facially different.

For a long time, I let my facial condition define me. I would pour over the *New York Times* men's fashion supplement and fantasise about wearing those clothes, when at the same time a voice in my head was saying I was not worthy. After years of working on myself, I wear those clothes. My facial disability did not disappear; rather, the role I had assigned it had changed, as did the perspective I had on how I saw myself.

KAPIL KAPUR

I was born with a cleft lip and palate. As I am fifty years old, some of the medical procedures that are now available to repair this condition weren't in existence when I was born. Despite my parents' wonderful support, no amount of surgery would result in me having the perfect face. Growing up was challenging, to say the least – having to cope with racism in the seventies as well as being made fun of for my looks. However, these hurtful remarks paled into insignificance when I went in search of a life partner.

Quite simply, in Indian circles, no matter how educated you are (MSc from Oxford), what career you have carved out for yourself (IT consultant), if you don't have the Bollywood look, then just forget it. Don't go knocking on doors – they will literally get slammed in your face (happened on more than one occasion). I have been fortunate though that I am now married to Kaye and have two young sons, Hari and Krishan.

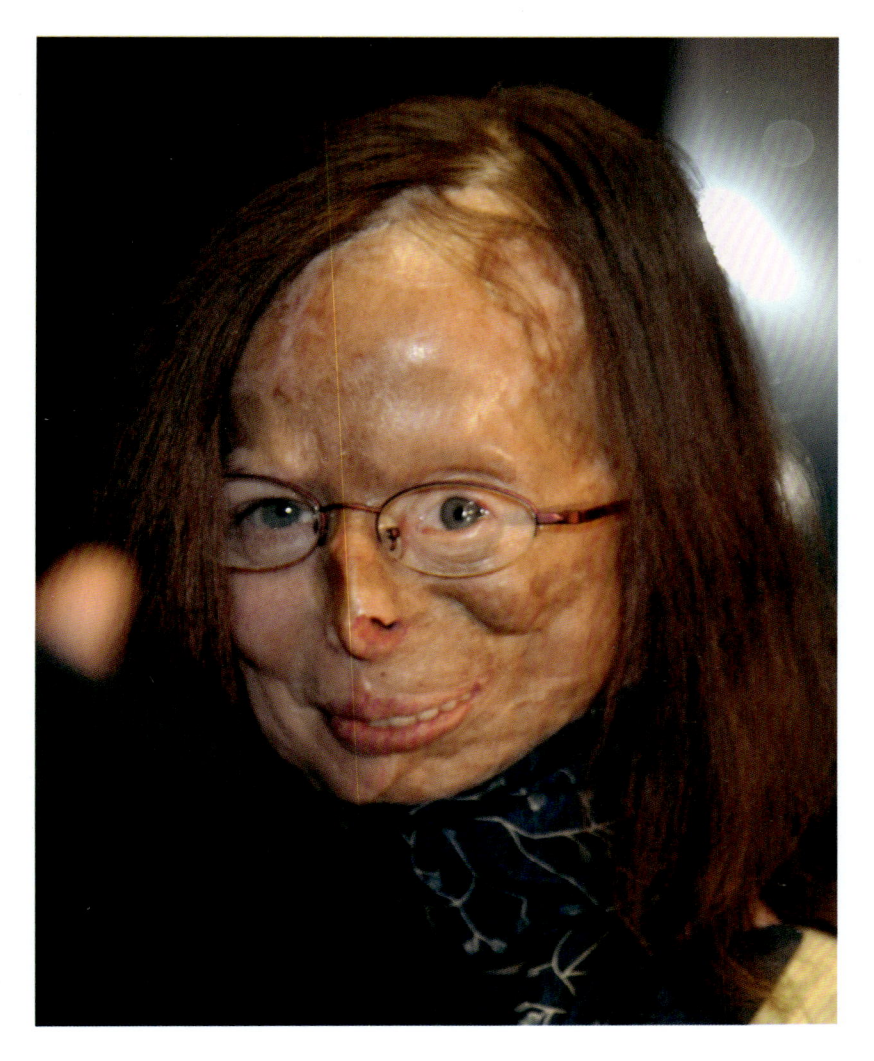

PATRICIA LE FRANC

Following an acid attack, I lost my face. Now I can only face the world by imagining I look like I used to. My face has strengthened me in some ways. Having an acid-burned face with an eye prosthesis is scary. People look at me with horror or pity and they don't know what to say.

So I decided to stand up to people's staring and start talking to them: 'Do you want to know what happened to me?' Some people say yes, others slink away. If it's an adult, I tell them my story and they often say: 'Oh, I've seen you on TV; you're very brave.' I say I have no choice.

If it's a child, I make up a story about a barbecue catching fire or something. That's kinder than telling them the full horror of what happened. And parents are usually grateful, as it reminds their children to be careful with barbecues and fires.

MIKE OKNINSKI

I had surgery for a facial skin cancer, DFSP or dermatofibrosarcoma protuberans. When I saw the dressings on my face after the surgery, I knew life had changed forever!

I was fifty-two, and had recently taken early retirement to set up my own management consultancy. I was petrified of what my friends, current clients and particularly the ones I hadn't yet met would think about my new far-from-perfect looks. Somehow, I felt I would be less valued now that I was 'damaged'.

Well, I found my pals and old clients didn't care! But I still lacked confidence with new contacts. I developed coping mechanisms, like the early introduction of the story of my unusual face into conversations and the use of self-deprecating humour. My experience of life was helpful, and I shudder to think of how the teenage me would have coped. But why should I have to do this coping at all? Is this what society has done to me? Surely can we change this?

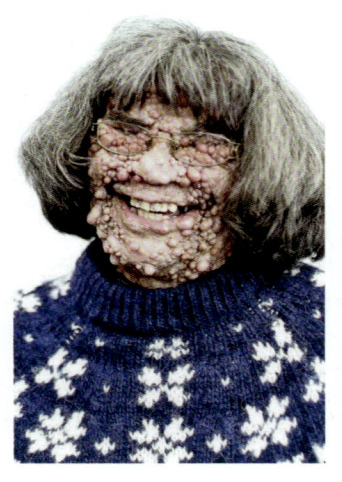

MARGARET SOARS

My disfigurement is caused by a form of neurofibromatosis, which has led to tumours growing over my body. Despite this I still held a customer-focused job until I retired in 2014. My general experience is that the majority of people are too busy, as indeed am I, to worry about what I look like. However, it always seems that if you have had a really enjoyable day, something will happen to spoil it, or if you are feeling extra low for some reason, something will happen to make it worse. If that happens, I try to count to ten before reacting and, something recommended by Changing Faces, smile.

PHYLLIDA SWIFT

In 2015 I was in a car accident in Ghana, which left me with a large scar from the top of my head down to the bottom of my cheek. At the time I was twenty-two, and like any other twenty something woman, I subscribed to a culture that sought perfection by way of perfect skin, immaculate complexion and flawless make-up. This was no longer possible for me, and I struggled with my identity. I no longer felt like myself, because I didn't look like myself. I was often stared at, whispered about and feared being pitied – until I made it my mission to embrace my scar and show that there was more to me and more that I had to offer than just my face.

JENN WALLACE

Growing up in the woods in the 1970s, I remember being four or five years old wearing bright pink corduroy pants and brown shoes with tassels, lying on my stomach on my living-room floor, chin in my hands, mesmerised by the Academy Awards playing on our big console TV. We knew nothing about Hollywood. We knew dogs, horses, ploughing the winter snow, chopping firewood.

But when the Oscars were on, I was in bliss. Every film the presenters described transported me. I knew at some intuitive level that this was the world I wanted to play in when I grew up. But as soon as I was completely immersed in those feelings of joy and excitement, I would see a gauzy reflection of myself in the glass of the TV screen. There I was, with my scarred face, the result of a massive hemangioma tumour, superimposed on the scene of perfect-looking beautiful people who got to play in movies. Seeing myself in that reflection, such a contrast to their perfect-looking world, yanked me back to reality quickly. That world was off-limits because of how I looked.

As a child, I couldn't even go to the grocery store without someone walking across the aisle and pointing at me and telling her child that that would happen to her if she didn't behave herself. If I couldn't even do mundane things like run errands, being allowed in to Hollywood was – well, forget about it. Seeing my reflection in the TV screen, my heart would break. I would turn off the TV and find something else to do, trying to forget that my stupid face, my frustrating, it's not fair, why me, the kids pick on me, boys will never like me, scarred-up, were you in a car accident, did someone hit you, Frankenstein, freak, *Scarface* of a face would be the barrier to my dreams coming true.

As an adult, I found the courage to step into the world of film-making, taking a risk to speak my truth. What I gained from my sadness as a child is what sets me apart and now gives me a unique perspective in this industry.

FACES: THE PRINCIPLES OF EFFECTIVE PSYCHOSOCIAL CARE

a book or two. It is amazing the variety that we humans have – and none of the skills are set in stone, despite what you might have previously thought. You can change the way you communicate!

'Social interaction skills training' classically takes the form of helping clients/participants in groups or in face-to-face sessions through three steps:

1. To acquire an understanding of what can go wrong in their social encounters and how that affects them.
2. To be introduced to a new set of effective strategies, behaviours or activities.
3. To practise and experiment with those strategies, often through graded exposure, to gain more control.

Here's how we set about designing our social skills training at Changing Faces:

1. An analytical framework to understand the problem

From research and the experiences of many clients at Changing Faces, we know that the problem, as stated above, revolves around many everyday social encounters. And a key insight in understanding why this happens is to realise that many people have never met someone with a disfigurement before, or if they have, only in an ill-at-ease way. They will be nervous about saying or doing the wrong thing.

It is very important, therefore, to be able to identify when this is happening to you and to understand its impact. At Changing Faces we created an analytical framework that can help you to understand what happens when you meet people – it's called the SCARED Syndrome.

In any such interaction, even the most trivial, there is a risk that you, the person with the disfigurement, will feel and act 'scared' – and the person you meet may do so too.

A person with a disfigurement may:			
Feel:			**Behave:**
Self-conscious	S		Shy
Conspicuous	C		Cowardly
Angry, Anxious	A		Aggressive
Rejected	R		Retreating
Embarrassed	E		Evasive
Different	D		Defensive
Other people can:			
Feel:			**Behave:**
Sorry, Shocked	S		Stare, Speechless
Curious, Confused	C		Clumsy
Anxious	A		Ask, Awkward
Repelled	R		Recoil, Rude
Embarrassed	E		Evasive
Distressed	D		Distracted

2. Your communication strategy

So, what to do when we meet SCAREDness?

The key principle that comes through from all the communication skills literature is that to create the best prospect of positive interactions as a person with a disfigurement, you need to be willing to take the initiative in most social encounters, especially first-time meetings of any sort. You can learn, practise and perfect new (possibly) proactive cognitive and behavioural strategies that will enable you to do this.

Taking the initiative means that, as the circumstance dictates, you can be/are the first to introduce yourself, the first to make eye contact, the first to offer information about yourself... but you have to be clever, too, in reading other people's cues, reactions, mood and

FACES: THE PRINCIPLES OF EFFECTIVE PSYCHOSOCIAL CARE

other information, and then lead the conversation forwards with new questions.

By using such skills, you control the encounter to such an extent that, for example, you can decide when you reveal information about yourself. And other people have the experience of seeing you as an interested communicator, first and foremost... and can get used to your face in the process.

We designed the REACH OUT toolkit to express some of the skills which you can learn, with the acronym being an aide-memoire:

R   REASSURE – it's important to show people, often through your non-verbal communication skills, that you are OK, not sad or needing help; it can be as simple as standing with your chin up or reading a newspaper.

E   ENERGY + EYE CONTACT – matching or slightly exceeding the energy exhibited by people you meet combined with powerful eye contact will help you to convey your personality before face-value judgements can be made.

A   ASSERTIVE – learning how to be firm but not aggressive if faced by intrusive staring, ridicule, etc. provides you with essential armour and will earn you respect – which often means speaking with a firm voice and using smart, short statements.

C   COURAGE – sometimes, you have to steel yourself to take a plunge into the unknown to face down a difficult situation – and you can learn how to do this, for example, by using strong self-talk – 'Go on, you can do this' – in less scary situations.

H   HUMOUR – learning how and when to use humour to ease a conversation, distract attention or make light of a subject can help others see you positively; some use self-deprecating humour, others wry comments; you can find your own way.

O 'OVER THERE' – instead of being self-conscious, develop 'other-consciousness', using open questions starting with the five Ws (who, what, where, why and when) and H (how), which distracts and provokes another person to talk.

U UNDERSTAND – sometimes other people are very confused and even upset at meeting you, and you have to be gently understanding (and not annoyed!); you can decide to share a bit about yourself, and then change the subject – over there...

T TENACITY – if you do not have success in a social situation try to analyse why, and then try again, when in a similar one, with a different approach – as Kathy Lacy used to say, 'There's no such thing as failure, only feedback.'

The need to be proactive doesn't stop once through the first few potentially awkward minutes of a meeting. No, by being super-aware of the subtle cues and signals of every person you meet, reading their mood and reaction to you and your face, you are then in a position to steer the conversation – it can become rather exciting!

REACH OUT isn't the only set of principles that have been developed, but they have been shown to be effective. There are more examples in the Changing Faces self-help guides here: www.changingfaces.org.uk/adviceandsupport/self-help/adults, and for young people and children, for parents and carers: www.changingfaces.org.uk/adviceandsupport/self-help/children-young-people.

3. Putting it all together

We recommend that these principles and strategies can be applied to deal with the common challenges faced by someone who is born

FACES: THE PRINCIPLES OF EFFECTIVE PSYCHOSOCIAL CARE

with or acquires a disfigurement. But they all take practice – graded practice. You shouldn't expect to acquire a PhD in a day or two. You can try them out in all sorts of everyday situations.

In the months and years after my accident, without a website or any kind of support to turn to, I had to learn a totally new set of behaviours by trial and error. It was like going back to kindergarten. People remember some of my attempts to learn new ways of managing the unfamiliar.

My brother David recalls: 'We went off to find a pub for lunch and you stood at the bar as we got our drinks... and I was aware of the stares of some characters further down the bar. Out of the blue, you offered, "Not looking my best today, I'm afraid." I was startled, but we didn't look long to see how your response had been received – probably with some embarrassment – but I saw a great surge in your resolve.' It wasn't the cleverest thing to say but, as an early ploy, it worked to some degree.

Shop assistants offered me many interesting encounters. Complete strangers, yes, and likely to remain so if I never shopped there again, so I could afford to take a few risks – and I often had to if I wanted to get served properly. So I started to use these tiny meaningless meetings to experiment with ensuring that they could see the real me. But I realise now that I got excessively involved sometimes, so I'd like to apologise to the many shop assistants and till clerks that I may have bored! Seven years later, when I first met my wife-to-be, she commented that it seemed to take me five minutes to pay for petrol when everyone else did so in a fraction of that time.

Gradually, I learned that I could take action to influence the way that the general public, strangers, saw me and reacted to my face. In fact, if I did not adopt proactive tactics, on almost all occasions I was at their mercy. As I got better and better at communicating, I discovered that it opened up so many new experiences, including making strong friendships and having amusing encounters.

FACE IT

So, your aim should be to be engaging, friendly and sometimes assertive in all your encounters... and if you are, you will almost certainly start to experience a positive feedback loop:

Positive Feedback Loop

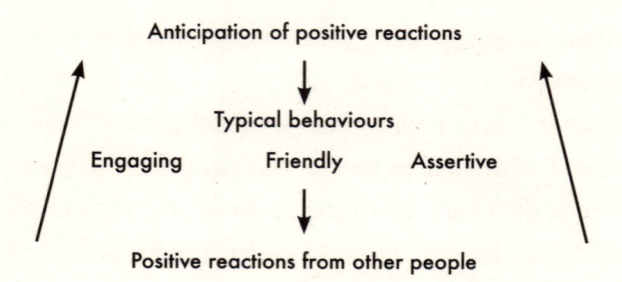

Anticipation of positive reactions

Typical behaviours

Engaging   Friendly   Assertive

Positive reactions from other people

It is also important to remember that as with learning any new skill, these new communication skills are bound to feel strange to start with, but with practice, they can become second nature.

The cycle of learning that applies to learning French or baking bread is also relevant here: initially you feel unconsciously incompetent, then consciously incompetent and, as you practise new skills, you will become consciously competent and then unconsciously competent.

Summing all this up, here are a few principles for being a good communicator if you have a distinctive face:

How you think:
- Discipline your self-talk to send yourself positive, affirming messages.
- Be in command of the factual details of your condition.
- Be understanding of others' difficulties with your face.
- Do not misinterpret others' avoidance behaviour as malign or hostile, but rather as indicative of their lack of understanding.
- Be prepared to help people understand more about you and your condition, but at a time and in a way that you choose.

FACES: THE PRINCIPLES OF EFFECTIVE PSYCHOSOCIAL CARE

And how you behave:
- Try not to hide your disfigurement, because it will almost certainly be obvious to others, who will then see it as something to be hidden.
- Show your face openly/strongly as far as you can – 'chin up'.
- Make effective eye contact as soon as you can – and sustain it throughout encounters.
- Use your voice, energy, humour, dress, make-up, body language, etc. to convey yourself and let your personality show/shine.
- Use your intellect to ask questions about the people you meet so that they talk about themselves – and then offer snippets about yourself too.

But before I finish 'S' for social skills, I need to deal with one common objection: 'This is all just unfair. It adds an imposition, an unfair burden, on someone with a disfigurement. Why should I/you have to make the effort? Because it is an effort.'

Agreed. Until the campaign for face equality is successful, it will be an effort. But there are three good reasons for making it – if you don't, you'll be floundering; if you do, you will feel more in control and get good vibes from those you meet; and, perhaps best of all, if you do, you will also be an educator about disfigurement and a champion for respect.

THE FACES PACKAGE IN PRACTICE

The FACES package is, effectively, a disfigurement-specific Cognitive Behavioural Therapy (CBT) approach with a strong emphasis on social skills training. It can be best described as 'brief intervention', and the goal is that everyone who enrols in the CFP sessions – child, young person, adult or parent – leaves feeling more confident, with a higher sense of self-esteem and better able to manage other people's reactions to their disfigurement.

Every element of FACES is important – some will be more so to one person compared to another, and that depends on their situation and experience.

There is a risk in listing the strands in an order; not least because I am often asked, 'Which is the most important?' – to which I reply, 'They are all equally important. Each person needs to be able to choose the ones that enable them to make progress.' I would have devoured every strand! As would my parents, siblings and family.

You can now do FACES yourself through online programmes like www.faceitonline.org.uk and, through gradual or graded exposure, tackle such tricky problems as:

- 'I can't stand the sight of my face in the mirror so I avoid it – and photos too.'
- 'I don't engage on social media because I don't like to post photos for fear of abuse.'
- 'My expectations of my future have been badly dented by the facial surgery I've had.'

The principles of the FACES package can enable you to grapple with the psychological and social impact of having a less-than-perfect face (or body). Please use this part of the book as a self-help manual if you wish, adapt it to your circumstances and add your own insights and flavours! Or seek help from a professional who can guide you through it.

16.
MAKING FACES AVAILABLE TO EVERYONE

Looking back over the last almost thirty years, I am very proud of what Changing Faces achieved – and many donors should be rightly proud too. My aim in setting it up in 1992 was for the charity to be innovative and groundbreaking. In particular, I wanted to create new types of help to enable people with less-than-perfect faces to cope better in our look-perfect world. By evolving the FACES package, we created a proven blueprint and set high standards for what should be offered by a comprehensive health care system *as a matter of routine* to someone whose face is or becomes unusual-looking for any reason. Without such help, living and contributing to British society is made that much more difficult for thousands of people every year.

But, much as it grieves me to say this, the fact is that it will take many years before the very high bar created by the UK's NHS for all innovations can be overcome – in fact, it probably won't ever be. The level of scientific evidence required has to be obtained through randomised controlled trials (RCTs) so as to demonstrate that this sort of help really does 'work', and to specify exactly what should be offered by psychologists at what precise moment in a person's 'journey' to adjusting to a less-than-perfect face. This is unlikely ever to be gathered. Such research is too expensive to undertake, takes too long to conduct and is disproportionate for the type and scale of service being considered.

I dispute that RCTs should be required before such short-duration interventions like FACES are considered valid. They are very cheap compared to high-tech medicine and surgery and are so fundamental to a person's future that they should be deemed essential. Just like bandages. But that's the evidence base that health service policymakers now demand in order to justify providing such psychosocial interventions using public monies.

Sadly, it's not just in the field of disfigurement that there is a lack of attention to mental health problems. The failure to provide psychosocial care alongside biomedical treatments for people with disfigurements is a symptom of a systemic failure of health care around the world; it is not one that can be put down to the behaviours of a few clinicians (many of whom are very supportive of mental health interventions). It happens in every health system in the world.

With the exception of a few isolated pockets in some countries – I'm thinking of cleft care in the UK, for example – disfigurement-specific psychosocial care is usually sporadic, half-hearted and done without adequate resources, making it dependent on charitable or volunteer efforts. And this is true not just for conditions like burns, vitiligo and facial cancer but for a whole raft of conditions that impair a person's mobility, sensory awareness or intellectual development. In all those categories there is poor support, both emotional and social, to allow a person (patient) to live a full life with their impairment (or after treatment for it).

The reasons are multifactorial and interrelated, and the impact is that mental health problems associated with disfigurement (and other impairments) are far too often left unnoticed and unaddressed – and therefore fester.

The first reason is that the focus of medical and surgical science and training is on finding cures for the conditions the human population suffer from, and on developing functional and pharmaceutical interventions. Which are very laudable goals. But they are pursued with far too little attention given to the everyday emotional and social concerns that people and families have to live with. My hope is that the next generation of health care practitioners and researchers will overturn this obsession.

Secondly, researching cures and fixes is often presented (including in charity research documents) as the most effective way – sometimes as the only way – of addressing mental health and psychosocial problems. Sadly, research into psychological methods for tackling intangible issues like emotional reactions and coping mechanisms is not yet attracting donors; but there are signs that attention to these issues is starting to increase. It was encouraging to see the British princes, William and Harry, set up their Foundation and Heads Together initiatives.

Thirdly, there has been far too little investment in the research needed to evaluate psychological interventions. In the 2000s, Professor Richard Layard of the London School of Economics conducted a seminal review of such interventions and concluded that only Cognitive Behavioural Therapy had sufficient evidence of cost-effectiveness, and this led to the development of a new programme in the NHS based on that approach (IAPT therapy). All other approaches were questioned and deemed 'not proven cost-effective'.

Since then, health economic studies of psychological treatments have increased in number, but the evidence base remains weak. And that's not entirely surprising, because bar CBT, which is extremely structured, none of them have clear definitions. Unlike a specified course of drugs, psychotherapy and psychoanalysis are variable by definition because their practitioners tailor what they do according to their clients' needs. It is therefore almost impossible to conduct RCTs of those treatments.

And, because the scientific evidence of impact is sketchy and by no means watertight, it's too easy for clinicians and policy-makers to deem psychological help something of an optional extra, a distraction, or even a waste of resources.

This is extremely frustrating and made the more so because, as many clinicians (especially surgeons), are willing to admit, a great deal of medicine and surgery lacks any credible evidence base; procedures continue to be undertaken because 'we've always done it that way' – and, of course, patients have to believe they work and are rightly very grateful when they do.

Lastly, there has not been sufficient sustained pressure from informed people and organisations to push for changes. Across the whole field of mental health, it has been a battle to get the right level of attention to the escalating mental health problems so rife in today's Britain – and across the developed world. There have, however, been some recent big strides forward: in February 2016, NHS England (the lead organisation in the UK) declared:

> The NHS in England today commits to the biggest transformation of mental health care across the NHS in a generation, pledging to help more than a million extra people and investing more than a billion pounds a year by 2020/21'.
>
> It is making the move in response to the final report of an independent taskforce, chaired by the excellent Chief Executive of Mind, Paul Farmer, set up by the NHS as part of its Five Year Forward View to build consensus on how to improve services for people of all ages.[1]

But realistically, it is highly unlikely that very much of this money will be directed to addressing the psychosocial problems of people with standing-out faces and bodies. Those problems are not seen as very significant compared to those of depression, adolescent self-harming, schizophrenia and the like.

To try to counter this dispiriting environment, in its first fifteen years, Changing Faces invested heavily in supporting psychosocial research so that our ideas – and those of others too – could be tested, refined, retested, etc.

Between 1992 and 2002, as well as providing lots of one-to-one help, Changing Faces ran three very important trial projects that were subjected to third-party independent evaluation: a study of the impact of our workshops, an audit of needs across many specialties, and a project to evaluate an NHS unit that we set up at Frenchay Hospital in Bristol. A later – and sadly, last – project evaluated the role of Changing Faces Practitioners (CFPs) in the NHS. Despite many practical difficulties in the research itself, it found that they can play a very effective role. However, it proved exceedingly difficult to sustain such projects as research funding dried up or was increasingly competed for.

The good news, however, is that those research projects spawned many others looking into the psychosocial needs of people with disfigurements in general and specific conditions in particular. So, I'm proud to say there is now a growing international body of literature that we can point to and draw upon which reinforces the need for and legitimises the value of this type of intervention. (I say 'this type of intervention' because Changing Faces does not have a monopoly over how it is delivered. We argued that the principles of our interventions should be included in all others.)

We also raised charitable funding for an online programme to be developed that became www.faceitonline.org.uk and was very successfully evaluated using an RCT methodology – a rare bird indeed![2]

We can also be proud that we created the Centre for Appearance Research in partnership with the University of the West of England in 2002. It has become the world leader (and only real research centre) in this work, with around thirty academics now attached to it. Its major biennial Appearance Matters conference attracts researchers from all over the world.

But I do see other trends that are less heartening. For example, it is depressing to see that the fix-it obsession has re-established itself:

where there is new money for disfigurement research, from the state or in philanthropy, it seems to prioritise cures for disfiguring conditions over the next decades rather than evaluating and embedding the practical, effective help we and others have pioneered and turning it into everyday health care.

Modern medicine and surgery have brilliantly supported that process – and reconstructive surgery, pressure garment therapy (to flatten out scars) and other interventions are hugely valuable. But scars are painful psychologically primarily because of our society's obsession with perfect looks. We should do much more to civilise that obsession and support people in the meantime.

I conclude sombrely that although there is now much greater clinical and professional awareness that people with less-than-perfect faces have psychosocial needs and that these can be effectively addressed if there is a will to do so, it is hard to see that happening in the near future.

The reluctance to invest in psychosocial treatments when combined with the economic constraints evident in all countries' health care systems means that most people with facial disfigurements will continue, largely unassisted, to struggle to cope in a society where the stigma of imperfection reigns untamed. They have to find their own way of living in this perfect-face world with their self-reliance and resilience at the fore, supported by their families and by charities like Changing Faces. They will remain stigmatised until face-ism is overthrown. Which is going to take a long time – as I explore in more detail in Part 3.

17.
THE PROFESSIONAL – A CONCLUSION

Setting up the charity Changing Faces in 1992 was a highly speculative venture in some respects, but its impact has been far beyond my wildest dreams. Only this week, I had an email from an American woman who had visited Changing Faces in the early 2000s hoping to plan a social skills study for people with Moebius syndrome (who have no facial musculature). She was a budding academic and I was delighted to enable her to adapt and evaluate our social skills programme. The great news was that not only was the programme quite helpful to her personally, but she's adapted it for many people with facial paralysis in North America and internationally. And sometimes I would hear from or meet people who had discovered that far from their disfigurement being a burden, it had become a force of liberation, freeing them from the unattainable and unreal expectations of today's society. This paradox was first pointed out to me by that guru figure of mine, Harry Williams, when he wrote in *True Resurrection*:

> [An] image of resurrection is found in the later paintings of Van Gogh. What from one point of view they portray is the horrific and poisonous power of destructive evil. The brushstrokes open

> our eyes to the hell and damnation which lie everywhere – in a field of growing corn, in the sky, in the chairs and tables of a café, in the wall of a house, in the features of a friend. Yet it is by means of this horror of hell that Van Gogh reveals his true affirmation of life. The paradox... was expressed by Sartre in terms of a nation's history when he said of his countrymen: 'We have never been more free than under the German occupation'. The brute fact of tyranny, the denial of all political and public freedom, made men aware to an unusual degree of their chains. And in this full recognition of their lack of freedom, men became aware of their true freedom which consists in the active acceptance of external reality with all its constraints, so that the constraint itself is made into the very context and milieu in which personal freedom is asserted.[3]

The reality that some surgeons and others find hard to contemplate is that people with disfigurements can come to realise that they are blissfully freed from the 'tyranny of the norm', as Bryan Appleyard has termed it.

How can people get to this state of 'active acceptance of external reality with all its constraints'? I described my own journey in Part 1, but there are many different routes. Some are inspired by a role model like Katie Piper. Others need a formal course in cognitive restructuring through which exaggerated or faulty beliefs ('nobody will like me because...' or 'people are staring at me because they don't like me...') are challenged and replaced by more positive thinking patterns. For others, debunking deeply held assumptions about how important appearance is frees them.

My hope is that Part 2 will help you – as an individual with the lived experience, or as a professional – to find ways to that active acceptance, which protects you against the stigma that a facial disfigurement carries.

MEZZANINE

Going 'political'

From the outset of Changing Faces in 1992, it was my intention – at some point – to start to raise awareness about the injustices and abuses faced by people with facial disfigurements in their everyday lives and to campaign 'to change the way we all face disfigurement', as our strapline put it. From the early days, the evidence began to accumulate that people with not-perfect faces were indeed disadvantaged by other people's attitudes and behaviours and by the actions – and inactions – of the media, schools, businesses, politicians and governments... and members of the public too.

Over the twenty-eight years since then, I have heard far too many distressing and anger-making stories of people being marginalised, discounted and treated badly.

But – and this heartens me daily – I have also been lucky enough to come across many, many strong-minded people who have been willing to become allies in bringing about change. They have demonstrated that life with a distinctive face can work out well – but you need bundles of luck, great social support around you and much more. None of them has found life straightforward. All have faced and struggled with facial stigma in its various and often insidious forms. All want to challenge those prejudices.

Before I explain how we came together to create the campaign for face equality, I've asked ten of them to share their stories. They are not a 'representative' group in the sense of perfectly reflecting all the myriad experiences that people have, but they come from a wide range of backgrounds and give a flavour of the challenges people with distinctive faces experience.

I thank them all for their willingness to share a little of their lives and show off their distinguished and outstanding faces!

FIRST TINY STEPS IN CAMPAIGNING

From the charity's earliest days, we knew that our first duty had to be to provide help and empowerment for the many people and families who made contact with the charity... Which explains the focus on all that is described in Part 2.

It wasn't until 2002 that we could start to develop our 'changing minds' work, as we called it, in earnest. By then, we had the necessary team in place to handle all the requests for 'changing lives' help that come in, and to develop new self-help resources for the embryonic internet.

Which isn't to say that we did no 'campaigning' in those first ten years. Far from it. Our media coverage to raise awareness of the issues was consistent, and we often gained attention from mainstream broadcasters too. And in 1995, we had a real breakthrough (described in more detail in Part 3) when, after much pressure from Changing Faces, the Disability Discrimination Act 1995 provided legal protection for people with 'severe disfigurements' as if they had a disability.

It was a landmark moment, the first legal recognition worldwide that someone with a distinctive face could be disadvantaged not by the lack of physical access nor the presence of barriers but by people's negative attitudes. It gave a lot of confidence to Changing Faces' clients and everyone else with a disfigurement – and in the years that followed, we had a steady stream of employers wanting to know how to make a 'reasonable adjustment' for someone with a facial disfigurement in their staff teams, as the new Act required.

How to survive
bumping into

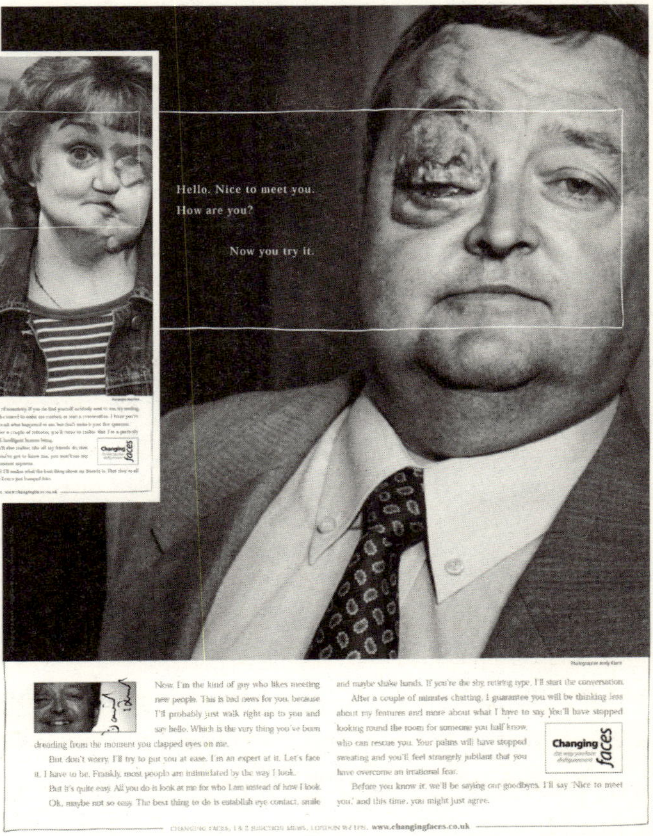
Hello. Nice to meet you.
How are you?
Now you try it.
Now I'm the kind of guy who likes meeting new people. This is bad news for you, because I'll probably just walk right up to you and say hello. Which is the very thing you've been dreading from the moment you clapped eyes on me.
But don't worry. I'll try to put you at ease. I'm an expert at it. Let's face it. I have to be. Frankly, most people are intimidated by the way I look.
But it's quite easy. All you do is look at me for who I am instead of how I look. Ok, maybe not so easy. The best thing to do is establish eye contact, smile and maybe shake hands. If you're the shy retiring type, I'll start the conversation.
After a couple of minutes chatting, I guarantee you will be thinking less about my features and more about what I have to say. You'll have stopped looking round the room for someone you half know who can rescue you. Your palms will have stopped sweating and you'll feel strangely jubilant that you have overcome an irrational fear.
Before you know it, we'll be saying our goodbyes. I'll say 'Nice to meet you,' and this time, you might just agree.
Changing faces
www.changingfaces.co.uk

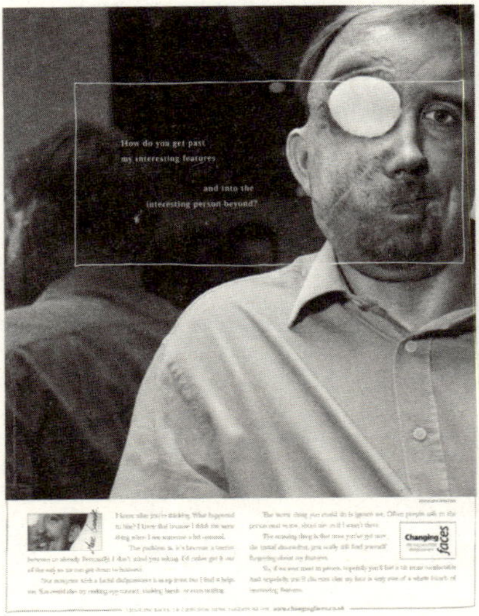
How do you get past
my interesting features
and into the
interesting person beyond?
Changing faces
www.changingfaces.co.uk

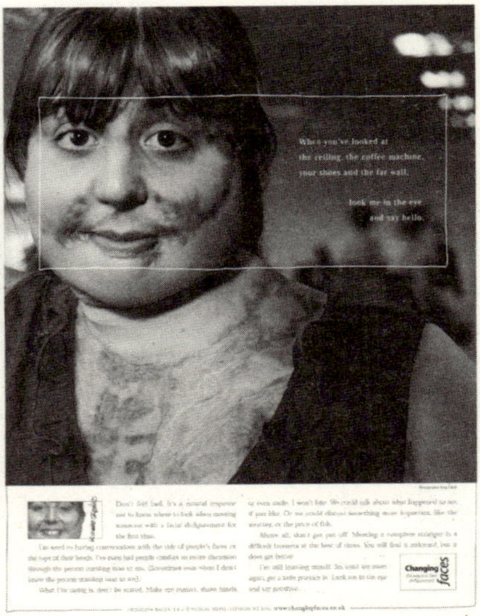
When you've looked at
the ceiling, the coffee machine,
your shoes and the far wall,
look me in the eye
and say hello.
Changing faces

Important as that breakthrough was, however, it was buried deep in a huge Act, and without social media to disseminate the news, we could not use it to challenge the wider public's attitudes.

Then, out of the blue in the winter of 2001–02, we were offered the brilliant pro bono support of an advertising agency, WCRS, led by one of our trustees, Stephen Woodford, to invent a really eye-catching public campaign. Four posters were created and then displayed throughout the London Underground system, on other billboards across the country and in many magazines too. And they made a big impact!

The four billboard posters had strong 'twists' in their short texts – like the one of David Bird, who has a complex birthmark over one eye, which says: 'Hello. Nice to meet you. How are you? Now you try it.'

The magazine versions carried longer and no less challenging narratives, and I'm deliberately including all four here because they demonstrate beautifully how it's possible to convey relatively straightforward public education messages about how to think and communicate when we meet someone with a distinctive face.

One was of a woman with facial burns, Michelle Syms:

When you've looked at the ceiling, the coffee machine, your shoes and the far wall, look me in the eye and say hello.

Don't feel bad. It's a natural response not to know where to look when meeting someone with a facial disfigurement for the first time. I'm used to having conversations with the side of people's faces, or the tops of their heads. I've even had people conduct an entire discussion through the person standing next to me. (Sometimes even when I don't know the person standing next to me.)

What I'm saying is, don't be scared. Make eye contact, shake hands, or even smile. I won't bite. We could talk about what happened to me, if you like. Or we could discuss something more important, like the weather, or the price of fish. Above

THE PROFESSIONAL – A CONCLUSION

all, don't get put off. Meeting a complete stranger is a difficult business at the best of times. You will find it awkward, but it does get better. I'm still learning myself. So, until we meet again, get a little practice in. Look me in the eye and say goodbye.

Marc Crank, a man with neurofibromatosis, starts with: 'How do you get past my interesting features and into the interesting person beyond?'

I know what you're thinking. What happened to him? I know that because I think the same thing when I see someone a bit unusual. The problem is, it's become a barrier between us already. Personally, I don't mind you asking. I'd rather get it out of the way so we can get down to business.

Not everyone with a facial disfigurement is as up front, but I find it helps me. You could also try making eye contact, shaking hands, or even smiling. The worst thing you could do is ignore me. Often people talk to the person next to me, about me, as if I wasn't there.

The amazing thing is that once you've got over the initial discomfort, you really will find yourself forgetting about my features.

So, if we ever meet in person, hopefully you'll feel a bit more comfortable. And hopefully, you'll discover that my face is only one of a whole bunch of interesting features.

Susan Duncan, a woman whose face had been damaged by radiotherapy she'd been prescribed as a child, offers advice on 'how to survive bumping into me'.

Let's be honest, I don't look like your average passer-by. I like to think of myself as unique. I have a facial disfigurement, that's all. Apart from that, I'm perfectly average. I go to the shops, the cinema and even to the pub, just like any other average person.

I'm simply out there, getting on with my life. Naturally, people are going to look at me. I don't mind this; I'm used to it. I do feel uncomfortable when they stare and I absolutely hate it when people shout rude names at me.

I'm just like anyone else with a facial disfigurement. I'm just looking for a degree of sensitivity. If you do find yourself suddenly next to me, try smiling.

Don't be scared to make eye contact, or start a conversation. I know you're dying to ask what happened to me, but don't make it your first question. After a couple of minutes, you'll come to realise that I'm a perfectly normal, intelligent human being.

You'll also realise, like all my friends do, that once you've got to know me, you won't see my disfigurement anymore. And I'll realise what the best thing about my friends is. That they're all people I once just bumped into.

Those scripts illustrate how very positive we were trying to be in 2002 about unblocking the excruciating 'communication channel' between people with disfigurements and those they meet in the first moments of social encounters.

Millions of travellers on the London Underground and on the buses in London and around Britain saw the posters – and I know they are still remembered today. Because nobody had ever done something like this before! The acclaim for the campaign was huge, and the WCRS agency won a national award.

There's a nice story attached to this poster campaign too. I'd managed to persuade Moira Stuart, the BBC newsreader, to do a photoshoot in front of one of the posters on Oxford Street. It was a cold morning and she and I went by Tube shortly after rush hour to do this and sat opposite a pair of canoodling lovers who were kissing as if there was no tomorrow. They too got out of the train at Oxford Circus and, as we went up the escalator, the young woman waved at

THE PROFESSIONAL – A CONCLUSION

me as if she knew me. What I loved was that she quite clearly had a bilateral cleft lip and palate! Moira loved it too – and we felt it was a great omen for what turned out to be a very successful campaign.

We followed that early poster effort with two more smaller ones featuring children in 2004, but knew that in order to get our 'campaigning' off the ground properly we had to find a unifying theme. And that came in an unexpected way.

In October 2004, a major exhibition was opened at the Science Museum in London called 'Future Face'. Curated by Sandra Kemp, it brought together a very eclectic and thought-provoking array of artefacts, images and articles from prehistory looking right into the next millennium. Fascinating! And happily, Changing Faces had a small but significant part in the exhibition, with our posters displayed and some agreed commentary too.

As part of the festival triggered by the exhibition, a big debate was held at the Royal Geographical Society's lovely wood-panelled lecture theatre, entitled 'Future Face?'. I was honoured to be part of a panel of scientists, ethicists and futurologists. It was a big occasion and I took a lot of time and care over my ten-minute presentation and slides – we were still in the era of making up transparent slides which had to go through a projector. In that lecture theatre, this meant that all speakers had to climb up into a booth near the ceiling to talk to the projectionist – who just happened to be a man with a very significant facial birthmark.

Inevitably, we got into a conversation about our respective lives. He said he was interested in what I was going to say, and I gave him a preview. Critically, he said that his jobs had always been 'behind the scenes' – and that gave me renewed determination to make my points. This was the first time I had ever suggested a campaign for 'face equality'. Here's a tiny snippet of what I said:

> While some may be thinking that we have come here tonight to eulogise about the coming age of designer faces and the market

for them that might result if science rolls on relentlessly, I want to engage you in a different way...

I will argue that our present cultural and social mindset about faces is unhealthy and unjust to millions of people on the planet... 'Face-ism' is a new concept for a very old process – and challenging it would have huge benefits for our entire culture. We believe that we must start a campaign to create face equality, and if you think I am barking, replace the face with race as I am speaking...

The response I received that evening was very interested and positive, but it was nearly four years before Changing Faces could launch the campaign for face equality. We were 'going political' at last.

THE LAUNCH OF THE CAMPAIGN FOR FACE EQUALITY

The campaign was launched at London's prestigious Mall Galleries to a crowd of over 200 people in May 2008. We set out ambitious goals – to promote fair and equal treatment, to raise public awareness, knowledge, skills and confidence, and to challenge negative attitudes towards people with facial disfigurements.

Why? Because, as our literature said, every single day, everyone with a facial disfigurement is vulnerable to unfairness. In Britain alone, that affects the lives of over half a million people who have distinctive faces because of birthmarks and congenital conditions, scarring after accidents, burns or cancer surgery, facial asymmetry or paralysis or the effects of a skin condition.

The reports from our supporters had showed us that they were fed up with the thoughtless prejudices and actions of individuals, professionals and private and public institutions – and, perhaps most starkly, with the imagery and words used in the media.

THE PROFESSIONAL – A CONCLUSION

But was that really happening? Were they just imagining it? The charity commissioned COG Research to objectively assess public attitudes towards people with disfigurements in the run-up to the campaign's launch. COG conducted a standard questionnaire and found that most people claimed *not* to hold any prejudice whatsoever. However, they then ran an Implicit Attitude Test (IAT), a method developed at Harvard University in the 1990s to measure 'unconscious bias' towards people based on their race, gender or sexuality. And the results were startling.

The IAT found that nine out of ten people had unconscious bias against those who had a facial disfigurement, finding it difficult to associate positive attributes to them like being happy, successful or fun to be with. This scale of bias was even larger than that revealed in the Harvard studies of racism in the 1990s.

We didn't gain much media coverage that day, but we nonetheless received much acclaim, and many leaders of like-minded organisations supported the call for action:

> The Cleft Lip and Palate Association (CLAPA) fully endorses Changing Faces' Face Equality Campaign. We know there are many, many people with clefts who find it difficult to relate to other people in both social and work situations as a result of looking – and sometimes sounding – different to others. We hope this campaign will increase awareness of facial difference and ensure that familiarity with appearance issues will lead to a far greater level of social acceptance.
>
> Gareth Davies, CEO, CLAPA

> We are conditioned to make rapid assessments of people from their appearance. A person with a facial difference can often be adversely affected by this instinctive reaction. This campaign will help us all to reassess how we perceive others

and therefore the Vitiligo Society fully and wholeheartedly supports this initiative.'

Jennifer Viles, Vitiligo Society

The Royal Association for Disability and Rehabilitation (RADAR) supports the Face Equality campaign because we want a just and equal society whose strength is human difference. That means rooting out discrimination in all its forms – from insidious prejudice to outright bullying. We wish the campaign every success.

Phil Friend OBE, Chair, Liz Sayce, CEO, RADAR

And, most pleasingly in light of the need to make this a human rights issue, Nicola Brewer, CEO, Equality and Human Rights Commission, said:

Only the bravest organisations talk about subjects that most people would rather ignore. Changing Faces is one of those organisations. It does a remarkable job raising awareness of this important issue and challenges negative attitudes to facial disfigurement. We welcome this positive and inspirational campaign which shows that how you look should be nothing to do with what you can achieve.

The campaign was kicked into action.

Part 3 now looks at its underlying rationale and how it can and should be mushroomed in the future.

PART 3

The Political

18.
'FACE-ISM' UNMASKED

Living in societies that obsess about the importance of perfect faces, as we virtually all do in the twenty-first century, imposes strains on everyone – and those with not-perfect faces especially so. It took me a full seven years after my accident to build a new, strong, resilient me, able to tolerate the intrusions and assumptions that go with living in what was then twentieth-century Britain.

Brilliant surgery gave me a noticeable but no longer shocking face, which I then had to integrate into a new identity. I gradually came to respect myself, to like my face and to find ways to persuade others to do so too – as soon as they met me, or even beforehand! The instantaneous facial stigma that I faced – and still face – did not change, but it could not touch me. Within seconds of meeting me, people realised they'd got it all wrong. And some found that very troubling.

Psychosocial support and empowerment for those of all ages with newly acquired not-perfect faces are now in existence (as I have described in Part 2), but it is very far from being widely available. In fact, it is only so through the not-for-profit sector in most countries. This means that the vast majority of people with distinctive faces are fending for themselves – which in most cases means having to accept, grudgingly, the facial stigma imposed on them. Millions of people in Britain and around the world live with it every single day.

I do not accept this. I hope you don't either. Here's why...

I believe we can successfully challenge the prejudice and discrimination of what amounts to 'face-ism' and disavow the culture of perfection. We can – and must – promote the human rights of, and equal opportunities for people with less-than-perfect faces.

This is a long-term project, no doubt, but it has started already.

Every one of us can contribute to it at micro-level, often using the social skills I outlined earlier: in small everyday incidents like staring in public places, ridicule on social media or awkwardness in a job interview, you can inform, reassure and sometimes, with gentle assertiveness, challenge – and, above all, help the other person to see you and your face in a new way. You will have educated one person, and they will take your teaching and pass it on.

At macro-level, too, we can work together to transform the daily experience of so many people disadvantaged by face-ism – just as campaigners against sexism and racism have done. A hundred years ago it was thought ridiculous in many circles to challenge the accepted inferior position of women or black people in our societies. It's happening... still a way to go, but...

This sort of macro change will require us to be much more assertive, because overthrowing face-ism is about justice and fairness. We have to argue strongly that existing ways of thinking and behaviours are faulty and lead to very undesirable outcomes – widespread unfairness, pervasive low expectations and diminished lives. 'Just' because of the way a person looks. It's not just at all.

This third part is therefore about unpicking face-ism and figuring out what we can do together to change it. Facial stigma comes in many forms and is caused by a number of factors, which we'll explore in the next chapters. Let's start by disabusing a few myths.

Facial stigma is not inevitable or biologically programmed. It doesn't kick in all the time – thankfully. When you are with your family or close friends, you are likely to be respected for who you are, irrespective of what your not-perfect face looks like.

But those moments may be short-lived, and there may be people quite close to you who observe your face without the open-minded respect you hope for. They may well think sadly about your face... and then they go on to make other judgements about you. In so doing, they are being sucked down, unwittingly perhaps, into the quagmire that is facial prejudice... and they may well show it in what they say to you, or how they behave, perhaps avoiding talking to you altogether.

Everyone with a less-than-perfect face is vulnerable to facial stigma and discrimination, and that includes people with wrinkles, eye bags and all the normal signs of ageing. We now need to call it out for what it is: face-ism – an insidious and highly damaging force in our global society.

We need to understand it so that we can grow a movement to challenge it. In its place, we must promote respect, fairness and equality for everyone, irrespective of their facial appearance.

WHAT DO I MEAN BY FACE-ISM?

This might be a rather academic sociological section, but stay with it, because you need to be able to use the right words to describe what's going on.

Years ago, back in the late 1970s, I read a brilliant and insightful article by two sociologists, Robert Bogdan and Douglas Biklen, entitled 'Handicapism', which has provided me ever since with a structure for understanding the experience of people with disabilities.[1] Their taxonomy has enabled me to get beyond the analysis of stigma provided by Goffman.

Paraphrasing Bogdan and Biklen: 'Face-ism is a set of *assumptions* and *prejudices* that promote the differential and unequal treatment of people because of their not-perfect faces that amounts to *discrimination*'.

Their taxonomy would suggest that facial stigma has two elements:

- '*the facial stereotypes or assumptions* that are attached to facial disfigurements', and
- '*the facial prejudices or beliefs* that people hold on the basis of those stereotypes'.

How people *discriminate* will be determined by what assumptions and beliefs they have.

Psychologists say that human beings need assumptions to allow them to negotiate the unexpected in human encounters without embarrassment or committing faux pas. So when someone meets a person with a distinctive face for the first time, they rely on their assumptions and beliefs to guide their behaviour so as to avoid embarrassment.

Where do they get their stereotypes/assumptions about facial disfigurements? Maybe from hearsay, family history or a media story. Sometimes from real life, of course. And their prejudices/beliefs? Similarly. They may be informed, or based entirely on speculation.

So, if someone meets or sees a woman with facial scars, their *assumption* could be that the scars came from a violent attack and their *belief* could be that she is from the criminal fraternity. On those premises, they would think themselves justified in treating her differently by avoiding her and telling others to do so too – effectively stigmatising her, more or less however she behaves and whether or not there is any truth in their assumption.

Or their *assumption* could be that she'd been the unfortunate victim of a car accident and their *belief* could be that such scars make her a rather sad case, worthy of compassion. Those reflex thoughts would cause them to treat her with words of sympathy, perhaps. Which she may well find irritating and patronising – stigmatising – despite their good intentions. The unintended consequences are negative.

Enough jargon, but you get the general idea. Using these words – assumptions (or stereotypes) and beliefs (or prejudices) – helps us to define everyday face-ism.

'FACE-ISM' UNMASKED

Most people are, entirely understandably, uninformed about facial disfigurements because there are a very great number of reasons why someone's face may be less-than-perfect. It could be a congenital condition or a traumatic cause... or a facial cancer... or a skin condition... or a facial paralysis... or... the list goes on. So, again not surprisingly, people have to rely on assumptions gleaned from hearsay or media stories that may well be untested and fallacious – and the beliefs they hold as a result may be similarly flawed.

This matters hugely more in the twenty-first century than it did in the past, when human beings moved in very limited social and geographical circles. Back then – and it is still true in small local communities – everyone came to know why a child or adult had a not-perfect face.

That knowledge may not have been sound – too often, old wives' tales dominated ('your mother must have played with hares' about a child with a cleft lip and palate and the like) and harmful prejudices were allowed to fester, often with nasty consequences, such as the child or adult being hidden away out of sight. Family shame took over.

But in today's incredibly visual and interactive world – far more visual and interactive than any previous era – the vast diversity of faces necessitates a very great reliance on stereotypes/assumptions. This reliance is much more marked than in dealing with other human characteristics like someone's race or ethnicity or their sexual orientation, the variety of which is much smaller.

This then influences how people with distinctive faces are treated. Even with all the mass communication and transportation that characterises the world today, it's relatively uncommon to meet someone with a less-than-perfect face – and so, naturally enough, people have to rely on assumptions and beliefs to determine how to behave. Unconscious bias kicks in.

Back in the 1990s, an American social anthropologist, Frances Cooke Macgregor, who studied, extremely insightfully, the lives of facially injured American veterans from the wars in Vietnam and Korea returning to civilian life, concluded that people with what she called 'deviant faces' experienced 'a loss of the civil inattention most of us take for granted'.[2]

That sums it up beautifully: a loss of – or lack of, to extend this to people with distinctive faces from birth – civil inattention is what the assumptions and beliefs that constitute facial stigma deny those of us with not-perfect faces. It is a human right denied.

Face-ist discrimination in modern society can take many forms, some subtle and unconscious, some blatant: people may avoid you or ask if you are feeling OK or look at you with sympathy, writing off your prospects of being a socially interesting person. They may stare at you, reject you for a job, avoid you at a party, talk about you loudly on public transport or write nasty things about you on social media.

It manifests itself in uncontrolled staring and intrusive questions, name-calling in playgrounds, harassment and bullying at work, ridicule and pointed jokes, patronisation ('so brave'), avoidance of social interaction and especially of eye contact, poor customer service, ostracism and discounting.

Add to that the media's loaded descriptions of 'sufferers' and 'victims', the evidence of low expectations in schools, rejection in job interviews and the resultant underemployment, and you have a picture of the exclusion that facial stigma imposes.

The loss or lack of civil inattention can take a serious toll on people's psyches and chances in life. People with less-than-perfect faces have to remain 'on guard' every single minute they are in public – and when they are using social media, too, because of its heavy focus on photographic imagery, which can so easily be abused. And the sometimes thoughtless imagery and words of private and public institutions, especially the film industry and some parts of the media, rub salt in the wound such as the portrayals of 'scarred' people as baddies in films.

'FACE-ISM' UNMASKED

On the UK's first Face Equality Day, 26th May 2017, Changing Faces published *Disfigurement in the UK*, the most extensive study of the lives of people with disfigurements, based on over 800 replies to an online survey. It described a vastly unequal playing field in almost every aspect of their lives, leading them to have lower aspirations and expectations, and to be resigned to the inevitability of abuse and injustice.

The key findings were:

- 80 per cent experienced staring, harassment or abuse from members of the public.
- 50 per cent experienced discrimination because of their disfigurement.
- 40 per cent said that their appearance affected how well they did at school.
- 80 per cent decided against applying for a job because they thought their face wouldn't fit.
- 67 per cent had experienced a health professional making an assumption about their emotional health.
- 75 per cent were denied medical or surgical treatment because it was deemed unnecessary.
- Almost 100 per cent had seen a meme or post on social media mocking disfigurement.
- Of those who complained to a social media company, 0 per cent had their complaint upheld.
- 92 per cent of those who'd used online dating had had unpleasant comments about their looks.

The conclusion has to be that the lives of people with disfigurements are disadvantaged by attitudes and behaviour towards them. The perpetrators are no one specific group. It's something that happens across all sections of society.

But, I hear you say, do people *really* hold such negative beliefs? Surely you are exaggerating. People don't really think like that.

Which is what an independent survey of public attitudes in 2008 found. When asked if they thought about or treated people with facial disfigurements differently, the answer was a clear 'certainly not'. Nobody thinks they think or behave badly.

But in a subsequent Implicit Attitude Test adapted from the one developed at Harvard University to test racial prejudice, nine out of ten people found it very hard to associate positive characteristics with someone who has a facial disfigurement – like being successful, having a fun life, being happy or good to spend time with. And that was the case even though the people with disfigurements in the test didn't just have not-perfect faces, they had smiling faces too!

However, whilst many people are not aware of this disfigurement bias and would claim that they bear no hostile intent, the fact is that the unconscious bias exists. It is a fact of life. And the danger is that until the bias is challenged by convincing counterarguments, it's also a self-fulfilling prophecy.

My contention is that face-ism is a global phenomenon of massive importance to millions of people. And it is worth noting that there is common ground here with the millions of other people who have a slightly large nose, wrinkles or a less-than-perfect complexion. All of them are feeling the effects of face-ism too. Not surprisingly, many now resort to expensive make-up, cosmetic surgery and facial fillers to ward off other people's face-value judgements.

The evidence piles up every week. Reports from organisations such as Girlguiding and the National Union of Teachers have come out of how women – and men too – are feeling inadequate about their looks. Research from the Be Real campaign (February 2018) called *In Your Face* exposed how widespread young peoples' fear and anxiety about their appearance has become.[3] They are increasingly looking for facial cosmetic surgery – and other statistics confirm the lengths to which people will go to make their facial imperfections less obvious.[4]

'FACE-ISM' UNMASKED

Facial stigma is increasingly expressed, too, even in cosmopolitan, informed and supposedly tolerant Britain. Comments below press or online articles reveal the unfettered nastiness that now prevails, particularly towards 'ugly people'. We have to put a stop to it.

19.

WHERE DOES FACE-ISM COME FROM?

I have spent many years at the front line tracking down where these assumptions and beliefs around distinctive faces come from and trying to counter them. Here's a brief summary of my detective work on the origins of face-ism.

Face-ism has deep and complex roots – like the enormous flax plant in my garden. It started life fifteen years ago as a single small plant, with pretty flowers, one amongst many others. It didn't affect anything else in the garden. But over the years the plant spread and spread. What had been one became three – and together they invaded other plants' space and overshadowed their growth until the others shrivelled and died. The flax we had admired had become a brute, and we decided that it had to come out. And we had to do it by hand.

That's when I came to understand the true meaning of 'entrenched'. The roots of the three flax plants were 'entrenched' in the ground by a densely intertwined and invisible root system. It gave the plant such a secure foothold as to be seemingly unassailable. It took us a fortnight of pickaxing, digging and hacking to wrench the thing in all its nastiness out of the ground.

Face-ism's roots lie deep and entrenched in the human psyche and modern culture. And they are invisible to the human eye, accepted as 'facts of life'. As a result, face-ism has been allowed to extend its roots unchallenged all around the globe, stifling other civilised and healthy thinking.

Face-ism actually consists of three strong stigmas towards people with not-perfect faces, which I've already referred to in Part 2 – see the section on attitudes (pages 169–173). Each stigma has a complete and coherent set of stereotypes, prejudices and discriminatory actions, and each has its origins in past or current cultural practices. These three stigmas are themselves severely intertwined, too, which allows face-ism to proliferate and spread unchecked. It's become entrenched, embedded.

The three stigmas and their seemingly coherent root systems are:

1. the 'You are sad and second-rate' stigma.
2. the 'You are morally deficient' stigma.
3. the 'Why don't you fix it?' stigma.

The next three sections look at each of these stigmas in a bit more detail, and the impact of believing them.

1. YOU ARE SAD AND SECOND-RATE

Probably the most ingrained face-ist stigma is that having a less-than-perfect face will mean you have a second-rate or third-rate existence. Your access to success and happiness in friendships, in intimate relationships, in work and in every aspect of life will be frustrated, however hard you try. One or two people with distinctive faces will slip through the barrier, but they are 'forces of nature', heroines, freaks, and viewed as 'exceptional'.

First-rate lives are the preserve of those with perfect faces who are more appealing to be and work with because of their 'good looks', and so have greater opportunities and chances of success. Their faces make them very attractive to others, and biologically, very desirable as a mate.

WHERE DOES FACE-ISM COME FROM?

This stigma is unquestionably embedded in the minds of the vast majority of the world's 8.1 billion people; 'unquestionably' both in the sense that nobody doubts the assertion that everyone believes this, and in the sense that most people do believe it without questioning it.

It is reinforced continually, unrelentingly and daily by massive commercial forces too: the daily visual diet that we all devour whilst going about our lives in twenty-first century British, Western and indeed global society is soused in it – marinated and cooked in it! Perfect faces are everywhere, telling us what to do, think and feel – 'Look like me and life will be happy ever after...'

That visual culture is more important today than it has ever been as everyone lives their lives through screens – TV screens, monitors, tablets and phones. The screens have become the perfect marketing platform for companies the world over. Add to the screens all the billboards and smart digital displays we see wherever we travel – in buses and at bus stops, in trains and in the underground metro/tube systems and through airports. It's a bombardment!

Thousands of glamorous, spotless (samey?) faces entice us not just to buy specific products and services, but cleverly hint that having a perfect, spotless and symmetrical face will bring so much more.

The most glossy of the adverts are for luxury goods and cosmetics using the faces of celebrities, chosen for their facial appeal – 'attractiveness', in the trade. Some admit afterwards that the photos have been airbrushed of all their deviance and flaws, but many just take the money – the big money that comes with being a fashion model.

If you think this is just hyperbole, consider airbrushing.

One of the most disturbing statistics I know is that millions of people across the planet are daily using airbrushing apps to touch up their face in the photos they are going to load onto social media platforms like Facebook and Instagram.

Here's one selling proposition from Huda Beauty's website:

> Let's face it, we all want to look like the hottest versions of ourselves! We're surrounded by airbrushed magazine covers and adverts, and reflecting on your filterless selfie is sometimes a bit of an anti-climax. Why shouldn't we all get to look as incredible as the celebs do? I mean thank the app gods for Snapchat filters, but sometimes that annoying spot or terrible lighting just doesn't do our flawless selves justice. So, here's our rundown of the top apps to get you front-cover ready, so when you don't have an extra five minutes to get your brows to their normal fleeky standard, these apps will help you fake it – no Photoshop course necessary![1]

There are many such apps now available, and they are big money. One popular one is ModiFace. A financial website says this:

> ModiFace powers a number of websites focused on facial visualization and virtual modification. ModiFace's story starts in 1999 at Stanford University, where Parham Aarabi initiated research on automatic face analysis. His work continued at the University of Toronto, where he worked on face processing algorithms (work which later won a world-wide innovation prize from MIT). In 2006, ModiFace Inc. was born.
>
> Today, ModiFace is the world's largest (performing nearly 750,000 makeovers per day) and most advanced (based on the number and technical complexity of the visualizations) virtual makeover platform, with nearly 100 websites in North America, Latin America, Europe, and Asia using ModiFace technology.[2]

ModiFace is just one. Others include Perfect365, 'a free app that lets people instantly smooth skin, excise zits, highlight eyes and even resize noses before sending their image out on the Internet',

WHERE DOES FACE-ISM COME FROM?

according to an article in the Huffington Post in 2013.[3] There are also Facetune, Pixtr and Visage Lab.

What this tells me is that there is a terrible worldwide fear about having a distinctive face, which is stoked by commercial forces. Every single human being is now vulnerable to what could be called 'the stigma of the not-perfect'.

Studies to test whether it is true that 'good' facial looks do actually improve a person's prospects at work or chances of success in life are few and far between – and are rarely convincing, not least because they use questionable methodologies. For example, some researchers have shown photographs of people with perfect and not-perfect faces to potential employers and asked them to rank the likelihood of hiring them. Hardly surprising, given the strength of the stereotyping, that people who 'look good' appear to have a better chance. What this misses is that when recruiting is done in the real world – and I am not counting e-recruitment, with its inherent risks of unconscious face-ist bias creeping in – people are chosen for their ability to do the job, and their social skills are critical in demonstrating their desire to do it well. People with not-perfect faces often have superb social skills!

But however weak the evidence for perfect faces meaning happy lives – and the divorce rates in Hollywood and amongst celebrities with supposedly perfect faces aren't exactly encouraging – the stigma of the not-perfect has us all in its vice-like grip.

This face-ist stereotype is also perpetuated by the lack of people with distinctive faces in British or international popular culture or public life. The fact that you or I may know lots of people with less-than-perfect faces living successful happy lives is irrelevant, because if there aren't any such role models in the online newspapers or celebrity magazines, they don't exist. It's hard to imagine an alternative. Rather like the early feminists: they were doubted until a critical mass started to form.

Many such people I know are happy in life, high flyers at work and in their chosen profession or trade and in fulfilling relationships if that is what they have decided upon. But frustratingly, the only ones I can cite as being well known are the Falklands soldier Simon Weston, the acid survivor Katie Piper, the actor Adam Pearson and Richard Morris, the former British Ambassador to Nepal. That's it. A few of the facially injured veterans from the Iraq and Afghanistan wars have also been seen performing heroic challenges to raise money so that others can get back to civvy street.

There have been even fewer role models internationally until really quite recently. Niki Lauda, the Formula 1 ace, was one, and there a few others, like film star Joaquin Phoenix (with a cleft lip), Winnie Harlow, an international model who has vitiligo, and Carly Findlay, a popular Australian writer with a rare skin condition (ichthyosis). And in India, some of the women attacked with acid are becoming known faces – one is even fronting up an advertising campaign for a fashion company.[4] More, please!

What effect can being gripped by this 'not-a-perfect-face means a sad life' stigma have?

There are many impacts, but let's look at three.

First, and in my view, worst: low expectations.

The worst setting for such thinking is in school, because if teachers hold such assumptions and beliefs and pass them on to other children, those with less-than-perfect faces may be seriously disadvantaged. Parents report teachers thinking something like this: 'I don't see many people with faces like your child's being successful, so it's not surprising that I don't push her to achieve academically… sadly, she's born to fail.'

The 2017 study of over 800 people with disfigurements by Changing Faces suggested that half of all schoolchildren who have a disfigurement experience discrimination because of it, and yet the ability of school leadership teams to deal with the problem appears limited.[5] Four in ten people say their appearance affected how well they did at school, and half said it affected their aspiration to stay in education post-sixteen.

WHERE DOES FACE-ISM COME FROM?

And those low expectations went on into adult life: four-fifths have avoided applying for a job because they thought their appearance would hinder them at interview, or because new colleagues would make them uncomfortable. More than half think their condition hindered their career, and 17 per cent had left a job or felt forced to leave because of reactions to their facial appearance.

The stultifying stereotype of low expectations is self-fulfilling, too. It is what the late Susan Daniels, the former Deputy Commissioner of the US Social Security Administration in the Clinton administration, famously called 'the soft bigotry of low expectations'. Daniels was responsible for the US government's policies towards disabled people and was rightly determined to draw attention to the unrecognised 'soft' sense that they were treated as inferior by large sections of the population – the bigotry – and were then not expected to work as hard or achieve much, which was then used to justify policies and a benefit system designed to prop them up. Being a disabled person herself, Daniels hated this unspoken belittling and riled against its insidiousness. It goes unsaid how many people with distinctive faces (and many with disabilities) are treated by others – and think about themselves too.

Low expectations can infect even your closest family. A good friend tells the story of how her mother fell into this trap. After she had acquired a disability in her teenage years, her mother said: 'I do hope you'll be able to get a little job sometime.' It was the snapping point for my friend, who recalls thinking that she wanted a bloody great big job! She has become a very successful social entrepreneur.

Second, this stigma can be twisted into the idea that someone with a less-than-perfect face cannot be 'attractive'. In this trope, attractiveness is synonymous with beauty and perfect faces. Assumption: 'You can never be attractive with a face like that.' The associated prejudice is, 'That accounts for your failure to find friends and lovers'. You can find it being promulgated in cosmetic adverts that point people to 'facial beauty and attractiveness tests' like www.anaface.com, which claims to rate your features according to their appeal, usually in terms of a sexual relationship. The celebrity pages of the tabloids and popular magazines like *Hello!*, *OK!* and the like are similarly crammed with the blind assertion that a beautiful face is an attractive face.

I will argue later that we need to transform how we think and see beauty, but there is no doubt that what makes you 'attractive' *as a person* is much, much more than the look of your face alone. Your face conveys a lot about you – your age, your mood and personality – and it's where people look first and foremost when they meet you. But your attractiveness is to be found in the use you make of your facial features, especially your eyes; it's what you say and how you speak; it's in the way you move, your gestures and body language and how you dress. All of that will be in the melting pot when people meet, assess and respond to you.

Someone with what appears to be a perfect beautiful face may fail to be attractive if their interaction skills are unappealing – they may be shy or have very little small talk, or be dull or talk too loudly or arrogantly. Equally, someone with a less-than-perfect face may be stunningly attractive because they have so much elegance, charisma, eye contact charm and witty dialogue.

But don't get me wrong here. Having a smart appearance may well, probably usually does, count, especially in first meetings. Nor am I suggesting that it is wrong to 'beautify' your face and look smart. I certainly do – I put on my 'best face', and I like to wear colourful ties, especially as I think they are nicely paradoxical with my face. Putting on your 'best face' to present yourself to the world, especially if meeting strangers, going to a party or an interview, is important.

Facial appearance matters, especially in the first few minutes of meetings, but having a distinctive face need not be a hindrance as long as you have the social and verbal skills to create rapport. It is the way you walk and talk and gesture and use eye contact and communicate that makes you interesting and attractive – including in a sexual way.

The third impact of believing the not-perfect = sad stigma is excessive sympathy, which can sometimes reveal itself in patronisation, sometimes in uncontained staring and at other times, in avoidance or looking away.

Patronisation is rarely deliberate, but is nonetheless painful. It can range from 'You're so brave' through to 'I don't know how you do it' – and you are frequently left grimacing as you respond, 'Oh, how kind.'

Staring and looking away are endemic to our culture, as Rosemarie Garland-Thomson exposes in her brilliant *Staring: How We Look* – and yet, to the person on the receiving end, they are often excruciating. The act of staring effectively strips away a person's privacy and drills, intrusively and without permission, into their face and identity. Non-staring is similarly grim but for opposite reasons: the avoidance of looking renders you an alien, set apart from society, not worthy of consideration. Both actions diminish your self-respect and suggest to you that you are a sad person.

This stigma is particularly obvious in the popular press when children are involved or mentioned – the word 'tragedy' hovers over every article, documentary and social media posting. I will look at this more when we come to 'what has to be done'…

Tackling face-ism means exploding this 'imperfection is never associated with success' equation. It's not true. And given that the vast majority of people have imperfect faces, it's in *everyone's* interest that this should be debunked and ended.

We are led to believe that there are some evolutionary roots for it, but the reality is that it is maintained and perpetuated by huge commercial interests, so we will have to be clever.

2. YOU ARE MORALLY DEFICIENT

Back to 1971. My Face Day. 18th March. My first sight of my face after my accident. An almost instant and horrible thought: my face – and therefore I – was now tainted with moral failure. I couldn't articulate why, but I know now. Because I had been conditioned to think like that from a very young age. The Ugly Sisters in the childhood pantomime, the wicked witch, the scarred villain... Now me.

We have to accept that human beings are hardwired by evolution to react to sights and sounds that are unusual and unexpected. Fear, fright and flight are common reactions. As we grow up, we are gradually conditioned by exposure to be selective about what things really should be avoided or are truly scary, like a big animal – or fire, as it happens.

We learn that we do not need to fear a door opening, a new person walking into the room, a new sound, or meeting strangers as long as they behave in a civilised fashion. As a grandfather, I take delight in getting to know my children's children as they leave infancy, and know that my face has absolutely nothing to do with their giggling reactions to me – it's all love!

It matters what your surroundings are, of course. If you grow up in a hot climate, you may fear the cold. If you grow up with only white people, meeting a black person could be surprising but, in today's cosmopolitan society, most of us are socialised very early on to think that black skin is entirely normal and not scary at all.

The influences on us in our childhood also enable our moral compass to develop and we start to decide what we like and dislike, what is right and wrong, and to act accordingly.

The problem for people with less-than-perfect faces is that the physical appearance of facial scars and asymmetry has become tangled up with morality. People with not-perfect, unusually shaped, scarred, asymmetrical or strange faces – 'ugly faces' – have become associated with morally undesirable characteristics. They are believed to be unpleasant, scary, nasty, evil, odd, corrupt and/or mean. And, as a result, people behave towards them as if they are members of a different, even alien species and a deserving target for ridicule, disrespect and even hate.

WHERE DOES FACE-ISM COME FROM?

This moral debasing has not just happened. Umberto Eco's book *On Ugliness* traces the stereotype attached to 'ugliness' back to Greek culture. From very early civilisation, a strong correlation was made 'between physical ugliness and moral ugliness'. In the fifth century BC Plato wrote, 'ugliness and discord and disharmony go hand in hand with bad words and bad nature, while the opposite qualities are the sisters of good, virtuous characters and resemble them.'[6]

Greek mythology was challenged by the Christian world in which even evil and ugliness could be redeemed in some way through prayer and suffering, but in the Book of Revelation, the devil becomes a physical ogre and hell a place full of ugliness – and those images dominated thinking for generations after the new Bible was written. Other religions, too, link facial and body disfigurement, including leprosy, with 'bad karma', the untouchable and infectious. But not all. Buddhism has no visual stigmas.

Through the Middle Ages, the Renaissance and into the modern era, distinctive faces appeared in many art forms to signify the lowest form of humanity: in gargoyles, satires, fables (Aesop was apparently a very unsightly man) and plays (Shakespeare's witches are 'the hags'), and in paintings and frescoes. An art historian friend conducted a study of disfigurement in art and could find few positive examples (see page 319).

Madness, too, and lack of intelligence is also often associated with less-than-perfect faces, and the nineteenth-century obsession with physiognomy brought forth a steady stream of publications about so-called 'criminal types', with measurements of their faces' proportions purportedly linked to stains on their characters. The so-called science of 'face-reading', phrenology, emerges from time to time even in today's sceptical modern culture.

'From here to the encouragement of the prejudice whereby "ugly people are bad by nature" is but a short step,' says Eco – and that evil–ugly association was further facilitated by the link between the unhappiness of ugliness (e.g. in Shelley's *Frankenstein*, 1818) and with the damned (e.g. in Leroux's *The Phantom of the Opera*, 1911).

I finally got to see the musical *The Phantom of the Opera* in 2008, fourteen years after it was created. I winced at the painful lyrics – 'my hideous visage' or words to that effect – but unenthusiastically went along with it. But I comforted myself with the argument that, 'Of course, that was the nineteenth century, and things have changed so much since – there's much less stigma today about facial disfigurement.'

I had, after all, walked maskless through the front door of the theatre, not via the cellars.

Coming out at the end into the wet reality of central London, twenty-first-century style – with iPhones flashing and beeping – I found myself being stared at by a respectable middle-aged woman, who then blurted out loudly to her friends and everyone else milling around – 'Hey, look, there's the Phantom – over there, look...' My wife and daughter, who'd witnessed this, were as flabbergasted as I was. I tried to ignore it and then decided to seek out the perpetrator, but the woman had disappeared into the crowd. This is the photo we took!

WHERE DOES FACE-ISM COME FROM?

This evil—ugly stigma is proliferated, and has been for generations, by a whole raft of cultural entities: some religions (not all of them), mythology, nursery rhymes and the nasty villains of Aesop's fables, plays, movies – especially, but not by any means only, horror films – comedians (the not-funny ones), newspapers and now the online media. They've largely got away with it, unnoticed and unchallenged, for far too long.

You should look out for movies that continue to use this lazy shorthand: give a character a scarred face and he's automatically a baddie. Bond movies stand out as particularly nasty examples, but there's also Two-Face in *Batman*, Freddy Krueger of *A Nightmare on Elm Street*, and of course the many other horror movies that are full of ghouls. Then there are the sketches of stand-up comedians like Jasper Carrott (who has been hauled up for ridiculing people with cleft lips and palates) and the scripted face-ist remarks of stars like Jeremy Clarkson.

No one with a not-perfect face is immune from such ridicule, because what goes in the movies or on TV is quickly used in the street, playground and other public places. One of my most demeaning moments was being hailed, 'Hi, Freddy' by a man on some scaffolding in a busy high street. Every one of us has to be on our guard every day for it. The effects are deeply undermining because those incidents linger and fester in the mind, and you can become very scared, even phobic, about the obnoxious and insulting behaviour of complete strangers.

My own 'favourite' is the depiction of the nasty, evil and depraved orcs as facially scarred from fire and violence in the blockbuster Hollywood movies based on Tolkien's *The Lord of the Rings*. Tolkien himself described Orcs in one of his *Letters*: '...they are (or were) squat, broad, flat-nosed, sallow-skinned, with wide mouths and slant eyes'. Some face-ist and racist undertones here, no doubt, but not a mention of a scar. But the film director needed an easy way to identify them as the villains – give them unsightly facial scars. A whole generation of young moviegoers and TV watchers has been and are being systematically prejudiced into face-ist thinking by Hollywood.

Some sections of the British media cannot resist demonising anyone with a scarred face, even using pictures of nineteenth-century freak shows to diminish them. Every year Hallowe'en, too, gets more and more gruesome. Journalists and film directors may plead innocence and 'no intention to hurt', but we have to make sure that that just doesn't wash anymore. The fact is that viewers pick up on the message and think nothing of hurling abuse.

Some will say this is just human nature, but they are wrong. The hardwired evolutionary instinct that tells us all to be alarmed by something or somebody who is unfamiliar and different is 'human nature'. But, critically, such shock can be diminished to almost nothing if the society in which you live provides cultural education and affirmation that something unusual is actually OK. Such education is, as yet, lacking for people with distinctive faces.

And that's not the end of our moral problem, because there is also a very strong set of cultural stereotypes and beliefs that hold that those with perfect faces are not only aesthetically beautiful but morally good and superior, too.

This beauty = good stereotype and prejudice was first tested in a famous study by Karen Dion and colleagues from 1972 called 'What is Beautiful is Good'.[7] As social psychologists, they describe how people rate others' faces when shown photographs that consistently demonstrated that 'attractiveness' was thought to be associated with other socially desirable and 'morally good' characteristics.

The evil-ugly prejudice goes deep, as the worship and obsession with this era's perfect-faced celebrities demonstrates. If they occasionally veer off track, and aren't quite as good as they should be, the celeb-press soon forgives them.

The moral degrading of people with not-perfect faces is not confined to our culture's visual imagery but is reflected in the very words we use every day. Words like ugly, grotesque, monstrous,

WHERE DOES FACE-ISM COME FROM?

deformed and disfigured are deemed acceptable to make aesthetic judgements of many aspects of our lives, including buildings, landscapes and beasts as well as human faces. I can just about accept them in most cases, but never for faces.

Even medicine and surgery are not immune. Words that surgeons have used, unthinkingly, for generations in their clinical discussions and papers to describe facial conditions are actually deeply stigmatising if used in the public domain, like deformity and abnormality. This was brought home to me some years ago when visiting a surgical team's department at a major hospital. The sign above the door read 'The Department for Facial Deformities', and as I walked in, I could feel my blood boiling. I saw one family waiting in a corner and wondered how those words were sitting with them as they waited for their child's craniofacial condition – which is what it was – to be assessed and treated. I took the issue up with the clinical team and their reaction was along the lines of, 'We've never thought of that,' with a gasp of surprise. I'm not sure if it made any difference…

Another medical term misused in our culture is the word 'scar'. It describes the result of the human body's normal healing process as it acts on a wound. Biologically, the cut or open wound is gradually filled by the body's fibroblasts and collagen, incredibly powerful healing agents – and these tend to overdo their efforts and seem not to know when to stop. Good job, well done, body. The lumpy and red scars that often result ('hypertrophic' or 'keloid' scars are the technical terms) provide a very solid barrier to any further infection or breakdown. Interestingly, scars do not result if a wound is incurred in the womb; the foetus's healing process seems to know exactly how much effort is required to repair the damage – and of course, the risk of further damage or infection is far less in the womb.

So, a 'scar' is a 'healing mark', a technical shorthand for how the amazing human body heals itself – a brilliant process. As someone who carries a fair few scars, they should not be vilified, methinks.

But wait a second. Aesthetically, these healing marks look less than pristine, and apparently taint a person's complexion in today's perfection-obsessed society. And it's applied more widely – 'scar' is used to describe things that are unappealing to the eye, like a geographical feature: 'a scar on the landscape'.

The renaming of the Healing Foundation (a harmless, neutral name) in 2016 as the 'Scar Free Foundation' in the UK, with its aim of 'scar-free healing within a generation', was a sad day. The new name explicitly reinforces the stigma of disfigurement that the very people the foundation claims to be for are battling with every single day. The name implies that scars are unsightly, distasteful and should be fixed, removed from public view.

Nobody doubts that scarring can be painful, physically, psychologically and socially, and efforts are needed to minimise it and treat the consequences. But trying to imagine a society without scars is not just science fiction; it also stigmatises anyone who has them, chooses to have them, is grateful for having them. Not clever.

Similarly, carbuncle – a rather old word, but still wheeled out. In medical terminology, the word describes a severe skin infection with swellings and boils badly infected by bacteria. But it is often used pejoratively, most famously by Prince Charles to refer to the new Sainsbury Wing of the National Gallery: a 'monstrous carbuncle on the face of a much-loved and elegant friend'.[8]

I wince when these and similar words are used, because they are almost always used in a way that suggests that not-perfect faces are undesirable. We need to challenge society into a new aesthetic where faces of all shapes and sizes are respected – warts, scars, blemishes, carbuncles and all.

There is absolutely no truth in the belief that scarring or asymmetry on the face causes or is associated with moral depravity. On occasion, just like some people who are tall, stocky or have a black skin, someone who has a facial scar does get on the wrong side of the law. But it is wrong to think this is their natural state. I've met

WHERE DOES FACE-ISM COME FROM?

several people in jails who have told me that their childhood was so damaged by other people's reactions to their face that they became isolated and stigmatised and fell into bad company, resorting to drugs and crime to earn a living.

But by far the worst, most stigmatising word in the English language to refer to a face is 'ugly'. 'Ugly' is offensive and should never be used to describe a face. I particularly object to it being used in the media. There is one particularly horrid example that has to be called out.

The TV company Betty first used 'ugly' in 2011 with a programme called *Beauty and the Beast: the Ugly Face of Prejudice*. It starred Adam Pearson, a man with a very distinctive face due to his neurofibromatosis – and the 'ugly' in the title was deliberately used to refer (subtly?) to Adam's face. It would have been easy to use words like 'unacceptable' or 'offensive'. It wasn't a bad programme and it exposed facial prejudice in some parts of British society, but that does not legitimise the title. It was not shown at a mainstream high-viewing time, thankfully.

A few years later (2015), despite Changing Faces' protests, Betty persuaded BBC3 to broadcast a documentary about disability hate crime with the nauseating title *The Ugly Face Of Disability Hate Crime*.

It was a very good programme, as it turned out, and Changing Faces contributed significantly to make it so. But, with Adam Pearson again as the lead, its title was deliberately chosen to perpetuate the stereotype that it's OK to refer, albeit obliquely, to Adam's face – and that of anyone with outstanding and distinctive facial features – as ugly. It is not acceptable.

U**y is a word that perpetuates the evil-ugly face-ist stigma, that people with not-perfect faces have moral failings and undesirable personalities, and I would like to see it taken out of common parlance – just as the N word has been to refer to people with black skin and the P word has been to refer to people from Pakistan. We need to decide as a society to be much more watchful and respectful about our use of vocabulary.

Lastly, an extreme version of the 'ugly-discounted' stigma is seen in the ridiculing by comedians, sometimes mimicked by children, of people with unusual faces through facial 'gurning' – the distorting of facial features. This is usually done to suggest someone is intellectually impaired, often with the added label 'thicko'. Totally unacceptable.

To conclude, the second face-ist stigma is deeply rooted in the conditioning of people across the world, not just in Western culture, and it will require a concerted and sustained offensive to debunk it. But it can be done.

3. WHY DON'T YOU FIX IT?

The Cardiff University study of TV coverage of disfiguring conditions in 2009 confirmed my suspicions: that almost all British TV coverage of people with disfigurements is in medical documentaries or cosmetic makeover/face-over shows.[9] Disfigurement is often presented as an 'individual problem' that can be solved with biomedical, technological or practical solutions. Things have not changed since.

We live in a world where increasingly, scarring and disfigurement is being wished away, and can be fixed, we are told, by sophisticated cosmetic surgeons and clever beauty therapists – or should I say, magicians?

A very large proportion of human beings now live in a media, celebrity and advertising bubble that promulgates the immensely powerful message that 'You don't have to look like that.' Our visual diet is swamped by images of perfect faces and bodies having fun, finding love and being successful.

If you believe the hype, with a little effort and for a modest sum of money (or so they say), you can have all your facial imperfections removed, or at least hidden away, thanks to the deftness of a surgeon's

WHERE DOES FACE-ISM COME FROM?

knife, a clever little jab of Botox or an aesthetic facial filler, a quick hit of a laser and the like. And that's not just if you are a woman, either. We men, too, can enhance our faces to remove irregularities and our bodies to give them the desired 'harmony', hairiness and muscles. And here's the best bit: it will do wonders for our prospects of happiness and success.

They are such beguiling propositions. And they are obviously widely believed, because the global cosmetic surgery and aesthetics industries are now booming multi-billion-dollar conerns.

Whereas in past times, people had to accept the evolutionary lottery that gave them their face with all the inevitable built-in imperfections, today we are told that it's really easy to change what nature gave you. Permanently. Well, not quite, but... certainly if you use enough moisturisers, facial sprays and cosmetics, you can sustain 'the look' for years. Investment in finding and marketing new medical and surgical interventions now runs to billions of pounds/dollars every year and the belief in them has to be continually stirred up.

Not only is it really easy, you really ought to do it – it's your moral duty to look 'your best'. And as Heather Widdows argues cogently in *Perfect Me*, if you don't do your duty, you are thought to be a bit weird and almost antisocial.[10] And that goes for people like me, too. If you have a less-than-perfect face, you can and should get it fixed. And, of course, you are destined for the sad life predicted in the first face-ist stigma if you don't search for and go for it.

For people with facial burns, there is a tiresome irony in this stigma, because the techniques developed by medical and surgical science since the First World War to save lives and reconstruct faces and bodies have been adapted and developed for use in a totally different context – cosmetic surgery. During the twentieth century, plastic and reconstructive surgery advanced dramatically in Britain and many other countries, not only to keep patients alive – those with severe burns, for example, even with 95 per cent of their body surface affected – but also to reconstruct their faces and bodies. Microsurgery, laser and other technological developments have made possible free-flap transfers, maxillo-facial and craniofacial reconstructions, and cleft lip and palate repairs which were unheard of even fifty years ago.

Those very same surgical skills are now being offered to a wider population, thereby narrowing the norm of what is desirable and acceptable, which in turn has added to the stigma experienced by people with distinctive faces or disfigurements.

What is profoundly sad about this is that cosmetic surgery is primarily available to people in richer countries who are able to pay, whereas for millions of people with not-perfect faces in poorer countries, not even reconstructive surgery to improve facial functioning is available. There is a case for imposing a levy on every single cosmetic procedure that would go towards funding treatments in low-income countries.

So can surgery really 'fix' not-perfect faces?

There is no doubt that surgery and other aesthetic interventions have evolved greatly over the last hundred years, but anyone with a not-perfect face needs to view these developments with very considerable scepticism and perspective, for three reasons:

First, the claims about what cosmetic surgery can do are less than 100 per cent truthful. All surgery has its aesthetic limits and nothing can halt the ageing process. So, unhappily, many patients – consumers – may and probably will become unsatisfied with the results. But it is well-nigh impossible to go back to the surgeon and ask either for them to reconfigure your previous looks or give you your money back. It's not like taking a jacket that you don't like back to the retailer.

Unfortunately, too, there are cowboys in the industry, surgeons who do not have the necessary skills or training or have not carried out more than a few of the operations which they are now paid handsomely to do. Which sometimes leads to mishaps, and occasionally

WHERE DOES FACE-ISM COME FROM?

a surgeon is struck off the medical practitioners' list. Although the riskiness of surgical and non-surgical cosmetic procedures is well recognised by the established medical bodies, they seem to find it very hard to accredit the qualifications of all those who practise – UK efforts over the last fifteen years to establish an accrediting body for cosmetic practitioners have been very staccato and slow.

Second, the marketing and wider cultural promotion of cosmetic surgery employs all the undermining hyperbole about looking perfect being the passport to happiness, the beauty-success face-ist stigma. Every kind of advertising and airbrushing trick is used to convey the association – 'Get yourself beach-ready!' as one campaign exclaimed (to considerable criticism). Although the Advertising Standards Authority did eventually issue a negative assessment of this advert, it was months later and the moment had passed.

Attempts to regulate, even self-regulate, the excesses of the cosmetics industry seem to get nowhere fast. Witness the UK government's puny response in 2014 to the excellent Keogh Review published the year before to advise how best to ensure patient safety after the Poly Implant Prothèse (PIP) silicone breast implants scandal. The Review brought forward some tough recommendations for improvements to be made across the whole industry, but the only real changes made five years on were in some minor tightening of regulations on premises where the industry practises. Nothing meaningful on qualifications of practitioners or the provision of objective consumer information has been done.[11]

Third, public understanding about the limits of cosmetic and reconstructive surgery remains less than fully informed – the idea that someone with a less-than-perfect face is only a few operations away from achieving near-perfection is rarely challenged. One or two plastic surgeons are willing to break the profession's cover and publicly explain these limits and the risks of Botox, lip fillers and implants etc., but for the most part it is in their interest to keep quiet.

Despite these reservations, the scale and growth of the cosmetic surgery and aesthetic industry is amazingly strong. Billions of dollars are spent worldwide in pursuit of facial (and body) perfection, a big business which gallops ahead unfettered by governmental attempts to regulate or contain it. This despite unintended consequences like anorexia, which damages the lives of young people who get obsessed with the search for the illusive 'perfect'. It is a stain on our culture.

It is not just the hype of cosmetic surgery that perpetuates the 'fix-it' face-ist stigma. Ever since the early 1990s, media interest worldwide about the prospect of 'face transplantation' becoming the answer for people with facial disfigurements has mushroomed – and with it the idea that it is *the* fix-it solution everyone with a disfigurement has been looking for, and should definitely consider.

I have been invited into many media studios since the day in November 2005 when the first face transplant operation on Isabelle Dinoire was announced, and the main reason why I have accepted these invitations is to contain the expectations of prospective patients and the wider community.

Face transplantation is a medical procedure to replace all or part of a person's face for both functional as well as aesthetic reasons by using the face of a deceased person whose blood type and other characteristics are a reasonable match with the recipient. It is an extremely complex and risky microsurgical process requiring a huge team of surgeons, nurses, immunologists and many other transplant specialists.

The first partial face transplant was carried out in 2005, the first full face one in Spain in 2010, and, at the time of writing, there have been about forty-five procedures worldwide since then on patients with burns, facial trauma and neurofibromatosis. This very small number shows that the technique is still in its research phase, which is no longer the case with hand transplants, which have now become quite commonplace and for which research has allowed robust protocols to be developed. Face transplantation is very far from being the fix-it panacea some were suggesting fifteen years ago, and it raises significant ethical issues – as I explore in more detail in a reflection on the subject in Annex 1 (see page 333). I thoroughly recommend the discussion of face transplantation (and much else) in the American sociologist Heather Laine Talley's book, *Saving Face: Disfigurement and the Politics of Appearance.*

The third face-ist stigma is now woven into the way in which twenty-first century human beings view their faces and bodies – as things which can be moulded and changed at will. The advertising and hype around this fix-it culture reinforces face-ism from an ever-younger age – which adds to the pressure on all of us to avoid not-perfect faces.

20.

THE VISION OF A WORLD THAT RESPECTS FACE EQUALITY

These three stigmas and the negative behaviours they legitimate besmirch the lives and prospects of millions of people with distinctive faces across the world. And I mean 'millions'. In the UK, a recent estimate suggested that one person in about 111 in the whole population had a psychologically and socially significant facial disfigurement.[1] Applying this same statistic to the whole world's population would suggest 66 million people are vulnerable across the planet. There are cultural variations in how the stigmas are imposed – and in some cultures, other stigmas, such as the belief that disfigurement is bad karma, add to the disadvantage.

And if each of those 66 million people with a facial condition or asymmetry experienced just one stigmatising incident a week, that adds up to 3,432,000,000 incidents of facial discrimination every year... yes, over 3 billion insulting moments in a year. And, actually, it happens to most of us at least once a day, not once a week.

There can be no doubt that face-ism, with its three interconnecting stigmas, is a scourge of our age. To challenge it, we must be prepared to dig out the roots of those stigmas, expose them to public disapproval and then eliminate them from our culture.

But we also need in our everyday lives and thinking to be able to describe the kind of society we aspire to live in. Being explicit may be a bit scary to start with – like saying that the world should eat less meat – but it will enable us to see a better future.

What would success look like if face-ism and the stigma of non-perfection were removed from our cultures? It sounds so unlikely, even crazy, to countenance, but unless we think the unthinkable, we will continue to be oppressed. And if you look at the history of other social change movements, most of them had colossal and unimaginable goals at the outset too.

'I have a dream,' said Martin Luther King in 1963 – and what a speech that was, raising up a whole nation, black and white, to overturn the oppression of racism.

I have a dream too. This is what success would look like through two lenses: what we'd like to see done differently, and what we'd like to remove from our cultural experience.

WHAT WOULD BE DONE DIFFERENTLY?

We want a world in which all human faces are celebrated in all their glorious uniqueness. I've used this word, uniqueness, deliberately here, but 'for all their diversity' or 'for all their differences' would be good too. Uniqueness is a wonderful attribute of faces from which stems the diversity of our human race.

In place of the narrowing cultural norms that prize 'perfect faces', societies across the world would savour and delight in everyone's face, making no judgement that one is better than another. Signs of uniqueness such as each individual's facial colouring, anatomical features, wrinkles and eye bags – now so scorned – would be interesting, indeed fascinating.

Commercial companies in the beauty and cosmetic industries would market their products as a means by which people could 'enhance their unique faces', making them stand out – highlighting

THE VISION OF A WORLD THAT RESPECTS FACE EQUALITY

the glory of their face rather than suggesting that there is a perfection they should be aspiring to. Their advertising would also be transformed as faces of all shapes and sizes would be displayed as evidence of the brilliance of their products.

What counts as 'beautiful' would not be defined by an airbrushed image in a one-dimensional photograph but would acknowledge and embrace the way a personality shines through in a human face.

There would be far more public information about the reasons why people's faces are so varied, and why some have irregular features, scars and asymmetries. There would be a David Attenborough-inspired major TV series on faces.

Aesthetic face values would be broadened to embrace and celebrate unique faces of all kinds. Dynamic moving photos would replace static ones on social media – and companies would compete as to which technology makes personalities shine best through faces.

The film industry would also open its eyes to using people with faces that have the whole gamut of facial variability – and Bollywood, rather than seemingly promoting skin whiteness, would make stars of Indians with skin tones of all kinds.

The global celebrity culture would embrace facial uniqueness in all its manifestations – prominent features, asymmetries, wrinkles and all – and would celebrate celebrities' real talents and attractive qualities.

Cosmetic surgery would be marketed as a means of sharpening up and enhancing your features so that you could display them, rather than as a means of excising perceived weaknesses. Surgeons would refer patients with low self-confidence or self-esteem to appropriate empowerment programmes – having sampled them first themselves.

Businesses and employers would never recruit or promote on the basis of appearance but would seek to embellish their workforces with the widest range of unique facial features. The commercial benefits would soon stack up, not least because the most important impact would be felt by everyone whose face had previously failed the perfection test.

There would be facial liberation!

We would all thrive unfettered by messages that we don't look good enough. People would be judged on their personality, talents and qualities and would be met by others with open minds and arms and with civilised twenty-first-century face values. Their employers would notice the change. Our whole society would. It would make a world of difference.

WHAT DO WE WANT TO ELIMINATE?

To create a society that respects face equality, we would expect to eliminate the three stigmas of face-ism identified earlier. Specifically:

People with not-perfect faces have sad and second-rate lives: the simplistic link between perfect faces and happiness would be completely discredited. Its corollary, that having a not-perfect face means a sad life with second- or even third-rate prospects, would be dismissed as utter balderdash. Anybody or any company suggesting such equations would be ridiculed – and possibly even taken to court, with hefty penalties being available for judges to hand down.

People with not-perfect faces have moral failings and undesirable personalities: not-perfect faces would never be used in film or media to signal any inadequacy or immoral actions or characteristics. Bad examples from the past of such associations would be mildly castigated but not censored. It is only by seeing the nastiness of the old that the new culture will be appreciated. Depictions of evil or villainy by people with not-perfect faces in the new era would be fiercely challenged, ostracised and possibly legally outlawed.

The fact that there will be many more faces previously thought of as 'not-perfect' in the public domain will help to establish this as the new norm.

Not-perfect faces aren't necessary and can be fixed: the aesthetic limits and risks of modern plastic and cosmetic surgery would be very widely understood – and plastic surgeons would lead such

THE VISION OF A WORLD THAT RESPECTS FACE EQUALITY

public education. Unrealistic expectations would be disputed, and people with distinctive faces would not feel any social pressure to have more surgery. And because they, like anyone who wants to gain more self-confidence, would have easy access to effective psychosocial help, they would face their futures with assurance.

It would also be vital to eliminate any social awkwardness that people feel towards those with distinctive faces. Public awareness would rise as more and more people with not-perfect faces were seen in public places, on TV, in advertising and in the public eye.

Social skills programmes on how to think without prejudice and interact normally with people whose faces are distinctive would be available on the internet and be an integral part of primary and secondary school education and citizenship programmes.

In addition to a transformed set of public attitudes, there would need to be stronger anti-discrimination protection for people with not-perfect faces. Human rights legislation around the world would recognise and protect people with facial differences and disfigurements from low expectations, discrimination at work, on social media and in public places.

'FINE WORDS BUTTER NO PARSNIPS'

Nice ideas. Nice writing. But you can't be serious.

Oh, but I am. Deadly serious.

And one reason I am is that if you replace 'not-perfect faces' with 'black', you will see that our aspiration is not an impossibility – even if it may take as long as or much longer than it is taking to achieve the freedoms inherent in race equality.

Black people were treated appallingly as slaves and excluded for generations. The civil rights movement set out to change that. People with distinctive faces are at risk of becoming similarly excluded – possibly increasingly so, unless we take action to raise public awareness of the injustice.

I am also uplifted by the increasing number of people around the world with distinctive faces who are willing to come forward and go public in support of this vision. At the launch of our Changing Faces campaign for face equality in 2008, two people were invited to say what a world that respected face equality would mean for them. Here's what they said.

> **Kellie O'Farrell, who experienced severe facial burns as a child, said:**
> Face equality would mean that:
>   When I walk into a room where people don't know me, I wouldn't have to witness everyone going quiet and observe their shocked expressions.
>   I would never shy away from doing sport because I have scars on my hands and face which tend to make others think that I am somehow inadequate or less able.
>   I wouldn't dread a new college year knowing that I have to spend the first few days being stared at by all the new students. It's hard enough starting a new college year without any other added stress.
>   I would be able to embrace my disfigurement and use it as something to be proud of – not something to be feared or unwanted.
>   I would be treated the same as any other young adult and not pitied by people. I am a burns survivor, not a victim; I don't need or want anyone's pity. Just because I have scars I can still be stylish and look as well as any other person.
>   Other people would not be afraid to speak to me just because I look different.
>   When I'm buying something in Topshop, I'd know that the staff wouldn't have a problem serving me just because I have a disfigurement.

THE VISION OF A WORLD THAT RESPECTS FACE EQUALITY

When I finish college and start a new job as a social worker, my new colleagues would accept me for who I am – not exclude me just because I look different.

Finally and most importantly, face equality would mean that any person, with any disfigurement, no matter how noticeable, would feel happy within themselves and have the confidence to lead their lives and not encounter any discrimination based on the way they look. Please stand out, like me, and show your support for face equality.

A parent, Chris Vezey, said:
I have been asked to talk for a couple of minutes on what Face Equality means to me, my daughter, and the rest of our family. Rebecca is five feet tall and twenty years old and was the second of our three children. The day she was born, I thought she looked a little strange and was told later that they thought she had Crouzon Syndrome, a problem confirmed four days later at Great Ormond Street Hospital in London. Nothing Mr Hayward, the neurosurgeon, said that day could have prepared us for what was to come over the next twenty years.

The worry of so many operations to correct internal and external craniofacial abnormalities is one thing, but the attitude of others is something else.

When Rebecca was small our children had plenty of friends who were in and out of our house and knew Rebecca as herself. Knowing her was the key – they discovered she wasn't really any different to them – I even remember taking a gang of them to bring her home from a hospital stay. But a visit to the park would be a totally different experience of kids asking what's wrong with her, and the continual routine in shops and the street of people going out of their way to stare quite blatantly. People made assumptions (wrongly) within seconds.

As she has grown older with wonderfully improved looks thanks to the plastic, dental and craniofacial teams, the problem would appear to be ever there – the pointing and laughing by others in restaurants (even whole families), students at college not wanting to be seen associating with someone who doesn't look the norm and more recently being totally abused by schoolchildren younger than herself on a bus. Let's take that incident…

How do you take on a bus full of teenage schoolchildren who mock and abuse you every day, from waiting at the bus stop until they get off? The word retard started to be used loudly until one day one of them came right up to her face and shouted 'HOW DO YOU SPELL RETARD – RETARD???' Unfortunately, the law in this country prevents you taking your own action – I know what I would have liked to do – but instead…

I called the headmaster of the school and hauled him over the coals, and he promised to do something about it – but when it happened again I felt it necessary to wake him up – 'What if my daughter was black?' I asked. 'What if she belonged to a different faith – she would be protected by the law – and YOU would have to take immediate action.' He fell silent and said he would contact Changing Faces, as I requested, while Rebecca, thoroughly traumatised by the event, takes buses outside school hours or has to be delivered or picked up from college by her mother.

By launching this campaign, Changing Faces has finally brought these prejudices about disfigurement out into the open and they will have to be talked out and debated – not just swept under the carpet.

THE VISION OF A WORLD THAT RESPECTS FACE EQUALITY

> The fact that Changing Faces is launching this campaign for face equality gives me and I am sure many other parents here tonight the hope that one day Rebecca will not have to live with being pre-judged every day of her life because of her face, that she can walk down the street or get on a bus and no one will give her a second glance – unless it is for all the right reasons.

We all need to have that goal in our minds... 'One day' we will create a world in which Kellie and Rebecca and millions of others with less-than-perfect faces can walk tall and be received with complete respect.

The good news is that the campaign for face equality launched in 2008 has already made some progress – and is yielding some results, too.

The 2007–08 Implicit Attitudes Test (IAT) (referred to on page 209) which showed the huge scale of the bias against people with facial disfigurements has been done many thousands of times since 2008 via the Changing Faces website. Exposure to all the positive stories on the website reduced the bias to six out of ten people. Which is encouraging. And in 2017, the IAT test was done again on the general population; this time, two-thirds were found to be negatively biased. Again, some encouragement, and suggestion that the charity's campaign for face equality is bearing some fruit.

But, let's be honest, at that rate of progress, it will take more than thirty years before only a single digit percentage of the UK population are found to have this bias.

Making facial prejudice and discrimination a thing of the past will take many years – and as we have seen, there are cultural and commercial forces that are making this very difficult. So, we are going to have to ratchet up our efforts, be clever and learn as much as we can from other (successful and unsuccessful) movements for social change.

First, let's look at what has been done to date to pursue face equality.

21.
THE CAMPAIGN FOR FACE EQUALITY IN THE UK TO DATE

What has happened since 2008? In the early years after the launch, Changing Faces created a series of productive efforts in Britain with a tiny team of staff and volunteer champions – but as the world recession caused by the sub-prime credit crunch gathered pace, with the UK adopting a ferocious austerity programme, finding funding to sustain such efforts became harder and harder. Despite this, by 2020, the charity could point to many successes in challenging the media, schools, employers, lawyers, artists, film-makers, the cosmetics and fashion industry, advertisers, MPs and, of course, the public at large.

But it wasn't just a campaign in the UK. A charity in Taiwan, the Sunshine Social Welfare Foundation, decided in 2011 to make the campaign a major part of its efforts, and in November 2018, I launched an international alliance, Face Equality International, to turn the campaign into a global movement.

We can look at the highlights of these efforts in brief – with internet links and additional annex materials for those who want to explore them in more detail – by focusing on challenging the three interlocking stigmas of face-ism and then describing the more general activities.

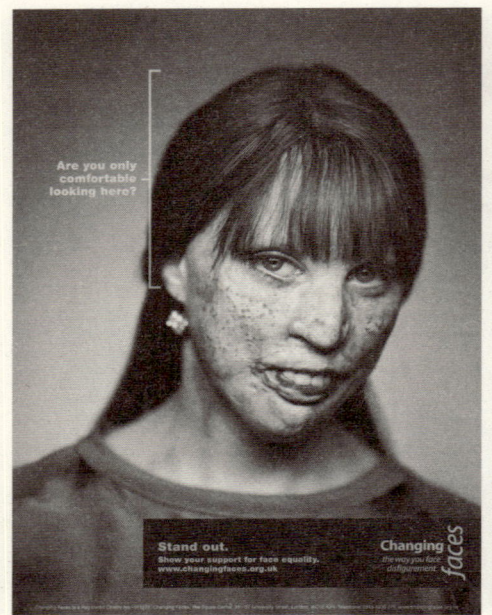

Are you only comfortable looking here?

Stand out.
Show your support for face equality.
www.changingfaces.org.uk

Changing faces
the way you face disfigurement

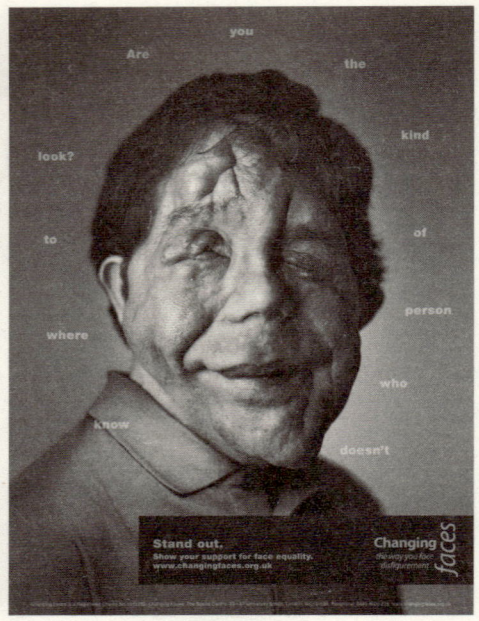

Are you the kind of person who doesn't know where to look?

Stand out.
Show your support for face equality.
www.changingfaces.org.uk

Changing faces
the way you face disfigurement

To anyone who looked at me and thought I'd never achieve anything
look at me now

Changing faces
the way you face disfigurement

See why Lucas chose to star in our face equality campaign at
www.changingfaces.org.uk

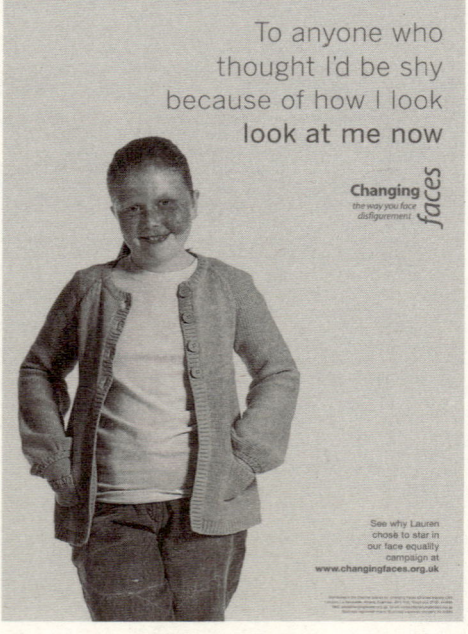

To anyone who thought I'd be shy because of how I look
look at me now

Changing faces
the way you face disfigurement

See why Lauren chose to star in our face equality campaign at
www.changingfaces.org.uk

THE CAMPAIGN FOR FACE EQUALITY IN THE UK TO DATE

CHALLENGING THE STIGMA OF THE SAD AND SECOND-RATE

The launch of the campaign in 2008 revolved around images designed to influence public consciousness. Thousands of Face Equality posters were displayed on London Underground and British Rail stations and billboards.

These posters were deliberately quite hard-hitting – definitely 'in your face' – and the call to action was clear: *Stand up for face equality*. We put out an agenda for change across society, and were delighted that the posters won high acclaim in the advertising press and opened doors for discussions with interested companies, schools and the media. A good start.

More directly aimed at challenging the low expectations stigma was a second poster campaign in 2010, featuring children with facial disfigurements with the strong strapline: 'If you don't think people like me can do this, think again'.

> **A brilliant BBC film called *Billboard Kids* about the making of these adverts was broadcast shortly afterwards in March 2010. One of the stars of that campaign, Lucas Hayward, told his story at the launch event:**
>
> Hello everyone. I'm Lucas, and I'm thirteen. My nose is wider and flatter than most people's. It's something I was born with, and the long name for it is frontal-nasal craniofacial dysplasia. I use this name when I want to confuse people!
>
> The first time I realised I had any kind of condition was when I was four, and I went to my local village primary school for the first time. The other children stared and asked questions like, 'What's wrong with you?' or 'What happened to you?' They

didn't understand, and neither did I. It was confusing and scary hearing them say those things, because I didn't understand I looked different. It was shocking to realise I wasn't the same as everyone else.

After that, I was bullied for most of my time at primary school. Boys would punch me and try to wrestle me to the ground and the girls called me cruel names like 'pig nose' or 'elephant man'. The physical bullying was the worst, and most of the time I was in tears and too scared to go into the playground.

They were so out of touch in my primary school that the teachers kept me inside until I felt better and told the children to stay away from me, so I ended up on my own. They suggested I see an educational psychologist when it affected my schoolwork. They were thinking I had learning difficulties, but when the report came back from him it showed I was actually very able, but in an oppressive environment.

One day when I was nine years old I'd had enough, so I just got up and went home.

That caused a quite a stir, and it was soon after that that my parents got in touch with Changing Faces for help and advice. Someone from the charity came to the school to help the teachers and thankfully things got much better from there on.

My next school got it right from the start. They had a meeting with people from Changing Faces and my mum. They know that looking different is like having something extra to deal with, and that it is support that I need to cope with other children's behaviour and reactions. Curiosity about my appearance is now treated appropriate to the manner in which it is asked and I'm pretty happy there.

But it's not just children who react to my appearance in a negative way. Adults do, too, and as I've grown older I have

THE CAMPAIGN FOR FACE EQUALITY IN THE UK TO DATE

had to learn how to handle people's reactions so that I can feel good about myself. When I was younger I remember thinking that all adults were angry because of the way they used to look at me. Now, if someone stares too long, or keeps looking back, I often smile and mouth the word 'Hello'.

Strangers tend to have low expectations of me; they assume that because I look different I must have learning difficulties. I still get asked if I need the help sheet by new or supply teachers, and some strangers give me nervous sideways glances and speak to me in a way that suggests I might not understand them. Now if I see someone wondering about my IQ, well, generally using an enhanced vocabulary sorts that out for them.

People sometimes ask me when I will have plastic surgery 'to put it right'. It doesn't seem to enter their heads that I might not want any more surgery or that I might be happy with the way I look. There is more to a person's 'image' than just their physical appearance and surgery is not a solution to other people's attitudes.

But to grow up constantly being thought of as abnormal, when I simply have an unusual face, does have an effect. I became lonely, self-conscious and felt I was worth less than normal-looking people. I stopped doing anything at school and was so very sad, I would come home and pretend to my parents that everything was fine and go to my bedroom and cry.

Changing Faces showed me, my family and teachers how to deal with this long-term negative pressure, and that's why I got involved with the Changing Faces children's campaign for 'Face Equality', because I want to help other children like me by changing people's beliefs about disfigurement.

It's been a lot of fun so far. The BBC filmed us all at home for a documentary about our involvement, but the most exciting

> bit was when the posters were up in the London Underground and we went on a 'search' to see whose poster was in which station. When we came out of one station, just as it was getting dark, we saw ourselves on this giant illuminated display. It was bigger than a double decker bus.
>
> I never dreamt I would see myself up in lights in the middle of London. We all felt like film stars! But it's not always easy to feel like this given people's assumptions about us.
>
> So, if you're looking at me tonight and thinking that I've got a bit of a sad life, I'm not likely to achieve much at school or that I don't have the confidence to make friends, you need to think again.

Those two poster campaigns gave the campaign for face equality real public profile in the UK and enabled Changing Faces to question many expressions of the 'sad and second-rate' stigma. One such opportunity arose in the aftermath of a research study from Cardiff University's School of Journalism, which examined the coverage of people with disfigurements on mainstream TV; the lack of such studies, given their importance in normalising less-than-perfect faces, had long been a cause of frustration.[1]

The research showed categorically that there were hardly ever any 'ordinary appearances' – of the 8,650 hours of television footage examined, people with disfigurements were shown on just 293 occasions. And if they did appear, it was usually in the context of face-over programmes or medical documentaries. In fact, 85 per cent of representations appeared in factual genres such as documentaries and the news. Only 15 per cent were in fictional programmes such as dramas, comedies and soaps.

We decided to convene a powwow of influential figures in the TV and broadcasting industries, chaired by the well-known BBC journalist Sarah Montague, and out of the blue, this tiny and highly unlikely exchange happened:

'What we really need is to normalise people with not-perfect faces on British TV. Wouldn't it be great if someone were to read the news, for example?'

'Great idea! Maybe I could get James to read it on Sky or Channel Five...' So said Simon Bucks, who was then one of the news directors at Sky. He was as good as his word.

Within a few months, through his good offices, I was in discussion with Channel 5 – and amazingly, they committed to it. I was to fill the space left by one of their regulars, Natasha Kaplinsky, who was on maternity leave – and it was a terrifying experience! Reading an autocue is far from straightforward, especially with other instructions coming at you, an ever-changing script and the need to provide interest in your voice at all times.

But whatever I felt like – and my son said that I actually managed to blink on the third day – the reaction from many quarters all over the world was astonishingly positive. I particularly liked a completely spontaneous and well-argued piece by the columnist Catherine Bennett in the *Observer* the following Sunday – see Annex 2.

A more factual report appeared in the *Telegraph* under the headline 'News reader with facial disfigurement is broadcasting phenomenon':[2]

> James Partridge, who was badly burned in a car accident as a teenager, was invited to present the lunchtime bulletin on Five in an effort to break down stereotypes. But he has developed a regular following, with thousands of people also downloading clips of his bulletins on the internet.
>
> The broadcaster said that it had received hundreds of emails from viewers hailing the initiative, many calling for him to be invited back. It has also disproved fears in some quarters that viewers would simply switch channel rather than watch a news reader with a facial disfigurement. Daily viewing levels

Reading the Channel 5 news, November 2009.

remained constant at around 250,000. Bulletins posted on YouTube, the video sharing website, have also attracted more than 10,000 hits.

The 57-year-old former farmer said: 'I've found it fascinating. People want to discover how they will react. There is nothing more everyday than watching someone read the news, and I wanted to prove my face can fit. It's the ultimate test because if someone who is disfigured can be accepted on TV, they can be accepted anywhere.' He admitted there was a 'risk' that the channel had encouraged voyeurism, but added: 'The aim is to make it seem normal.'

That was 2009, and I believe those initiatives sowed good seeds amongst some TV producers who have enabled people with unusual faces to be more commonplace on TV: witness Adam Pearson and Katie Piper, who have become almost household names and faces. But there is far to go – and there have also been a few disturbing trends in the opposite direction, with older TV stars with their

THE CAMPAIGN FOR FACE EQUALITY IN THE UK TO DATE

not-perfect ageing faces such as Nick Ross and Moira Stuart seemingly being deleted from the main TV channels in Britain.

Challenging the stigma of the sad and second-rate will take many years, although the prevailing current of opinion is driving attitudes increasingly towards it. Some years ago we produced a website (no longer active) called 'What Success Looks Like' and encouraged people to join it, but the feedback we got was that people were loath to put their faces above the parapet for fear of being harassed; what an appalling stain on twenty-first century culture that is. The explosion of social media should allow more distinctive faces to be seen, and I believe that is slowly happening. But until the epidemic of unfettered abuse they are vulnerable to is outlawed, the opportunities of the internet will be hard to take.

But let us not be too downhearted. There are some great examples that need replicating and magnifying in the years ahead.

First, people with distinctive faces like Winnie Harlow, a fashion model who has vitiligo, are becoming recognised for their talents – and, in her case, becoming bigger stars as a result.[3]

Along similar lines, Changing Faces and the Katie Piper Foundation have held catwalk displays and portrait exhibitions to show people with disfigurements being successful, happy and confident in their faces and skins. And Katie Piper herself, an acid survivor, has become a celebrity in Britain with a significant role fronting up Chanel 4 programmes and appearing in the celebrity press.

Second, in Britain and India, people with facial scars and unusual looks are appearing in corporate advertising and marketing campaigns more than just once a decade. Take the example of Laxmi Agarwal, who has been the face of a major fashion house's new range of clothes – and has become a TV news anchor too.[4]

In 2018 Changing Faces launched a campaign called #PledgeToBeSeen to challenge beauty brands to position people with disfigurements in their branding and advertising. Avon was the first to commit, with burn survivor Catrin Pugh fronting, and the hope is that others will follow suit.[5]

Third, some film-makers are showing themselves willing to take the risks of casting people with less-than-perfect faces in major parts: stars with cleft lips, for example, like Tom Burke and Joaquin Phoenix are now more commonly seen.

CHALLENGING THE STIGMA OF MORAL FAILINGS AND UNDESIRABLE PERSONALITIES

This stigma has remained barely challenged for so long, and that says something of the power of folklore, children's nursery rhymes and pantomimes, and Hollywood movie-makers. For far too long, intelligent, creative people have idly resorted to using facial scars to portray villains and nasty people.

In 2010, in an effort to draw attention to this abuse, Changing Faces produced a one-minute film, *Leo*, starring Michelle Dockery of *Downton Abbey* fame, designed to draw attention to this. It featured Leo Gormley, who survived a fire in his childhood and carries the scars to prove it. He's a successful entrepreneur in the north-east of England. In the film, he is seen in what are contrived to appear 'suspicious circumstances' arriving at Michelle Dockery's flat on a cold wet night, and the viewer is asked, 'What did you think was going to happen?' It's been viewed over 86,000 times on YouTube and by many thousands of people in Odeon cinemas around the country.[6]

Changing Faces ran another campaign in 2018 with a similar message. Led by young people, #IAmNotYourVillain prompted a breakthrough in the form of a commitment from the British Film Institute (BFI) to not having negative representations depicted through scars or facial difference in the films they fund.

Ben Roberts, Film Fund Director at the BFI, is quoted as saying:

Film has such a powerful influence on society; it enables us to see the world in new ways, enriches lives and can make a vital contribution to our well-being. It is also a catalyst for change and that is why we are committing to not having negative representations depicted through scars or facial difference in the films we fund.

It's astonishing to think that films have used visible difference as a shorthand for villainy so often and for so long. The time has come for this to stop.

The BFI believes that film should be truly representative of the UK, and this campaign speaks directly to the criteria in the BFI Diversity Standards which call for meaningful representations on screen. We fully support Changing Faces' I Am Not Your Villain campaign and urge the rest of the film industry to do the same.[7]

And there was further good news when one of the first films to receive BFI funding after they made their pledge, *Dirty God*, starred a young woman who really does have burn scars from a childhood accident, playing an acid survivor.

Challenging such imagery is far from easy. A 2013 Disney film, *The Lone Ranger* starring Johnny Depp, used just such a lazy shortcut to depict a nasty villain: Butch Cavendish. A toy made by Lego of this character to coincide with the film's launch described him on its website as 'a ruthless outlaw whose terribly scarred face is a perfect reflection of the bottomless pit of depravity that passes for his soul'.

We challenged the Disney film-makers, but to no avail. Lego on the other hand apologised profusely – 'no offence intended' – and took down the website description immediately, replacing it with a wording which Changing Faces was asked to approve.

And lest you think this is a problem of the past, the Bond movie franchise announced in December 2019 that its latest offering, *No Time to Die*, is going to feature not one but two villains with facial scarring. Hard to believe... Are the directors and casting teams living in a vacuum?

We should be less surprised that the remake of *The Lion King* in 2019 again made the villain carry the name 'Scar', but I was pleased to see that a strong warning to parents was issued by a leading team of cognitive neuroscientists:

> The idea that moral corruption is expressed by physical anomaly is woven into many popular movies. In [many films facial scars or burns]... point to a cheap Hollywood prop for villainy. The audience knows implicitly: these are bad people, Scar is a bad lion.
>
> Recognising such built-in biases is a first step to overcoming them. A person with a cleft palate is not inherently bad. A person with a facial acid burn is not inherently bad. A person with skin cancer is not inherently bad. A person with a port wine birthmark is not inherently bad. A person with an orbital fracture is not inherently bad. Despite what the movies would have you believe.
>
> If you must take your child to see *The Lion King*, use its messages as teachable moments. Do not settle for 'Hakuna Matata' ['no problem' in Swahili]. There *are* troubles. There *are* worries. This is no problem-free philosophy.[8]

It's not just films that perpetrate this stigma – TV shows do too. One example I was at the centre of challenging in 2011 came in an episode of the fantastically popular BBC programme *Top Gear*. In a scripted section of the show, Jeremy Clarkson and his fellow hosts deliberately poked fun at a car which they described as 'an elephant car', one that they wouldn't want to meet at a party... with allusions to John Merrick, who became known as the 'Elephant Man' in Victorian freak shows. The so-called stars of the show even lisped and spoke in imitation – and the whole studio audience was encouraged to join in.

THE CAMPAIGN FOR FACE EQUALITY IN THE UK TO DATE

Changing Faces challenged this affront immediately. I received an email from the then-Director General of the BBC to the effect that he had concluded, after taking soundings from the show's director, that there was no case to answer because there was no intent to harm. I disagreed strongly and appealed to the BBC Trust, the oversight body. After much pressure and legal submissions from us, I was delighted when the Trust upheld our complaint and required the BBC to apologise.[9]

BBC directors had to take note – and there has not been another incident since, as far as I know.

Unfortunately, it isn't just the film and TV industries that can perpetrate such stigma. Two other examples illustrate this, one from children's games and the other from advertising.

In 2012, Changing Faces very publicly challenged a then-flavour-of-the-month tech company called Mind Candy when our attention was drawn to the set of baddies in Moshi Monsters, their online game played by over 100 million children aged between four and eight years old worldwide.

The baddies were all lumped into one family (i.e. were all congenitally linked), the Glumps, with names like Freakface, Fish Lips and Bruiser, all with nasty face-ist descriptions attached, such as, 'Fish Lips is a one-eyed blob of badness.'

We created a petition signed by over 2,000 people, raised questions in Parliament and created a coalition of respected professional associations which put our case to the makers of the game. But to no avail; Mind Candy made no changes to the game. The surrounding media coverage might, however, have had a small part to play in the downward-sliding sales of Moshi Monsters.

Another very face-ist corporate offering became apparent in 2015 when the conference call phone company PowWowNow concocted an advertising campaign under the banner of 'Avoid the Horror', which suggested that people could avoid rush-hour commuting by using a conference call facility.

Autumn 2015, yet another insensitive advertising campaign.

THE CAMPAIGN FOR FACE EQUALITY IN THE UK TO DATE

We went public with our complaint:

People with facial burns criticise 'offensive' advert
A poster for conference call firm PowWowNow shows a man on an underground train surrounded by zombie-like characters in masks. Changing Faces says the adverts are 'insensitive' because of the similarity to masks worn by people recovering from burns.[10]

Initially, the company accepted our challenge and removed the offending advert, but then, over a weekend, it had a rethink and we were therefore forced to take the case up with the Advertising Standards Authority. Their conclusion was unsatisfactory:

Further to our previous correspondence, I can now inform you of the outcome of the ASA Council's assessment. They have now carefully considered the ad and the issues raised, but have concluded that there are insufficient grounds for further ASA intervention on this occasion.

As you are aware, the complainants raised concerns that the ad was offensive to those with facial disfigurements, as they felt zombies could be seen as resembling people who had sustained burn injuries. The complainants felt that the image, combined with the use of the words 'AVOID THE HORROR', was irresponsible and might promote discrimination against those with facial disfigurements. In this case, whilst the Council recognised the strength of feeling of the complainants, it considered that in the context of an ad for a conference call provider it was generally likely to be seen as a light-hearted representation of what commuting on a busy train to a meeting might be like and how the advertiser's service could help you avoid it. It did not consider that the ad was likely to be seen as trivialising real facial disfigurements, nor would it encourage discrimination or bullying of those affected. The Council therefore did not consider the ad was likely to cause serious or widespread offence, be seen as irresponsible or to cause harm.

As the Council has concluded that there was no breach of the Code, the ASA will not be able to take further action on this occasion. We appreciate that this will not be the outcome you'd hoped for, but we have informed the advertiser of the issues raised to us.

We disagreed with the judgement, but there was no appeal. It's a voluntary code of practice anyway. So no brake was applied to the advertising industry.

Lastly, there are frequent occasions when the media, online and hard-copy, perpetuate the face-ist stigma of moral failings and undesirable personalities. Changing Faces decided to keep a close eye on such imagery and reporting in the media and we encouraged our supporters to do so too. One particularly nasty headline we successfully challenged accompanied the photograph of a young woman with neurofibromatosis in the *Daily Express*. It read: 'World's Worst Disfigurement? Young woman born with NO FACE hopes for surgery'.

We complained to the newspaper and the headline was changed within twenty-four hours to: 'World's worst disfigurement? Young woman with obscured face hopes for surgery'.

Although still far from ideal, it was an improvement. On the strength of this, the independent press regulator (IPSO) accepted our media guidelines as best practice and promised to put them on their website – which was never actually done.

To try to prevent further abuses, Changing Faces produced and widely circulated media guidelines to journalists and broadcasters on a daily basis. They contained the principles and best practice in reporting and covering the lives of people with facial disfigurements. (See Annex 3: International Media Standard.)

THE CAMPAIGN FOR FACE EQUALITY IN THE UK TO DATE

CHALLENGING THE STIGMA THAT NOT-PERFECT FACES AREN'T NECESSARY AND CAN BE FIXED

Changing Faces was constantly on the lookout for overblown claims about cosmetic and reconstructive surgery, but we were not alone in doing this. Other charities like Which? and Action Against Medical Accidents (known then as Action for the Victims of Medical Accidents) were very much on the case, and we added our support on suitable occasions.

In 2017–18, I was a member of a working party on the ethics of cosmetic surgery created by the highly respected Nuffield Council on Bioethics, and I fully endorse the report and its three main recommendations.[11]

First, we have in Britain (and in most parts of the world) a largely unregulated industry exploiting people – including children – by pushing often untested, unproven and unsafe products and procedures. Young women and teenagers are being encouraged – often through social media, apps and the 'selfie culture' – to have potentially dangerous treatments such as lip fillers. Insecurity about appearance and low self-esteem are being fuelled and nourished by the industry, celeb culture, media and peer pressure.

We need much better evidence regarding the claims made about the safety, effectiveness and long-term effects of these products and procedures.

Second, we need much better regulation of the efficacy of these products and procedures, the people who carry them out and where they're carried out. Fillers, for example, should only be available on prescription after being approved by regulators. We need to ensure people don't provide cosmetic procedures to children unless it is part of multidisciplinary health care. And anyone offering cosmetic invasive treatments, such as fat freezing, Botox, fillers or breast implants, must be certified and trained. Procedures should only take place on licensed premises.

And third, people should be able to make informed choices – these are risky, serious 'medical' procedures, not consumer goods like a trip to the spa. We should be able to be guaranteed responsible advertising that does not pressure people to conform to unrealistic body shapes. Ofcom, the communications regulator, should look at makeover show rules. We need to put a stop to cosmetic surgery makeover apps that target children.

People need easy access to quality information about the risks, benefits and safety in the long and short term. Companies making these products need to improve this information. And we should expect the likes of Facebook, Instagram, Snapchat etc. to fund independent research on the impact of social media on anxiety about appearance – and act on it.

CREATING 'BEST PRACTICE' RESOURCES FOR SCHOOLS AND EMPLOYERS

Challenging instances of face-ist stigma is very important, but long term, preventing it is a much better strategy. Changing Faces created a whole range of resources for teachers, disseminated Face Equality teaching resources for secondary schools, gained the support of the inspectors (Ofsted) to promote face equality and outlaw disfigurement discrimination and has been very active in anti-bullying campaigning. With employers, too, we developed guidelines for recruiting people with not-pretty faces with a parallel set of guidelines for them too. Let's look at what research and experience suggest as best practice in each arena:

Education – with support from Jane Frances

Jane Frances is a teacher, researcher, writer and psychotherapist who worked for Changing Faces in several educational roles over nineteen years from 1998. Her book Educating Children with Facial Disfigurements: Creating Inclusive School Communities *was*

THE CAMPAIGN FOR FACE EQUALITY IN THE UK TO DATE

published by Routledge in 2004 and is a seminal work on this subject. I am delighted she agreed to help me write this section.

Each and every child needs a good education, and this is enshrined in the United Nations Convention on the Rights of the Child. Article 28 focuses on all children's right to an education that respects their human dignity. Article 29 outlines the aims of education, which include the development of the child's personality, talents and mental and physical abilities to their fullest potential.[12]

This is no less true for children who happen to be born with a birthmark, a cleft, or a cranio facial condition that affects the way their face or head looks, or whose facial appearance is changed by an injury like a burn or an illness like cancer or its treatment.

When at school, children's development of social skills, self-esteem and confidence is as important as knowledge, skills and qualifications, for without good self-esteem it is harder to learn, and without social confidence it is harder to interact with your peers and, when the time comes, to step out into the world as a young adult.

In order to ensure that all children have the best educational and social experiences at school, teachers need some knowledge and understanding of the way people of all ages respond to an unusual facial appearance. This is where research comes in. Understanding how children respond to each other's differences, and how they are affected by what adults say and do, enables effective interventions to be developed that will give all children what they need to do well, both in school and beyond school.

What does research tell us?

Facial appearance and educational attainment

For children whose facial appearance is affected by a condition or injury, school brings particular challenges. To meet and overcome each new challenge calls both for preparations and ongoing attention to a range of indicators:

1. Teacher expectations

Along with establishing the curriculum and growing a team of good teachers, laying the foundations for children's success at school means ensuring that all staff have high expectations of each child. Numerous research studies reveal a link between teacher expectation and pupil attainment.[13] When a teacher believes a pupil is capable of good or very good educational outcomes, the pupil does well. When a teacher believes a pupil is never going to achieve much, the pupil does not do well.

Teacher expectations include a kind of 'negative compassion' in response to a pupil who has an unusual facial appearance. The teacher may be almost unaware that their response is along the lines of, 'Poor child, what can the future hold for them?', but this kind of thinking reduces this pupil's chance of success at school.

Authenticity and realism are important. If a teacher pretends to have high expectations when really they do not, the pupil will tend to underachieve.

To raise teacher expectations of a child whose appearance is affected by an injury or condition, it is important to become familiar with examples of other people – older children and adults of all ages – who also have a facial condition or injury and who are living positive, satisfying lives.

A child who looks unusual is much more likely to do well at school if their teachers think in terms of, 'You may have to face some extra challenges, but I'm sure you can do it and I will do my best to get you on your way.'

An important exception to this will arise when a child returns to school after a traumatic illness or injury or serious surgery in hospital. A child may seem on the surface to have recovered well from their traumatic experience, but research in Australia, New Zealand, Norway and the USA has found a high incidence of post-traumatic stress disorder (PTSD) affecting children, and other family members, after these kinds of experiences.[14]

These kinds of experiences invariably lead a child to *regress* for a while as they recover. During this time they may be unable to do the things they could do, and even do easily, before the traumatic event set them back. In this case the child will need to spend some time refamiliarising and reassuring themselves with earlier, 'easier' schoolwork before they can start catching up on more challenging work that they have missed. This may be managed by offering carefully set up choices to enable them to make up their lost ground at their own pace. In some cases, specialist psychological support may be required to prevent the development of deeper, more long-term difficulties.

2. Medical or surgical treatment

Here there are two main issues that can affect children's educational progress: (a) time away from school due to hospitalisation and recovery, and (b) the psychological and emotional aspects of invasive or painful or prolonged medical procedures.

(a) Across all age groups, children who miss school lose out, and the extent of the loss appears to increase with age as lessons are more and more focused on crucial exams. In England, research shows that pupils with no absence are 2.2 times more likely to achieve five or more GCSEs or equivalent at grades A*–C, including English and mathematics, and 4.7 times more likely to achieve the English Baccalaureate than pupils missing 10–15 per cent of KS4 sessions (between fourteen and sixteen years).[15] This research, based on data from over 1 million pupils in state-funded schools in England, found that, whereas almost 80 per cent of fourteen, fifteen and sixteen-year-old pupils who missed no school achieved top GCSE grades, for pupils who missed zero to five days this fell to below 70 per cent, and for pupils who missed more than twenty days, only about 15 per cent gained GCSE grades A*, A, B or C.

To ensure a pupil does not lose out educationally, if their facial condition or injury takes them away from school, even for one day, teachers must ensure that the child is enabled to make up missed schoolwork. For longer absence, they will need to liaise with parents and, if there is one, the hospital school or hospital teacher to ensure that when the child feels able to do some schoolwork, there is interesting and useful work lined up for them to do.

Facial appearance and social experiences

1. What shall we tell the other children?
A member of the child's specialist clinic or burns unit may offer to give the children 'a talk' about the injury or condition that affects the child. The child's parent may suggest this or offer to do it themselves. *Surely* giving the children a talk, sharing some basic information with them, about the condition or injury that affects their classmate's appearance, will reduce staring and make it easier to make friends. But does giving a talk promote inclusive attitudes and behaviour?

Perhaps surprisingly, research suggests that giving the children such information about a classmate has the opposite effect. In the early days of disability integration in the USA, a research team looked into what would help integration to go well. For this research, the integration of a number of profoundly deaf children into mainstream school settings was thoroughly researched: experiment groups were established where carefully and imaginatively devised information and play sessions were run to inform the mainstream children about the deafness of those who were to join their classes; a control group ran alongside, where no information was shared with the mainstream pupils before the deaf children joined them.[16]

Upon integration, the research team counted 'social initiations' (any mainstream child looking, speaking, touching or gesturing to any deaf child). The mainstream children who had learned about the new children's deafness showed many *fewer* social initiations towards their deaf peers than the 'control' group, who had no prior information about the new pupils' deafness.

THE CAMPAIGN FOR FACE EQUALITY IN THE UK TO DATE

Has this completely unexpected research finding been replicated? Yes, it has. Also in the USA, researchers used images of children with and without a facial scar, combined with a range of different scripts describing the child in the image, to evaluate each participating child's like or dislike for the child in the drawing, and whether or not they would like to play with them.[17] This research showed that it was positive information about the skills and abilities of the child with the facial scar in the drawing that increased the children's acceptance and inclination to play with this child. More detailed information about the scar was not a significant influence. In fact, the most effective script was: *This is Mary. Mary loves to run and jump. She likes to talk and laugh and play. If you sit at the table with Mary, you two can play games together. She is good at playing with blocks or doing puzzles or colouring at the table.*

If we give the children a talk about their classmate's injury or illness, they are likely to know more about that injury or illness; but to promote friendly interest and readiness to play together, it is more useful to know what this unusual-looking child likes doing and is good at. If nothing else, instead of focusing on what makes a child 'look different', this approach will emphasise what the children share in common.

In the integration research with the deaf children, one of the control group children who knew nothing about deafness asked the new boy, whose speech was unusual, if he was French. The new boy (perhaps lip-reading 'French' as 'deaf') nodded. The classmate then gestured playing football and they went off to play football together.

Instead of giving a talk, there is much value in supporting the child in question to respond to classmates' curiosity, looking, and questions. They will need to figure out an answer that they are comfortable with. For example, at lunchtime, a young child might answer another child's question – 'What happened to your face?' – with something like, 'It's just the way my face is. I've got peanut butter in my sandwich. What's in yours?' This might take some careful preparation and practice beforehand, but if a child can manage this even once, their facial condition or injury will become less important and the ordinary things that keep school days moving along socially will gain momentum.

2. How does appearance affect children's social choices?
Research suggests that children may show negative reactions towards a classmate whose appearance is noticeably affected by a condition or injury, especially when first meeting them.[18] But there are also some studies that offer perhaps unexpected findings.

A research team based in Switzerland asked if children with a squint are less likely to be invited to birthday parties.[19] Children from three to twelve years old were shown a selection of paired photographs of boys and girls of their own age and invited to choose who they would like to come to their birthday party. Some of the images had been modified so that the children were choosing from a range of peers with and without a squint (strabismus). The research team found that children below the age of six years showed no significant preference for children with or without a squint. However, children above six years showed a significant preference for children without squint. This research concluded that 'negative attitude towards strabismus appears to emerge at approximately the age of six years' and that children with a squint are likely to be invited to fewer birthday parties.

Teachers need to be aware that even though a child's facial condition or injury may look minimal to them – a squint is surely a very minimal facial condition – it can nevertheless very significantly affect the way other children respond to this child; not being invited to birthday parties is a horrible slight to experience.

Also concerned with children's preferences regarding aspects of other children's appearance, a researcher based in the USA collated and further extended a large body of research into eight- to twelve-year-old children's responses to images of peers with a range of

THE CAMPAIGN FOR FACE EQUALITY IN THE UK TO DATE

different injuries and disabilities.[20] These research findings, gathered over many years in many different parts of the world, show that (able-bodied) children would like to play with (in order of preference):

1. a non-disabled child (most liked)
2. a child with crutch/brace
3. a child in wheelchair
4. a child with hand missing
5. a child with facial disfigurement
6. a child with obesity (most disliked)*

Teachers need to be aware that even though a child with a not-perfect face may be able-bodied and apparently well able to join in all the usual playtime activities with classmates, they may nevertheless end up standing alone on the sidelines because 'facial disfigurement' is disliked by other children.

Denis C. Harper, the researcher in question, writes very interestingly about some of the children's thoughts on playing with different-looking children:

> The comments associated with the least preferred ranking of the child with a facial-oral cleft were uniformly negative... The generally negative attributions reported toward the depiction of the child with a facial-oral cleft reflect an illogical 'spread' of negativism that engulfs the individual with facial disfigurement (e.g. 'She can't play because of her mouth' or 'He wouldn't know how to play the game,' suggesting that those with such facial differences have other limitations as well). [This may very occasionally be the case at school but was not the case in the images used in the research.]

---

* In cultures where a large body size is a manifestation of high status, obesity was not a characteristic that the research children disliked.

Other comments reflect how the child with facial-oral disfigurement makes the observer feel (i.e. 'awkward, dirty, or scared') and how others see the appearance ('He looks like cat lips,' 'She looks bad,' or 'He's not good-looking'). References were made to functional communication problems as well, which also reflect concern with the level of comfort in communicating with children with a facial disfigurement. Several comments, however, included an awareness or sensitivity of social difficulties; one child noted: 'People like that go into themselves.'[21]

Perhaps here we glimpse a mix-up between cause and effect: if the child with the repaired cleft is the other children's last or last-but-one choice of playmate, then perhaps they will, thus isolated, 'go into themselves'.

Returning to Harper's reportage of his conversations with children about their play preferences:

> … children who selected the child portrayed with facial-oral disfigurement as their first playmate – a rare occurrence – reported a combination of positive affirmations. Attributions identified or affirmed positive personal characteristics (e.g. seems friendly) and an awareness that the child with a facial-oral cleft could engage in functional activities (e.g. 'could climb a tree, could play, and could do the game'). These responses reflect a positive awareness of skills for peer interaction, and as one child affirmed, 'Because her face is different doesn't mean she can't do things.'[22]

Such responses reflect a move beyond more common negative attributions to a positive spread of visible differences.

The children who participated in this research included, in the USA, some children with cerebral palsy and spina bifida. Harper notes that the attributions of those who themselves had mobility impairments were very different from all others studied, in that their responses reflected an awareness of personal functional problems and a sensitivity to such differences; the person with the facial-oral cleft might feel 'hurt, and kids make fun of her nose'. Clearly, those with mobility impairments have a unique perspective towards peers with facial disfigurement.

It seems possible, therefore, that more fully inclusive classrooms may give teachers more opportunities to use classroom discussions to draw upon wider experience and different perspectives in order to increase children's access to face equality at school.

3. How does appearance affect children becoming friends?

Children whose facial appearance is affected by a condition or injury tend to have fewer friends than their classmates whose appearance is more familiar and ordinary.[23] To try to understand why this may be, Urie Bronfenbrenner, a USA-based developmental psychologist, offers a very useful analysis of the different qualities that characterise different ways that two people can relate or be together (two children = one dyad), and also analyses the processes through which dyads develop, grow and change.

The process of becoming friends can be seen to fall into distinct stages:

- Stage 1: two young children pay attention to one another's activities – an *observational dyad*.
- Stage 2: observing the other's activity leads to becoming engaged in the activity together – a *joint activity dyad*.
- Stage 3: engaging in joint activity leads to more differentiated and enduring feeling towards one another – a *primary dyad*.

A primary dyad 'is one that continues to exist phenomenologically for both participants even when they are not together'.[24] So, when two young children at school form a 'primary dyad', they will feel the benefit of each other's presence in their life, even when they are not together at school – they are friends.

Thus, Bronfenbrenner shows us the importance of children looking at each other. Observation. Just looking appears to be an essential precursor – perhaps *the* essential precursor – to becoming friends.

However, when a child has an unusual facial appearance, just looking can be problematic for their classmates. When we first see someone whose face is an unusual shape or colour, who is missing an ear, say, or whose skin is affected by scarring, we as humans seem to need to *look harder* and to *look longer* – to stare. Societies and cultures vary in terms of the social acceptability of staring. But being stared at is not a pleasant experience. This may be because the longer, harder look – the stare – focuses on the outward appearance only, whilst the *person* whose face it is remains unseen, and feels unseen.

Staring can also make a child feel horribly visible, with nowhere to hide. When one's appearance is affected by a condition or injury, one is forever on the receiving end of *unwanted attention.* Children whose facial appearance is unusual and noticeable often ask the teacher to stop the other children staring. Wanting only to help, teachers invariably set about prohibiting staring. Children learn that 'it is rude to stare'.

Then how is a child to look – to make a start on that vital *observational dyad* – if staring is rude, and is prohibited? Can small children distinguish between looking at or observing a classmate whose face happens to be interesting and unusual, and staring at them?

Children will try and be good, and you will sometimes see them looking firmly in the other direction to prevent themselves from staring. Less often, a child will deliberately break the no-staring rule, because the urge to look is irresistible, or perhaps just because it's an exciting way to cause a stir.

Returning to the initial question, we now know that if children are discouraged from looking then it will be much harder for them to become friends.

Nevertheless, being stared at is not pleasant. So, if prohibiting staring turns out to be an unhelpful intervention then the task is clear: to find other ways to deal with staring that allow children at school to form *observational dyads* – to look at each other.

Conclusions

This overview of some key research findings helps to highlight some tips and interventions that will better enable teachers to work effectively with all the children in their class, however they may look. In summary:

- High expectations of what each child can make of their life will help them to do well at school and work towards a satisfying life for themselves beyond school.
- Familiarise all children (and school staff) with positive role models of older children and adults with all kinds of unusual faces, to balance the widespread media preference for 'perfect-face people' who are conventionally judged to be happy and successful.
- Make sure all pupils make up schoolwork missed through medical appointments, hospitalisation, convalescence etc. As children get older, even one day's absence risks harming their access to good exam results, so they always need support to cover what they've missed if they possibly can.
- Don't give the children a talk about the condition or injury that affects their classmate's appearance. Instead, coach the child whose appearance is unusual to understand that other children will be curious and ensure that they have an answer ready, an answer that goes on to flag up something else about them as a person, and perhaps ends with a question. 'I was in a fire but I'm OK now. I support Man U – what's your team?'

- A seemingly very slight appearance variation such as a squint can make classmates want to avoid and exclude. Teachers should therefore keep an alert professional eye out for any child who is left standing on the sidelines, who doesn't get 'picked', who has no friends. This can take some turning around, for example through setting up a Circle of Friends,[25] organising the class into carefully planned small groups for all kinds of different tasks so that each pupil can spend a significant amount of time working with classmates they don't usually engage with.
- Finally, and perhaps most important of all, do not prohibit 'staring', as this turns out, in practice, to prohibit looking, which makes making friends much harder. Staring can usually be managed quite effectively if it is understood as an unspoken question, which either the teacher, or the child being looked at, can then answer; (as outlined above) with a previously prepared and rehearsed answer such as; 'If you're wondering about my scar, it's called a cleft lip that the doctors mended in hospital. Have you ever been to hospital?'

That is a summary of the latest research, and it informed how Changing Faces sought to influence the teaching practices of schools and teachers around the UK. We also produced guidance for teachers about anti-bullying policies that should include reference to children with facial disfigurements.

Perhaps most importantly, we also created age-specific guidance for teachers about how to support students with distinctive faces in their classes and schools. Subjects include 'teasing, name-calling and bullying', 'moving on to junior/secondary school', 'practical support with social skills' and 'building self-esteem' – teachers are given straightforward practical advice based on years of work and research.

These can be found here: www.changingfaces.org.uk/education/education-resources/supporting-pupils.

THE CAMPAIGN FOR FACE EQUALITY IN THE UK TO DATE

Employers and business – with support from Henrietta Spalding

Henrietta Spalding trained as a teacher and headed up a language school in Spain for many years. She started to work for Changing Faces in the mid-2000s and became our Head of Advocacy in the run-up to the launch of the campaign for face equality. Her work in shifting employer opinion was groundbreaking, as she brought her personal experience of Moebius syndrome together with her understanding of business to bear on senior figures throughout UK business. I am delighted she agreed to help me write this section.

First, some history: when, in the early 1990s, I first started to make the case for employers to become fair and inclusive in employing people with facial disfigurements and serving them as customers, I found supportive allies in what would be called the soft or progressive section of the disability movement. Throughout the 1980s, that movement in Britain struggled to make its voice for full-scale civil rights heard. Despite many marches, protests and sit-ins – and many arrests of people with disabilities who'd chained themselves (and their wheelchairs) to railings – little progress was being made. In 1982, a commission supported the idea of an act and a body to enforce it, but the Conservative Party of the day led by Mrs Thatcher opposed any such change and the right-wing press continued to tar disabled people as scroungers.

The passing of the Americans with Disabilities Act in 1990 showed what could be done even with the business-friendly administration of President George H.W. Bush. But nothing similar happened in Britain and several private member's bills (such as one by Roger Berry MP) were rejected.

Then, in 1994, Sir Nicholas Scott, the Minister for Disabled People, used ancient House of Commons procedures to defeat the Civil Rights (Disabled Persons) Bill brought by Harry Barnes MP. This provoked a massive media storm stoked strongly by the minister's daughter, who was working for the Royal Association for Disability and Rehabilitation, and who went public using very strong words. By the spring of 1994, the government had capitulated and introduced the Disability Discrimination Bill, which was to become an Act in 1995.

But the Bill had absolutely no mention of people with disfigurements despite my strenuous efforts to persuade the officials involved in the consultation. Then, out of the blue, I was invited to address MPs in the House of Commons as part of the launch of a new *Guide for MPs on Disability* produced by the Employers' Forum on Disability, which despite being a voice of employers was in favour of the legislation. It was a terrifying occasion and I spoke after William Hague MP, the new Minister for Disabled People.

What I had to say went down well enough and, with the minister's officials standing just across the room, I 'went for him'. No holds barred. I explained the case for legal protection for people with disfigurements. He asked me to send him more details.

Imagine my shock and delight when the Act was published in early 1995: people with 'severe disfigurements' were to be covered as if they had a disability. They did not even need to demonstrate, as other disabled people had to do, that the impairment had a substantial adverse effect on their ability to carry out normal day-to-day activities.

History lesson over! The importance of this legal breakthrough (which was subsequently repeated in the Equality Act 2010) cannot be underestimated. From that moment on, people with disfigurements should have been judged fairly, without prejudice or bias, and treated fairly and equally at work, in shops, in restaurants, at school and in every walk of life. But, of course, it wasn't as simple as that.

The 1995 law was flawed in many ways, not least by being based on a medical model approach, requiring people with disabilities to prove they were disabled before any discrimination could

THE CAMPAIGN FOR FACE EQUALITY IN THE UK TO DATE

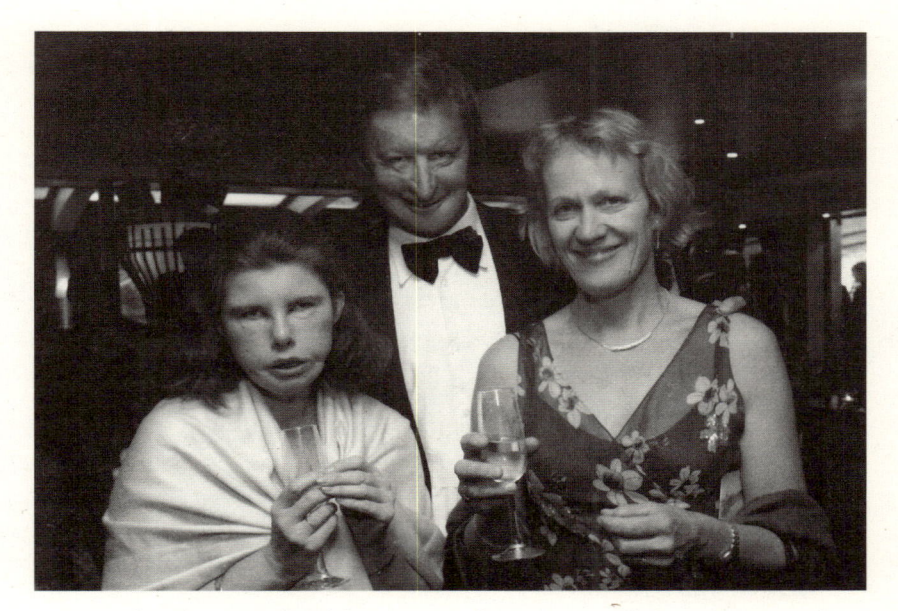

With Henrietta Spalding, my wife Carrie and me as guests of Camelot in 2004 as we started to nurture corporate relationships.

be considered. But it did provide unprecedented new legal rights for people with severe disfigurements and protected them from appearance-related discrimination. However, many people with disfigurements themselves, as well as employers and customer service representatives, remained unaware of the law or what it meant in practice. Indeed, we found that many employers hadn't a clue what it meant to make a reasonable adjustment for someone with a disfigurement.

In 2008 (as described in the second Mezzanine), we discovered that there was still immense implicit bias against people with distinctive faces: nine out of ten members of the public unwittingly judged them to be less attractive, less likely to succeed and less easy to work with. And the bias was consistent whatever the survey respondent's age or educational status. There had also been very few publicised legal cases that tested the Act's provisions, although several were settled out of court.

Which accounts for why, when we came to launch the campaign for face equality in May 2008, we knew we had to make a very strong case to employers of all kinds and sizes. Hence the 'Face Equality at Work' initiative. Over the next five years, despite the world economy freezing up in the wake of the credit crunch, the scheme influenced over a hundred leading companies and organisations serving millions of people. Household names like Barclays, BA, British Gas, Sainsbury's, BT, the 2012 Olympics, KPMG, Shell and many more signed up to the Face Equality at Work pledge, and we worked with many of them to inform their staff and influence their work practices.

What we learned is that influencing employers today has to have three components:

1. Making the case
2. Explaining what employers need to do
3. Providing training and resources to make it easier.

1. Making the case
No business in today's tough economic climate is going to respect face equality just because it sounds a nice thing to do. We have to make a strong business case as to why they should, and it starts from the idea that in an increasingly diverse world, they can't afford to miss out on recruiting the best people and tapping into new customer markets.

So, getting face equality 'right' enables organisations to make money and attract talent in the following ways:

- Customers who have facial disfigurements, one in every 111 people in the UK population, and their families and friends have spending power.
- Having members of staff with personal experience of a disfigurement shows a company values diversity, and they can be a great source of advice and insight.

- Businesses that demonstrate that they welcome and value diverse staff, customers and clients will enhance their reputation – and employing someone with a facial difference reflects the diversity of our population.
- Many people who have disfigurements have incredibly proactive and well-practised social skills, which they will have had to develop in order to encourage people to see past their disfigurement, making them an asset to any organisation.

Getting it 'wrong' can be costly: in litigation if discrimination happens, in loss of customers, in reputational damage, bad press or negative social media coverage. In 2009, for example, there was a very well-publicised – and helpful – legal case in which Riam Dean won a case for wrongful dismissal against Abercrombie & Fitch after she claimed that the firm 'hid' her in a stockroom at its London store because her prosthetic arm didn't fit with the firm's 'look policy'.

And organisations may find that failing in diversity can lead to high staff turnover too.

Any organisation that wants to be competitive must ensure that they are getting it right in terms of face and disfigurement equality, as it is a strong link in the chain of diversity.

2. Explaining what employers need to do

Truly respecting face equality isn't a quick process for any organisation, because breaking out of the facial prejudices and unwitting behaviours they engender takes time. But it can be done by sustained action – just as it can be on other equality strands too. Institutional racism or sexism is being broken down, but slowly.

Our experience is that the best progress can be made from getting top-table commitment from the board of directors or governing body of the organisation. So, we aimed at winning the support of one or two influential leaders of big companies at the outset – for example, John Varley at Barclays and James Smith at Shell. They were willing to sign a pledge, hold an event for their top teams and then drive the changes needed through their companies.

The pledge itself signalled that they had been made aware of the disadvantage that people with facial disfigurements experience and were determined to eradicate any barriers or stereotypes that contributed to that situation in their organisation. They also recognised that whilst the law required companies to make reasonable adjustments, their businesses needed to work hard to understand what this meant for people with disfigurements (since it clearly did not mean creating a ramp or improving IT access).

Signing the pledge led to the next stage: committing to review and make changes to all policies and practices within the company that could impinge on people with facial disfigurements. That included how recruitment was carried out – were photos required, for example? – and how interviews were conducted. Were staff given implicit bias training? Did it include reference to facial prejudices? And what about customer service training? And advertising – were any people with not-perfect faces included?

That review process pointed to ways in which the company could embed face equality, not just as a one-year 'initiative' but as a long-term change. Many decided that they had to bring about sustained culture change in how their staff teams felt about people with facial differences. So, they arranged 'lunch and learn' events, created company-wide screen savers, used the Face Equality posters.

In some cases, a whole industry got involved. On the back of one man being turned away from a pub because of his face, our #ServeAlex campaign came forward with new guidance and it was adopted and disseminated by the British Beer and Pub Association.

Another good example is the training given to BA's cabin staff which, we gather, still contains a section on interacting with a traveller with a facial disfigurement.

THE CAMPAIGN FOR FACE EQUALITY IN THE UK TO DATE

3. Providing training and resources to make it easier

At Changing Faces we developed a series of generic training courses which we could offer organisations – on implicit bias, for example. And on occasion, we were asked to create company-specific training. The best example was the induction training given to all Specsavers staff, which shows how to be sensitive and excellent in customer service whether the person concerned has a birthmark, scarring, a skin condition or whatever. This came about because one of Changing Faces' champions reported a negative experience in one of the company's stores. We then worked with Specsavers to design an innovative training module that was rolled out at all their franchises – after the training, 99 per cent of customer-facing staff reported being comfortable helping people with a disfigurement choose glasses. Leadership and responsibility in spades!

We also put together an online guide for employers for dealing with the challenges within the workplace – which we did in parallel with a best-practice self-help guide for people who wanted to find work or get promotion. See:

- www.changingfaces.org.uk/adviceandsupport/self-help/work/a-guide-for-employers
- www.changingfaces.org.uk/adviceandsupport/self-help/work/a-guide-for-employees

CREATING 'FACE EQUALITY DAYS'

To coincide with Changing Faces' twenty-fifth anniversary, we decided to create the UK's first 'Face Equality Day' in May 2017. Although it was a first-time effort during a period of highly-charged media coverage (with a snap British general election and terrorist outrages in Manchester and London), the day was a big success.

We called on individuals, schools, charities and organisations to support Changing Faces' vision of a society where all individuals with disfigurements are treated respectfully, equally and fairly, irrespective of their appearance. Our big goal was to remove the stigma, prejudice and discrimination that people face so they can have the same life choices and opportunities as everyone else and will be free to live life the way they want.

The first Face Equality Day was intended to raise awareness of disfigurement and its impact on people's daily lives, and promote the face equality campaign. Various activities were planned including illuminating public buildings with the charity's distinctive brand colours and logo, poster campaigns, and publicising the results of our major new report through media and social media coverage, with individuals sharing their experiences and celebrities speaking out. We also tried to get as many people as possible to wear the Changing Faces butterfly as a transfer on their faces to show their support.

We created two pledges, one organisational, one personal, for people, schools and companies to sign:

Organisational Pledge: *'At XXXXXXXXXX, we are committed to respecting Face Equality in everything that we do. We will challenge appearance bias and discrimination and treat everyone equally and fairly whatever the appearance of their face or body.'*

Individual Pledge: *'I'm committed to Face Equality. I will challenge appearance discrimination whenever I see it. I will help to create a society that treats everyone equally and without prejudice whatever their face or body looks like.'*

As well as signing the pledge, organisations such as charities, schools, companies and sports clubs were asked to support Face Equality Day by committing to review their policies and practice towards people with disfigurement, provide implicit bias training for their staff on face equality and hold an event to raise awareness amongst colleagues.

Individuals were invited to support Face Equality Day on social media with selfies showing them wearing the butterfly and to challenge unfair attitudes and behaviours towards people with disfigurements.

And it all worked incredibly well, as these numbers demonstrate:

- 84,300 butterflies were ordered by supporters, including 4,250 new supporters.
- 38,219 emails were sent to supporters along with more than 10,000 leaflets; 6,000 posters and 14,000 stickers were produced for schools.
- Changing Faces gave twenty-nine media interviews about Face Equality Day and news of the *Disfigurement in the UK* report was disseminated to over 19.2 million.
- On Twitter, the #FaceEquality hashtag had 23.8 million impressions, and our tweets reached 4.6 million unique users. Our Thunderclap campaign reached 218 per cent of its target, with a reach of 532,229, and supporters including Rory Bremner.
- Our new face equality film, titled *Tulsi's Story*, reached 431,642 people and was viewed by more than 227,000 people on Facebook alone.
- Our posts about Face Equality Day and *Disfigurement in the UK* reached 920,293 people, created 90,465 engagements and 947 new page 'likes'.

We also arranged events such as one outside the Scottish Parliament attended by thirty MSPs including the Scottish Deputy First Minister, the leader of the Scottish Conservatives, Labour Party and Liberal Democrats and the Deputy Leader of the Scottish Green Party, and more than eighty people attended a Face Equality reception. In Sheffield, hundreds of people attended events in the city's cathedral forecourt and botanical gardens, and more than 300 tiles were included in a 'Butterfly of Tiles' installation.' The town hall displayed a banner affirming the city's support for Face Equality Day.

There were five key things that went to make this first Face Equality Day a success:

1. Acquiring solid new evidence to make the case

On the day, 26th May 2017, Changing Faces published *Disfigurement in the UK*, the most extensive study of people with a disfigurement's lives, based on over 800 people's replies to an online survey.[26] It described a vastly unequal playing field in almost every aspect of their lives, leading them to have lower aspirations and expectations, and to be resigned to the inevitability of abuse and injustice.

Dame Margaret Hodge MP commented in her foreword that 'the report tells me that people with disfigurements have been left behind in Britain's progress towards being a fair and equal society. I commend it to you – and hope you will commit to help make the changes so very obviously needed.'

2. Generating rising social media interest in positive champion stories

We created a fantastic book of photographs called *Faces of Equality* that showcased twenty-two champions in all their glory, a book which epitomised what face equality means.[27] All the champions committed to being leaders of our social media campaign, and they were very impactful, as the statistics above show.

3. Creating an alliance with like-minded organisations and professionals

Changing Faces managed to secure the support of about forty organisations and groups representing people with conditions that affect the appearance of their faces and bodies – and, importantly, many of the professional medical associations involved in their care – and other organisations representing people with disabilities and gay rights groups.

The day provided a unifying call for organisations that had never worked together – such as those for people with cleft lips and palates, facial paralysis and psoriasis – which they all considered very strengthening.

4. Distributing a visual symbol for supporters to wear to signify their support

On Face Equality Day, thousands of people wore the butterfly on their faces in solidarity.

5. Gaining pledges of support from influencers, politicians and celebrities

We approached lots of VIPs, MPs and celebrities and gained many pledges. The most important of these was from the Chair of the Equality and Human Rights Commission:

Wearing my butterfly with pride on Face Equality Day, May 2017.

As individuals and employers it is vital that we recognise how unconscious bias prevents people from fulfilling their true potential. Changing Faces encourages us to confront uncomfortable truths about how society treats people with facial disfigurements. Their important work challenges negative attitudes that can profoundly impact on people's lives. At the Commission we are working to deliver a fairer Britain for everyone and we wholeheartedly support both Changing Faces and their Face Equality campaign.

Those lessons informed the Face Equality Days in the UK in 2018 and 2019. And the ones in Taiwan since 2011 have become increasingly impressive, with projects in schools, businesses and government departments. It was partly because of the example of Taiwan that I took another important step towards globalising the campaign for face equality in 2018...

6. Face Equality International

I set up Face Equality International in late 2018 to bring attention to the fact that disfigurement is a neglected global human rights issue. I argued that millions of people with disfigurements, wherever they live in the world, face many challenges in living confident, successful lives in the twenty-first century. Many report (and academic studies bear this out) feeling very self-conscious, isolated and friendless, facing teasing, ridicule and staring in public, low expectations in school, problems getting work, discrimination in the workplace, abuse on social media and stereotyping in the media just because of the way they look. In many countries, disfigurement goes hand in hand with poverty, prejudice and exclusion. You can find out more from the website: www.faceequalityinternational.org.

At the beginning of 2020, Face Equality International had already become an alliance of thirty NGOs/charities around the world that are supporting and representing people with many different disfig-

THE CAMPAIGN FOR FACE EQUALITY IN THE UK TO DATE

urements. Crucially, most NGOs for people with disfigurements are condition-specific (e.g. clefts, burns) but their members face very similar cultural and social barriers to living fulfilling lives. Working together on these common problems will create the critical mass and solidarity needed to gain global attention to tackle these injustices.

The alliance will be a powerful mouthpiece to enable the voice of many excluded people to challenge the cultural forces that are increasingly global concerns. It will raise the profile of disfigurement and put the issues people with disfigurements experience on the agenda of the UN Convention on the Rights of Persons with Disabilities (CRPD), international bodies, companies and social media outlets.

It will also enable the sharing of best practice and be an incubator (capacity builder) for NGOs to campaign for face equality in their own settings. It will be a learning exchange and set global standards on how to challenge disfigurement discrimination (e.g. on social media and at work) and promote face equality (e.g. in schools).

The first International Face Equality Week in May 2019 was a great start. Awareness was raised. On social media, for example, the Phoenix Society for Burn Survivors reached 100,000 people on Facebook alone. In Taiwan, the Sunshine Foundation arranged an island tour that generated 258 media reports – but the biggest outcomes there were:

- Nineteen cities and counties have pledged support for Face Equality and two, Tainan City and New Taipei City, have adopted measures to stop the practice of requiring a photo to accompany a CV/resumé when hiring government employees.
- Over 450 schools and 200 businesses across Taiwan have pledged support for Face Equality.

Two priority projects for Face Equality International in its early years deserve a mention:

First, members decided that the portrayal and treatment of people with facial disfigurements by the media and broadcasting industries was far too often biased, negative and in need of improvement. So, we decided to draw up the International Media Standard on Disfigurement, which was launched in early 2020 – see Annex 3. The standard will be followed by media guidelines reflecting the cultural nuances of Taiwan, Northern America, Europe, the UK and other settings.

Second, we are determined the improve the legal protection of people with disfigurements from discrimination and prejudice. Although in the UK, Taiwan and some other countries, such protection exists – but is far from ideal, as Hannah Saunders has expertly pointed out[28] – in many countries, there is absolutely no protection. Our first focus is going to be on getting disfigurement recognised within the UN Convention on the Rights of Persons with Disabilities, which has been ratified in 130 countries.

Face Equality International also chose as its logo a symbol that reflects the Japanese aesthetic known as *wabi-sabi*. This sees the beauty, profundity and authenticity in irregularity and imprecision and seems a perfect way of conveying the alliance's ethos. The logo is displayed with more explanation in Annex 5.[29]

CONCLUSION

The campaign for face equality has made considerable progress since its launch in 2008, especially in recent years, and it has certainly challenged and activated many thousands of people in Britain – and now in other countries – to think and act in new inclusive ways. BUT there is still *a very long way* to go.

We cannot be sure how much public attitudes have shifted so far, but they are changing. The campaign can be turned into a worldwide movement to give people with distinctive faces the human rights

THE CAMPAIGN FOR FACE EQUALITY IN THE UK TO DATE

they deserve. To achieve these goals we will need bigger platforms and stronger alliances than we have created to date – and we have new digital technologies and social media to use if we can: Facebook – yes, Face-Book – and all. But, on the flip side, the airwaves are incredibly crowded and competed for, and people's attention span is diminishing every year. We will have to be very resourceful!

22.
WHAT CAN WE ALL DO TO CREATE FACE EQUALITY?

The campaign for face equality is already well launched, the allies are gathering and the social media platforms are proliferating. The foundations of a global movement are there and can be built upon. And we can take lessons and inspiration from other social change movements that seemed highly unlikely when I was first reading Goffman in 1971.

Since then, I have watched many equality campaigns grow from a tiny germ of a very improbable idea through various stages of development to being full-blown movements that have successfully brought about change. Campaigns for feminism and for disability, gay and transgender rights have all made huge strides, if not fully achieved their goals.

Other movements, like #MeToo or to tackle climate change – notably, the school strikes and Extinction Rebellion – have gained great momentum and achieved some of their goals. But not all succeed: I was a great advocate of organic farming (still am) but, so far, it has achieved limited success, although public awareness is a great deal higher.

In Malcolm Gladwell's book *The Tipping Point*, he theorises about how it is that seemingly highly unlikely changes can and do occur.

It usually happens when one or more small ideas or actions accumulate until they become, often very suddenly, the order of the day – the new norm – and then spread like wildfire. With social media now connecting people at such speed and enabling great numbers of people to get together quickly, that accumulation is made easier.

Gladwell suggests that a tipping point happens when events build up so that something which seems highly unlikely doesn't just become a prospect, but an inevitability.[1]

How does that accumulation build up? Gladwell suggests that you have to make something you want to happen the obvious thing to do – and, crucially, the easy thing to do, too. The geniuses of the IT era like Steve Jobs, the co-founder of Apple, knew this instinctively – he explained what a smartphone would be able to do, made it happen and its popularity rose exponentially.

Here's an example that I was involved with tangentially. In the run-up to the UK adopting anti-discrimination disability legislation in the mid-1990s, it seemed highly unlikely that UK business could be persuaded to accept it – the usual arguments were being wheeled out: too much red tape, unnecessary because we already look after needy people through our charitable giving, impossible to provide accessible premises for all…

The UK minister responsible for looking at this subject, Nick Scott, then discovered the Employers' Forum on Disability. Started by Susan Scott-Parker in 1991, it had rapidly become a business voice for fairness and best practice towards disabled people. What's more, it already had over a hundred blue-chip companies as members – and they wanted new legislation!

With those enlightened employers on side, the minister's case for legislation was irresistible, and soon, employers across the UK were seeing the logic: provide good working arrangements and 'reasonable adjustments' for disabled people and businesses could tap into all their talents and skills – and their purchasing power, too. A Tipping Point had been created: the desired change became the obvious

WHAT CAN WE ALL DO TO CREATE FACE EQUALITY?

thing to do... although it has to be said that even after twenty-four years, there is much to do to make offices, shops and public places fully accessible. The law has proved too puny.

Tipping Points don't just turn up without a great deal of hard work and some luck – but you make your own luck.

And sometimes, even when you think you've made a breakthrough, change doesn't quite happen. I had hoped that my appearance reading the Channel 5 news for a week in November 2009 would create a Tipping Point. It didn't, though it probably added a little to the accumulation of effort needed to get people with distinctive faces to be positively accepted on TV. Why did it fail? Because there were no parallel follow-ups.

I have been amazed that a Tipping Point around transgender (trans) people has been achieved, because it was in the wilderness for years. Sixty years ago, when Jan (then James) Morris, the famous historian on the Everest expedition in 1952, announced her transition, British culture was shocked. She became an icon, but an isolated one. But, very gradually, the clamour for change grew louder. Medical science and public opinion started to acknowledge that some people wanted to transition, and safe and effective methods were evolved.

But what really made the difference was the strength of the coalition of voices pressing for change, supported by celebrities and leading public figures. The Gender Recognition Act was passed in 2004 after much lobbying of the Labour Government. Just six years later, trans people were more broadly protected under the Equality Act 2010 – and given the great legal significance of having 'a protected characteristic' like race, gender and age, each with its own set of legal obligations and requirements.[2] This is what we tried to achieve for people with unusual faces to no avail. There was no pressure for change. Then.

But it isn't just in the equality domain that people try to bring about Tipping Points.

Peter Singer, the moral philosopher, recalls a time – and I was there as an observer – when protesters about battery farming started to raise their voices on the streets of Oxford. It was not a Tipping Point, but it certainly raised public awareness significantly. Now, after years of angry protests at the factories which irritated as many as they persuaded, there has been a huge rise in food awareness; veganism and pescetarianism are on the rise... a Tipping Point is coming.[3]

Singer has also on more than one occasion cited the famous statement by Margaret Mead, the anthropologist, who is reported to have said: 'Never doubt that a small group of thoughtful, committed citizens can change the world. Indeed, it is the only thing that ever has.' Singer says – and I agree – 'The second part may not be true, but the first surely is.'

Can we apply these ideas to making face equality a reality? I believe we can – not least because if you say 'I'm in favour of face equality,' people get it very quickly. And you don't have to have a wonky face like mine to do this!

It is extremely difficult to predict when a Tipping Point is approaching, but I believe that if we press sufficiently and gather enough allies, a Tipping Point in the struggle to overthrow the vice-like grip of face-ism can be found.

Three other things stand out for me from successful social change movements:

First, we need a high-level manifesto for action, what we are for and against and how to make change happen. Not one that is prescriptive in all circumstances, but one that gives people the broad goals and principles on which to campaign.

WHAT CAN WE ALL DO TO CREATE FACE EQUALITY?

> **A Manifesto for Change**
>
> The campaign for 'face equality' aims to assert the human rights and improve the life prospects of any person anywhere in the world who has a disfigurement, a facial difference, a distinctive, scarred or asymmetrical face for any reason.
>
> The campaign aims to challenge facial prejudices and create a global culture and national societies in which everyone, whatever their face looks like, is valued for the unique contribution they can make, and is treated equally, with high expectations like everyone else.
>
> The campaign calls on:
>
> - Individuals to spread the word, to stand out and to support face equality.
> - Education systems to ensure that all teaching staff are adequately trained to develop a culture and practice of inclusion for children with disfigurements.
> - Employers to create a culture and practice of face equality for people with disfigurements as employees and customers.
> - The media, advertisers and the film industry to positively promote facial diversity, to adopt factual and unbiased portrayals of disfigurement and actively avoid language and imagery that create prejudice.
> - Politicians and policymakers to ensure that facial prejudice and discrimination are outlawed by improving anti-discrimination law and promoting best practice.

The means to share this is the internet, social media platforms and open source websites.

Second, success stems from having a very logical and coherent explanation as to why the campaign is needed, why people are disadvantaged and put at risk by current thinking and practices – an explanation that can be communicated effectively and therefore can be shared quickly, especially through social media across the world. Which is what the four chapters earlier on were intended to do: to dissect the origins, causes and characteristics of facial stigma into clean nuggets. Here's a summary:

> **Why is the campaign needed?**
> Because disfigurement is a neglected global human rights issue. People with disfigurements everywhere face many injustices and challenges to living confident, successful lives in the twenty-first century.
>
> The stigma of disfigurement is rooted in three false but deeply conditioned, unconscious prejudices that impinge on a person's self-worth – the ideas that…
>
> - Facial 'good looks' are the passport for success; without them, failure is inevitable.
> - Disfigurement is linked to meanness, lack of intelligence, immorality and evil.
> - Modern medicine and surgery can remove disfigurements completely.
>
> All too often, the stigma is self-imposed, too, with low expectations of success and a lack of aspiration leading to a resignation that this is how things will always be; consequently, unfairness and discrimination go unchallenged. And worse still, people with facial differences have reported that authorities who should stand up to prejudice (e.g. in schools) fail to do so even when alerted to it.
>
> 'Face equality' means being treated fairly and equally irrespective of your facial appearance.

WHAT CAN WE ALL DO TO CREATE FACE EQUALITY?

Third, movements can get off the ground without much organisation behind them – witness #MeToo and Extinction Rebellion – but it is very hard for them to be sustained without some coordination. That doesn't necessarily mean one lead or coordinating organisation – which can be divisive – but it is one way. The advantage is that it can raise funds, create events, coordinate campaigning and galvanise collective efforts.

I am hoping and intending that Face Equality International can be such an agent, at least initially. What I hope we can orchestrate is 'macro-level' efforts and individuals making lots of 'micro-level' changes too. Here's what I mean:

1. Working at macro-level

The macro efforts need both to create countervailing forces and to promote all manner of good examples and practices.

Countervailing actions

In this era of instantaneous communication and social media pressure companies, media, politicians and governments are increasingly responsive to how people think. Popular trends can arise, petitions can gain vast support and changes seem to be brought about very quickly. But I doubt the global grip that face-ism has on our minds can be broken that way.

There must be *countervailing forces* around which people with distinctive faces can gather, and to which the commercial and political forces are forced to pay attention.

I was strongly influenced in my university days by the wisdom of John Kenneth Galbraith, whose books on American and global capitalism enriched economics in the last century. His greatest contribution was to point out that without any countervailing power, giant corporations can manipulate consumers who, far from being free agents as described in economic theory and 'conventional wisdom', are actually liable to be persuaded by clever advertising and marketing. Facial prejudices we are dealing with are undoubtedly perpetuated in that way, through everyday hype and bombardment.

Galbraith believed that those commercial forces were not in the public interest and could be destructive, and that the way to contain them was to create strong countervailing forces – unions, consumer associations, NGOs and the like – and that governments had a role, too, in providing legislation and regulation, such as anti-monopoly laws.

That's how I see the challenge of overturning the cultural and commercial forces that perpetuate face-ism today. I do not want to see big cosmetics businesses collapse, for example, with all the loss of jobs involved. No, they need to be civilised into new face values – just as they are being into new gender and ethnic values.

The problem is that currently, there are too few NGOs making the face-ism case, and together we lack the resources at this time. So, we need to be smart in searching for more funding and more allies – such as organisations that are campaigning for race, gender and gay rights, and think tanks like the Nuffield Council on Bioethics. Their recent report on the ethics of cosmetic surgery procedures has much of value – and they have the ear of government. Some governmental agencies like the Equality and Human Rights Commission in Britain may be willing to give further support too.

It is also crucial that disfigurement receives international recognition in the UN Convention on the Rights of Persons with Disabilities, which has already been ratified by 130 countries. Although, in some eyes, disfigurement shouldn't be legally covered as a disability, the reality is that this is currently the best way of gaining legal protection from discrimination.

Similarly, countervailing actions are needed to prevent negative media descriptions and portrayals of people with not-perfect faces. The written media needs to be continually monitored and bad examples highlighted and challenged. It is often the case in newspaper culture that a journalist can write quite a sensitive article, but its

WHAT CAN WE ALL DO TO CREATE FACE EQUALITY?

impact is ruined by an offensive or prejudiced headline or captioning. Media guidelines need to be produced in different countries and regularly updated – Face Equality International is producing a template for such guidelines. There must then be a concerted effort to get those bodies that regulate the press, like IPSO in the UK, to strongly recommend their members adopt them, too.

The advertising of so many products and services these days relies on spotless, wrinkle-less faces doing the selling – that's bad enough, and changing that advertising culture so that people with real faces are regularly seen may take many years. But what we must do is to watch out for those ads that suggest that people with less-than-perfect faces have no need for such products or would not enjoy a certain service.

The advertising industry is a bulwark of face-ism and one of the hardest to regulate about anything. Which is not to say that it has not responded to the threat to regulate it on issues such as sexism or racism. We may need to press it to be aware of face-ism too.

An example of this that was particularly galling for Changing Faces came in the winter of 2004, before the campaign for face equality had been launched. We convened what we called a 'powwow' of opinion-leaders and influencers on how to tackle the unfairness in employment experienced by people with facial disfigurements and poor portrayals in the media. It was held at the House of Lords, with sponsorship from the British company BSkyB. The conclusion was that much greater corporate efforts need to be stimulated to promote awareness of facial diversity and respect for people with distinctive faces.

Imagine my dismay when, two days later, I found myself staring at an advertisement for the TV show *Nip/Tuck* (all about cosmetic surgery) put out by none other than Sky TV, a major company within the BSkyB conglomerate, with the strapline: 'Ugliness demeans us all. Invest in your face.' I was rapidly on the phone to my contact at BSkyB and she was as devastated as I was – and pleaded with me not to go to the press for twenty-four hours.

It turned out that the company's marketing team was operating completely without cognisance of its CSR, diversity and inclusion agendas. It didn't even take twenty-four hours for the company to decide to pull this 'offending' advert – much to Changing Faces' relief. Change was achieved without noise.

Persuading the global film and TV industry that face-ist casting, stigma and ridicule is no longer acceptable may not be as difficult as might have been thought a few years ago. The standard response of the entertainment industry has been that freedom of speech and artistic freedom are sacrosanct… and their defence is often 'no offence meant'. But in the last few years, campaigns like #MeToo and those from gay, black and ethnic minority communities have started to pressurise Hollywood and film-makers across the planet to respect their rights.

Which shows that countervailing force doesn't have to come from government or quasi-government agencies. No, face-ism can be acted upon using the power of social media and, where possible, celebrity culture. Companies are extremely concerned about sustaining their reputations, and we can use that to our advantage.

Another issue where countervailing power is needed is around cosmetic surgery and procedures. The global nature of the beauty industry complicates its regulation, because every territory has to enact its own laws and, even in something like the European Union, with its many member states, it has been hard to get agreement as to what should be done. Nevertheless, considerable regulation of cosmetic products has been achieved[4] and there is a willingness to look more closely at the training and accreditation of cosmetic doctors.[5]

An excellent article by Griffiths and Mullock ('Cosmetic Surgery: Regulatory Challenges in a Global Beauty Market') explains the challenge in considerable detail and concludes that whilst international regulation would be ideal, it is unlikely to happen, and so national governments need to step up their efforts, especially to stamp out cosmetic surgery hyperbole.[6] In doing so, they would send strong

WHAT CAN WE ALL DO TO CREATE FACE EQUALITY?

messages to the public to be more aware of the risks associated with the surgery and products and of the exaggerated claims that are so rife in the industry.[7]

On this issue, those supporting face equality can make alliance with many other groups, especially women's organisations. It should not be necessary for bad practice, like the illegal manufacturing of silicone breast implants in the late 2000s that affected hundreds of thousands of women worldwide, to force governments into action; but sadly, in an age of deregulation and free-market thinking, too many politicians have neglected their duty to protect their constituents.

One last example: the growing influence of social media platforms on everyday life needs to be carefully patrolled for abuse and negative imagery. The 2017 *Disfigurement in the UK* survey reported:

> … that people with a disfigurement experience shockingly high levels of abuse and 'trolling', and that there is very little faith in the ability or willingness of social media websites themselves to tackle the problem and provide help and support… Almost all respondents to our survey – 96 per cent of them – have seen a photo, meme or other content on social media that mocked someone's appearance… [This] could account for why three in ten (29 per cent) respondents said that their social media profile photo or avatar is not an image of their face.

It is vital that governments are persuaded to put pressure on the very powerful social media companies, which appear to be trying to wash their hands of responsibility for what is written or what images appear on their so-called 'platforms'. Governments around the world need to get together on this and enforce new codes – and there are signs in their efforts to outlaw child abuse that they are willing and able to do this effectively. But commercial pressures will weigh on all governments, so we need to give them all the support possible to declare these companies 'publishers' rather than just 'platforms' for people to give views, share stories etc. Once that happens, Facebook and others will be liable for what they 'publish' and will be bound to stamp out ridicule and offence.

Promoting actions
The flip side of countervailing efforts is all about getting positive change to happen in many different settings that promote new inclusive face values. Persuading major global corporates is key here. I once met Anita Roddick, founder of The Body Shop. Her crusading zeal was infectious. And she did indeed 'infect' other companies in the beauty sector – and in others too – to change the way they produced their products. She was ahead of her time.

We need to find corporate allies like her – and it's been good to see Dove, with its very inclusive advertising and Self-Esteem Fund leading the way. Avon, too, has come on board recently by featuring Catrin Pugh, a burn survivor, as the face of a new campaign for their Perfect Nudes beauty range. And Katie Piper, the acid survivor, is now promoting a new Pantene shampoo range. It's not just in the UK that this is happening: Laxmi, an Indian acid survivor, fronted up a fashion brand advertising campaign very beautifully.[8]

One of most promising models in today's culture is Winnie Harlow, who is using her vitiligo with great skill to show off her beauty – and is being paid a great deal, I hope, to do so! My favourite is Jo Corbin, a woman with a most beautiful birthmark, modelling for the I'mperfection range of the cosmetic company Illamasqua.[9]

More unique faces in fashion, please.

But we should take the faltering example of the Be Real campaign (for body confidence) in Britain as a warning bell, because it has found the search for supportive corporates to be very problematic. Although a few companies, notably Dove, have been willing to endorse the campaign, it's floundered partly for lack of corporate drivers.

WHAT CAN WE ALL DO TO CREATE FACE EQUALITY?

We need powerful allies amongst celebrities, too: women and men who are willing to 'come out' as having a not-perfect face – or whose children or family members do. Celebrities are such a dominant force in today's society all around the world and to acquire a growing band of them committed to face equality would be a big step forward. Put your hand up if you know any... and then approach them, sign them up and get them out there!

And then we need the leaders of the medical world to join us and actively promote face equality. We need more plastic surgeons, dermatologists and the like – and their associations – willing to tell the full truth about their speciality's abilities and limitations.

We should also look out for examples of films and TV series that promote public understanding and new face values. The 2017 film *Wonder*, after the book by R.J. Palacio, has undoubtedly been good for starting conversations about facial difference, especially in schools – and many NGOs produced school resources to help teachers get the maximum from the film and book.

Which isn't to say that it's perfect: I'm not happy about the patronising title, nor the report that the author did not speak to parents and children with Treacher Collins Syndrome before writing it. And the casting and making-up of star Jacob Tremblay as the 'wonder boy', Auggie, rather than a boy with a not-perfect face, was disappointing and an opportunity missed. The film directors denied this, saying they tried hard to find a suitable actor. I don't find that convincing. No doubt the part required a skilled child actor, but I'm sure a child with the condition could have been supported to play the role.

Reservations aside, such as the portrayal of Auggie winning a prize for the student whose kindness 'carried up the most hearts' rather than one for being the best at French or another subject, *Wonder* has definitely opened eyes and minds – and should be a must-see movie for all children in the ten- to twelve-year-old age group.

One of the most powerful ways to raise public consciousness and respect for people with facial differences is having them appear as regular contributors to today's visual culture. We need to see more people in the media. Great to see Adam Pearson, for example, becoming a respected actor (in *Under the Skin* in 2013 with Scarlett Johansson) and moving on from fronting TV shows about disfigurement and disability in Britain to appearing on quirky shows like *Tricks of the Restaurant Trade* and the like. Katie Piper is another in the UK who has become a mainstream personality. More Adams and Katies must and will emerge.

One of the biggest challenges we have to tackle in raising public awareness and commitment to face equality is that there are so many reasons why a person's face is 'not-perfect'. How on earth can we possibly provide straightforward facts about these conditions; facts that are seen by many as a prerequisite to normalising them? 'If I don't know why she looks like that, how on earth can I accept her?'

In my view, there are three main answers to this question: first, those of us with distinctive faces have to be willing to share some of the reasons why we look as we do. This is already happening through the plethora of blogs and social media posts across all platforms. Many of them start with 'I'm proud of my...' and that's fine. The important point is that other people can then read up on your cleft, your vitiligo or rosacea, your rare craniosynostosis (like Crouzon Syndrome) or your facial paralysis or whatever it may be. The objective facts provided in these 'lay' non-medicalised accounts help to bridge the familiarity gap and, because the facts are only a part of what the person is telling, they are very normalising.

We need more books written by people with the lived experience of disfigurement too. Three that I would recommend are Lucy Grealy's *Autobiography of a Face*, stark and ultimately very sad but not sentimental, *Imperfect* by Lee Kofman, and Carly Findlay's *Say Hello*, about her life with ichthyosis. I was also empowered by reading and looking at those adolescents who survived the Volendam café fire of 2001 in Suzan van de Roemer's superb *The Power of Resilience*.

WHAT CAN WE ALL DO TO CREATE FACE EQUALITY?

Second, the written and broadcast media has a big part to play in raising public knowledge – and again, this is already happening in many newspapers and TV programmes. Facial disfigurement is a fascinating subject! However, there are serious risks that the potential for normalising through the media is jeopardised by the way in which a person's story is told. Too often, we have seen journalists and broadcasters produce sentimentalised accounts with words like 'sad' and 'victim' dominating the narrative rather than objective facts and a 'this is how it is' attitude. Such stories are sometimes known as 'triumph over tragedy stories' (TOTS) and they have little value in bringing about face equality awareness. Which is why media organisations need to heed the International Media Standard on Disfigurement (see page 272 and Annex 3).

Third, it behoves every organisation that supports and represents people with facial differences to take every opportunity to explain in clear language why their 'members' look as they do. Such education can be incredibly powerful, as the experience of the annual and now international Face Equality Week shows.

But public information about disfigurement is not just the preserve of the media and social media. As I discussed earlier in this part, promoting new face values in schools and businesses is crucial. Doing so continually can raise awareness, challenge low expectations and demonstrate that people with distinctive faces are not dangerous, not to be avoided or excluded – they are good students, good employees and good citizens. They should be seen and respected as such.

Lastly, I think we need to take proactive action to enable people to meet someone with a facial disfigurement with confidence – because people often ask me, 'Where should I look?' and, 'What should I say?' If we want to get to a situation in which I have to make only 50 per cent of the effort whenever I meet someone, especially a stranger, and they do similarly – rather than the current 90 per cent–10 per cent split – a sustained campaign to instil new communication skills is required.

Yes, social skills training for all. All that's needed is a very public series of tips and tactics for when meeting someone with a scarred face like me. Here are a few to start you off:

- WHERE TO LOOK? In my eye – or the bridge of my nose; it has the same effect.
- TRY NOT TO STARE. It's OK to be interested, just not too much!
- WHAT TO SAY? Talk about the weather, say hello, perhaps, or find common ground.
- 'WHAT HAPPENED?' Try not to ask until you know me better… but I may tell you anyway.
- ACT 'NORMALLY'. Smile, shake hands… be as you would with someone you've not met before.

This all sounds so easy, but it isn't.

A few years ago, Changing Faces produced a set of posters that appeared in the London Underground and in magazines, with useful social skills tactics for first meetings – referred to in the second Mezzanine. There was one with a photo of a man, David Bird, with a birthmark (haemangioma) over his right eye, who said: 'Hello. Nice to meet you. How are you? Now you try it.'

It is particularly important that children and young people receive social skills training to handle meetings with people with distinctive faces – and these will help them meet people who look different in all sorts of ways.

Changing Faces' experience in schools suggests that even if they adopt equal opportunities policies, there is no guarantee that this will create an inclusive atmosphere. If staff and pupils/students are uninformed about people with disfigurements, and socially unskilled or unsure as to how to interact normally with them, sympathy, awkwardness and exclusion will persist.

I'd go further: engaging social skills for meeting imperfection and difference should be taught to HR professionals and customer-facing staff in businesses and public services. The increasing corporate awareness of the importance of implicit bias should open doors to such training opportunities – and using webinars and e-learning should make it possible.

Promoting non-face-ist thinking can also be done through other mediums, such as in short videos on social media, or in art exhibitions. Changing Faces gave a prize for that purpose for fifteen years at the prestigious annual art exhibition of the Royal Society of Portrait Painters. The prize winner was given a £2,000 cheque as a commission to paint a person with an unusual face. That resulted in some superb portraits being produced, which then appeared in the next year's exhibition – and some won awards.

As an interesting spin-off of those portrait exhibitions, a friend of mine, Mary Rose Rivett-Carnac, was motivated to do a survey of portraiture across the ages to explore whether and how facial disfigurement has been portrayed. The resulting thesis is fascinating. She concluded:

> There has been scant representation of facial disfigurement in portraiture through the ages. Reasons include the frequent emphasis in art on beauty, symmetry and proportion, the need for the artist to sell his or her work, and the widespread tendency in commissioned work for the artist to flatter the sitter to indicate wealth, status and power. Sitters with unusual faces often required artists to conceal or disguise any facial differences.[10]

2. Micro actions

It's not just at a macro-level that we must see action. Every single one of us can play a part in removing the oppression of face-ism from our lives, challenging perfectionist thinking wherever it appears and standing out for imperfection in all its glory.

Face-ism is deeply ingrained in people's minds and lives. Like sexism, it will not be eradicated without all of us being challenged –

and that means being challenged every single day. And like sexism, its overthrow begins in everyday living.

I grew up in the open-minded seventies, and so I know all the arguments for gender equality by heart – or so I think. But, much to my irritation, I am still, much too often for comfort, brought up short by my family for some thoughtlessness. My conditioning goes far deeper than I imagine, so that even though my rational brain knows not to think and act in chauvinist ways, I still do.

This was brought home to me when my daughters insisted – despite my protestations that I knew it all – that I had to read one of their generation's bibles on how, as young women, they can avoid being swamped by the sexist stereotyping that can hold back their lives and careers. *Lean In* by Sheryl Sandberg is a classic, and I did indeed need to read it. From the first chapter's entreaty 'Internalising the Revolution', it reminds and rams home time and again that we *all* have to be wary of falling into sexist elephant traps every single day.

I know all about face-ist prejudices, don't I? Well, yes, but I am still liable to impose those very same prejudices on myself. It's so easy to do so.

Every morning. Looking in the mirror. Thinking your face isn't good enough. Yearning for some magic to cover up or remove that scar or blemish. Imagining that you'll be less liked until you have some surgery or less appealing unless you put on your full-scale face paint. Or grow the beard to cover up. Or get a hair transplant. Or get your nose reshaped.

Catch yourself when you do this. Become aware of your face-ist tendencies.

Every time you look in the mirror or see a photo or yourself, don't make face-ist value judgements. Admire the uniqueness of your face, its maturity, its quirkiness or whatever you think makes it special. And make the most of it.

Face-ism has many parallels with sexism. It is passed on from one generation to another. And it is, as sexism has been and continues to

WHAT CAN WE ALL DO TO CREATE FACE EQUALITY?

be, perpetuated by media and culture. Feminists' distaste for much of the fashion world and pornography parallels mine for the cosmetics industry's hype about people with supposedly beautiful faces leading lovely lives, and the lazy use of facial scars to depict evil in iconography and movies. Many parallels.

Challenging face-ism also means we have to tune up our friends, children and families to be aware so that they can learn to counter their reflexes about their faces and looks too. For example, my children were 'trained' very early not to use gurning as a game, distorting their faces to come across as nasty or weird.

I am a great believer in the value of pebbles. Small stones can be very potent if well directed – sometimes hitting a target that seems impregnable, sometimes creating huge ripples that can trigger a tsunami of effects.

Another of Malcolm Gladwell's books, *David and Goliath*, is deliberately named to remind readers how, against all odds and expectations, a tiny shepherd boy with an innocent sling brought down the massive champion of the Philistines and all that went with him.[11] Gladwell's thesis is that 'Davids' are everywhere, finding ways every day to challenge oppression and injustice and the doubters who say, 'You'll never do that'. I would say more and more are active now as social media's power is harnessed for good causes. Davids use clever, smart and creative tactics that are totally beyond the consciousness of their opponents. And they win.

So can we, people with not-perfect faces of all sorts, be 'Davids'? Definitely, yes!

I believe that with lots of Davids working to take on each and every face-ist stigma, we can build up a body of opinion – a movement – that will increasingly become influential, both by promoting what we want to happen and acting on what we are against. We can use social media prolifically too, and gain lots of supporters along the way.

Maybe becoming a pebble-thrower isn't your natural instinct, but I urge you to learn how to do it – and to enjoy its impact!

So what is pebble-throwing? What would we do as budding pebble-throwers?

I can recall the first time I seriously picked up a pebble – a trivial moment, but it sums up an attitude of mind. It was shortly after I got married in 1978; Carrie and I were to go to my parents' house and collect some furniture in a hired van.

The Saturday morning came and we went to the hire car company and I filled in the forms. The guy behind the desk looked at them and then me and said point-blank, 'No way we can hire you the van.' I asked why and he said, 'You clearly have some ongoing medical and surgical issues and your left hand makes you unfit to drive – so you have lied in your answers to those questions.' Both fictions! I explained that I was nearly four years post-discharge and my GP had signed me off as fit to drive. But those points fell on stony ground. Carrie filled in the forms, got into the driving seat and off we went.

Although somewhat enraged at the time, I felt impotent. But, as we drove on, I decided to 'pick up a pebble'. Later that day, I wrote to the managing director of the hire car company, telling the story, not blaming the desk man for following the rules but suggesting he needed to prevent such an injustice happening again.

This was in the days before anti-discrimination legislation and email, but I received a speedy reply to say that he would look into it and, a few days later, a fulsome apology arrived. He had instructed a complete review of those rules from his management team. A few weeks later, he wrote again to the effect that whilst needing to assure themselves of a customer's credentials, never again would such (face-ist) judgements be made – because his staff were all receiving training to prevent it. A tiny victory but, for me at least, a very pleasing one. I like to think that my pebble-throwing with that hire care company influenced the whole industry.

Another analogy about pebbles is true too – and shows that sometimes it's fruitless.

WHAT CAN WE ALL DO TO CREATE FACE EQUALITY?

In the early years of Changing Faces, I took aim at Martini about an advertisement which, in my view, was blatantly face-ist – although I didn't have that word in my armoury then! The ad was full of hype about how people with perfect faces and a Martini in their hands were guaranteed the high life. It was a difficult case to make and I was probably stretching my argument, but it elicited a letter back from the chairman of Martini saying that he had not thought about this angle before – 'thank you' – and that he would ask his team to be more aware in the future. I heard no more.

But I don't want you to think that you have to throw pebbles to change big things or 'go viral'.

Much of my pebble-throwing has been deliberately but gently 'in your face' in everyday encounters. For example, when I'm standing waiting for the train and am conscious of someone inspecting me, I'll surprise them with a line like, 'It's an interesting face, isn't it?' and smile, disarmingly and non-threateningly. It often starts a conversation and I can gently get my point across – the smallest possible pebble is lobbed in their direction! You should try it. I encourage you to adopt this approach in getting your friends and work colleagues to think differently about faces.

So, what should be the targets of your pebbles? Here are some examples of the face-ist stereotypes to look out for…

Watch out for instances, in films or video games, for children particularly, where having a distinctive face appears to mean a life with second-rate prospects.

Keep a beady eye out for and draw public attention to all instances of unusual faces being used in film or media to represent baddies or bad actions.

Applaud examples of characters with scars on their faces being 'good', counter to cultural norms. For example, the 2017 BBC series *Rellik* featured a detective who had been attacked with acid returning to work – I saluted the BBC.

If you come across examples of face-ist casting on old films, point them out as outmoded and from a bygone era.

Check out the websites of the professional bodies of plastic surgeons and dermatologists and compare them with private sector adverts.

Get informed about the risks of aesthetic fillers, Botox and other face treatments – and be prepared to point them out to any friends who may be considering them.

Don't be afraid to challenge your friends, too. An attractive and intelligent young woman, whose face was pretty much flawless as far as I could see, recently told me she was seriously considering having 'some work done'. Why? I asked. 'Because I can...' and 'It might help me.' How? She couldn't define it... She was already married, but maybe in her career and life in general. 'Aren't you being seduced by false gods?' 'Oh, I know, but...' and her voice tailed off.

So deep is our conditioning that it is hard to imagine ever breaking free. But you can. Throwing a pebble into a pond can cause ripples whose reverberations can last for years.

FACE IT – SUMMING UP

FACE IT is my attempt to make living with a distinctive face in today's perfect-face society just a tad easier.

First, by describing my experience in considerable detail, I hope I've conveyed how multi-dimensional was my adjustment – and I do realise that everyone's experience is different, perhaps especially if they have had a facial disfigurement from birth. But my twenty-five years of leading Changing Faces tells me that the many dimensions of adjustment that I've laid out are remarkably common to other people.

Because our faces are so central to our self-image and social identity, all of us have to pick our way as carefully as possible, but often without any kind of a roadmap or advice and through a series of minefields: medical and surgical, emotional/psychological and socio-cultural. In each there are unexpected obstacles and hidden explosives that can blow you off track.

My journey through these minefields was immensely difficult at times. But I found a way out the other side by reinventing my understanding of my face and finding new insights into its meaning in my life, by carefully deciding what and how much surgery to have, by redefining my relationships with other people and by discovering a new energy from the respect I felt from others and gave myself.

The realisation that I was not alone in my struggle was probably not as important in the key years of my adjustment as it might have been today, because social media did not exist; but it undoubtedly played a part. What ultimately made the biggest difference was the revelation that my outstanding face did not mean that I had to be apart from other people. Far from it. By becoming a powerful communicator, I enhanced the quality of all my relationships.

Second, I hope I showed in Part 2 that effective psychosocial programmes can be pioneered and proven to work, contrary to one of the big myths surrounding facial disfigurement today – that only surgery can save you from oblivion and depression.

Such packages enable anyone with a standing-out face to strengthen their self-esteem, free themselves from the clutches of perfect-face thinking and evolve new proactive communication skills that break through other people's awkwardness in a millisecond.

We have to find ways to convince relevant clinicians and health care policymakers that taking a bio-psychosocial perspective on facial disfigurement has massive pay-offs – and resist the high-tech urge to 'fix it' as the only option.

Which led me to the third part of the book, where I talk about transforming public attitudes towards people with distinctive faces by calling out the face-ist culture in which we live and challenging us all to overthrow it in all its tyranny! Which is not going to happen quickly, I appreciate, but unless that dream is articulated, it cannot be shared and built upon.

One of the biggest obstacles to creating a world that respects face equality is the vocabulary we use as a society to describe people whose faces are like mine. I am against euphemisms, particularly when they suggest something inferior and undesirable, like 'different'. So I have generally used 'people with distinctive faces' or 'distinguished' ones or similar expressions throughout the book. I like the idea of being part of a community of 'people with faces of distinction' (thanks to Vicki McCarrell, CEO of the Moebius Syndrome Foundation).

I strongly believe that we can end the stigma of facial disfigurement during the twenty-first century, but it will not happen without a fight for facial inclusion that will upset some institutions and

FACE IT – SUMMING UP

entrenched interests. Face-ism should not be tolerated. It's a human rights issue and must be seen as such.

We need new twenty-first century face values that do away with the absurd norms of our global cosmetic culture and put an end to the hierarchy of facial looks that oppresses everyone across the planet.

People should be judged for their talents, skills and attractiveness as human beings, not by the look of their face.

The new face values would celebrate the amazing facial uniqueness of every single human being. They would allow for a healthy new definition of beauty, too, one that sees beauty in imperfection and does not confuse being beautiful with being attractive.

Face equality, impossible? I think not. Liberating? Doable? Essential? I think so.

None of us, on our own, can make this happen – but together we can.

You know, I know, we all know that the way we behave in every social encounter can rub off positively on those we meet. We can all change attitudes every day if we want to.

Every human face should carry the same value, because each and every one is fascinating and beautifully made and is owned by a person worthy of equal respect.

We all need face equality now. Let's make it happen.

LAST WORD

For the first eighteen years of my life, I lived in a near-perfect face which I prized and traded on. And for the last fifty years, I have learned how to live, thrive and love in a quirky and distinctive face which has distinguished me in my working and social life – and I have traded on that, too, in a very different way to how I'd expected or even dreamed I could.

Just occasionally I have wondered what would have happened had I steered successfully around the corner that changed my face and life forever. Which is why I love the film *Sliding Doors*, starring Gwyneth Paltrow and John Hannah.

It so brilliantly captures the sense of what might have happened if an Underground train door had not opened or closed. Like the Gwyneth Paltrow character early in the movie with her wonderful relationship, great job and near-perfect life, I fully imagined my future was on a plate. I would have a feast! But then the door closed and another opened.

A few years ago, one of my children asked: 'What would your face have looked like if…?' A tantalising question!

I sought out forensic artist Teri Blythe, who uses 'face-ageing' technology to try to track down missing people, especially children who have been kidnapped. It's not a precise science, more an art. I sent her lots of pictures of my childhood and adolescent face, photos of my parents and sister at various ages, and even my children. And she then composed – or did she create? – my 'lost face'.

Here it is…

*The 'lost face' I might have had,
created using face-aeging technology.*

Very different!

It's fascinating to imagine myself inside 'it', with that firm contoured chin with its impressive indent, the ice-cool eyes and pleasing smile.

Actually, I find it almost impossible to imagine what that 'I' would have been like. My eyes would have been the same, but I would have very different lenses on. I might have looked at the same world but I would have interpreted it very differently indeed, and would have had a radically different self-image.

Identikit pictures are notoriously inexpressive and it's impossible to know how that face would have worked, whether my voice

LAST WORD

would have been the same and how I would have communicated, what gestures would have brought me alive.

Had I met 'that' man, with his clean-shaven, cheerful, serious and friendly looks, I would have expected him to be very reliable, a pleasant, honest man, able to negotiate people and life with ease.

In contrast, when I see my face today in a photo, I don't notice its scars and asymmetry. Nor do I yearn for something 'better'. No way. I'm very attached to it.

And what did my children think of 'that' face?

'It's so *ordinary*, Dad!'

So right!

February 2020: my face today. High-level smiling!

ANNEX 1
A Reflection on Face Transplantation

I first became aware of the possibility of a face transplant in 1996, and my position was gently questioning and undecided. It still is. Was this really a 'magic' new technology that could be the 'answer' to facial disfigurement as some proponents seemed to be claiming? Here's my reflection twenty-plus years on.

The first face transplant procedure took place in the autumn of 2005 and over forty-five other such procedures have been carried out since, mainly in the United States and Europe. None have been attempted in the UK, despite a surgical team led by Professor Peter Butler at London's Royal Free Hospital being given permission by the hospital's research ethics board in October 2006 to carry out one to four full face transplants on adults.

Face transplantation's relative rarity indicates it is still very much 'in research and development' as a surgical intervention, and its very great cost (around $1 million has been quoted for a US operation) and the still uncertain long-term consequences for patients are likely to mean it stays in that category for a considerable number of years ahead.

Each face transplant procedure has been slightly different, with some involving only the skin envelope, others soft tissue, cartilage and palate, some cheekbone and nose, and in the most sophisticated ones, the whole face including eyelids and the tongue as well. Some patients have told inspiring stories in the press; some have preferred privacy. Data collection and the spread of good evidence about how the more than forty-five patients have fared has, however, been less than ideal.

A review in 2011 by Peter Butler and his team concluded:

> The initial experience has demonstrated that facial transplantation is surgically feasible. Functional and aesthetic outcomes have been very encouraging with good motor and sensory recovery and improvements to important facial functions observed. Episodes of acute rejection have been common, as predicted, but easily controlled with increases in systemic immunosuppression. Psychological improvements have been remarkable and have resulted in the reintegration of patients into the outside world, social networks and even the workplace. Complications of immunosuppression and patient mortality have been observed in the initial series.[1]

A five-year review of six patients of the Brigham and Women's Hospital in Boston, USA, published in 2019, found similar positive results regarding functional and psychological adjustment whilst also cautioning that immunosuppression is an ongoing issue.[2] However, a review of seven French patients found much less favourable psychological outcomes.[3]

It is also sadly the case that at least six patients have died, including Isabelle Dinoire, the first patient, after ten years with her transplant; most of their deaths have been associated with transplant failure and associated complications, including cancer. One patient has had a second transplant and, at the time of writing, another is imminent.

ANNEX 1

BACK TO THE BEGINNING

The first public discussion of face transplantation in Britain was in 1996 when a leading plastic surgeon, Jim Frame, speculated in the press that this operation was now technically possible and should be conducted. There was considerable media interest. I was asked for Changing Faces' view and did several media interviews in which I was cautiously supportive of further research whilst suggesting that there could be considerable risks, especially related to the immunology, and that more effort should be given to psychosocial rehabilitation programmes.

The media hyped the story: a 'medical miracle for everyone with a facial disfigurement is about to be available'. My face was morphed with Steve McQueen's in one tabloid newspaper – without my permission – to show what I would look like. I didn't like that press intrusion and I wasn't impressed with the morphed result, either. I anticipated more but it all went quiet.

Then in July 2002, an article in *The Lancet* reignited interest. Peter Butler and Shehan Hettiaratchy, research surgeons at the Royal Free Hospital, London and Harvard, Cambridge Massachusetts respectively, described their very initial thinking about how a face transplant could be done, and concluded:

> The idea of taking off a dead person's face and putting it on someone else appears to have come straight out of science fiction. However, recipient patients have serious physical and psychological problems that cannot be solved by conventional treatments. If face transplantation is shown to be the only effective way of treating these severely disfigured patients, then doctors would have a duty to use the technique.[4]

This triggered another wave of media interest around the world (nothing to compare with today's waves given the lack of satellites, internet etc.), and again we at Changing Faces were asked for an opinion, which had not changed.

But this time media interest did not wane. Throughout the autumn and winter of 2002–03, Changing Faces was receiving daily enquiries from journalists seeking information and advice. By February 2003, we were under pressure to open up contacts with clients to the press – which we strenuously refused to do. We did, however, consult a group of people with facial disfigurements on our advisory panels, and they supported our hesitant position.

On 23rd February 2003, *The Sunday Times* carried a large feature in which Prof Butler was said to be nearly ready to undertake the first face transplant, and was quoted as saying that a fourteen-year-old Irish child and three others were being 'assessed' in the next few weeks to establish whether one was a suitable candidate. This intensified the media's hunt for that first patient, whose name finally appeared in the *Evening Standard* the following Friday, only to be removed after parental legal threats.

Changing Faces' trustees and staff were furious about these developments, and that Friday evening I wrote to Sir Peter Morris, the President of the Royal College of Surgeons of England. I called on 'the Royal College of Surgeons as a matter of the greatest urgency to attempt to create a moratorium on further media coverage of the issue. We also urge that the College establishes a Committee, including scientists, surgeons, ethicists, psychologists and people with disfigurements, charged to investigate and report on all aspects of face transplantation prior to any experimentation whatsoever.'

The Royal College did indeed set up a working party, which reported in November 2003 and recommended that 'a much more incremental approach [be taken] than some of the current hype surrounding it has suggested'. Further research on immunological, psychological and ethical issues was needed before face transplantation should be attempted or offered to patients – a conclusion that we strongly welcomed. The report seems not to be available

ANNEX 1

online anymore, but a contemporary account in the *BMJ* is printed in Addendum 1.

I have a hard copy of that 2003 report, however; it still reads incredibly well nearly twenty years on, and we all owe a great debt of gratitude to Sir Peter Morris, a man of integrity and gravitas who assembled a strong committee. His scientific and surgical career, which had focused on transplantation with a major interest in the immunology, made him the ideal president for the moment.

The report calmed the atmosphere considerably in Britain. But the media knew that an international 'race' was on to do the first transplant. And so it was probably no surprise when in late November 2005, the operation was conducted on Isabelle Dinoire by a team in Amiens, France, which refreshed media interest – I did at least twenty-five TV interviews for the UK and international media in the space of twenty-four hours!

I wrote again to the Royal College in February 2006, asking that the working party revisit the issues so that British public opinion – and especially patients – could weigh up the latest developments. The second report was published in November 2006 and reviewed the three years of research done since the first, and the evidence after the first transplant.[5] It accepted that some patients were now likely to be willing to take 'the leap into the dark', but it defined fifteen preconditions that should be met before the procedure was undertaken in the UK (see Annex 2).

We at Changing Faces were again supportive of this view. We argued that the preconditions should inform all decisions made by patients, surgeons and ethics committees worldwide.

Since then, fourteen years ago, forty-five patients have taken that leap, but I still remain concerned.[6]

SIX CONCERNS

1. Technical surgical and functional issues

Long-term functional or aesthetic reasons

It is clear that face transplantation has been conducted for both functional and aesthetic reasons. However, given that it is not a life-saving procedure (as is a heart transplant), patients will have considerable difficulty weighing up the functional and aesthetic benefits and setting them against the risks (e.g. to life expectancy) until far more hard objective evidence is available.

Conventional surgery

There is no doubt that conventional reconstructive surgery (which has minimal side effects) is sometimes unable to achieve effective functioning and a 'non-shocking' aesthetic result. Such patients will understandably consider face transplantation instead of, or as well as, conventional surgery.

However, there have now been several 'immediate' face transplants – that is, without any conventional surgery being attempted – as was the case with Isabelle Dinoire. In such circumstances, it is essential that patients be fully and objectively informed about what can be done conventionally and be able to choose such surgery.

Face transplantation is now sometimes suggested before all conventional treatments have either failed or been discounted. This is acceptable as long as all reconstructive options are offered for consideration by patient and family.

Functionality

The evidence suggests that patients are achieving considerable facial sensation and mobility after transplantation, but how much is still unpredictable. The idea that such a procedure can bring near-normal functionality needs to be questioned, especially if the new 'dynamic' face is being promoted as a means to easier social interaction. Its appearance could still be a barrier to social interaction, although probably a lesser one than the status quo ante.

Post-rejection plans (Plan B)
Every patient and potential patient needs to be fully briefed about Plan B. A range of options (e.g. replacement transplant, conventional surgery) have to be described by clinical teams for implementation in the event of transplant failure. The ongoing problems publicised about Carmen Blandin Tarleton are a case in point.[7]

2. Immunology

After a face transplant, immunosuppressive drugs are necessary to suppress the patient's own immune systems and prevent rejection of foreign tissue. Long-term or lifelong immunosuppression increases the risk of developing life-threatening infections, kidney damage and cancer. The transplant surgery itself can result in complications, such as infections, that could damage the transplanted face and require a second transplant or reconstruction with skin grafts.

My understanding is that the current face transplant patients are receiving relatively low doses of immunosuppressants but that, if they have episodes when the transplant appears to be failing, this dose is raised quickly and very substantially, and then gradually reduced again if rejection is prevented. However, it is unclear, to date, whether (a) the risk of transplant failure has changed from the RCS's estimate (30–50 per cent within five years), (b) there are serious side effects from the drug regime (as has been reported by one hand transplant patient), or (c) the risk of reduced life expectancy (up to ten years, according to the RCS) has lessened since the early days of the procedure.

Patients need to be made aware of the risks of long-term use of immunosuppressive drugs, and this should be an important aspect in their decision to undergo face transplantation.

3. Psychological issues

New identity

Thanks to Professor Butler's team's efforts to publicly explain its proposed transplantation in full – including morphing his face onto his colleagues', and vice versa – it has been clear for ten years that a recipient of a transplanted face will not look identical to the donor. However, that point notwithstanding, there is no doubt that most patients who have had media coverage have spoken of the challenge posed by the fact that the face which they see in the mirror and with which they face the world does not resemble their old face/identity, but someone else's. This is a fundamentally different change from that experienced by those who go through conventional facial reconstruction after an accident or violent incident like an acid attack.

It is vital that face transplant patients receive long-term psychosocial support to address this fact and the other issues they are likely to experience, such as how to sustain their compliance with the drug regimes.

Patient selection

All clinical teams around the world have now been expected by their ethics committees to go to great lengths to outline their process and criteria for choosing a suitable patient for a face transplant. They stress the importance of identifying a psychologically stable recipient who is assessed as robust enough to cope with the lifetime challenges following the transplant and, unless they choose complete privacy, can handle (along with their family) the intense and probably lifelong media attention.

However, concern continues that teams themselves have an interest in conducting such procedures, and may not be completely unbiased in how they inform patients and families.

Psychosocial adjustment

Face transplantation carries with it a host of psychosocial adjustment challenges. The British team's preparation to support patients pre-

and post-transplant was led by clinical psychologist Alex Clarke, who worked with me at Changing Faces in the 1990s. She and her colleagues published a range of excellent papers describing how the Royal Free team would aim to support the long-term adjustment of the recipient and their family, and of the donor's family too (including privacy).[8]

I strongly believe that her guidelines should be used by all clinical teams.

4. Informed consent

Full information about all other interventions

I have been repeatedly assured by clinicians that all potential patients who are being considered for face transplants by surgical teams in the UK, USA, France and elsewhere are being, provided with full, frank and, as far as possible, objective information and a frank assessment of risks and benefits – not just of the face transplant procedure but of all alternative treatments, including those of a psychosocial nature such as social skills training. My concern lingers, however, that such information is (a) hard for clinical teams to assemble – a concern that would be somewhat allayed if such information were subject to public scrutiny, and (b) hard for patients to assimilate, fully understand or process (e.g. with regards to the impact of immunosuppressants).

Who counsels the patient

Clinical teams that have assembled to combine their skills to perform face transplant operations need to assure patients and their families that those responsible for acquiring their informed consent are sufficiently independent from the transplant team, to ensure that they are not influenced by any factors other than respect for and protection of the patient – as the RCS's seventh precondition requires.

I believe that potential transplant patients should have access to others with severe facial disfigurements who may be well adjusted thanks to alternative treatments, which may include counselling and communication skills training.

5. Media representation and coverage

Changing Faces was very concerned about the way in which some parts of the British and international media has occasionally portrayed face transplantation as some kind of miracle 'fix' for everyone who has a facial disfigurement. We frequently challenged over-simplistic media coverage that (a) suggests wrongly that people can't lead happy lives unless their disfigurement is removed, (b) reinforces the stereotypical view that a disfigurement is undesirable and disastrous, and (c) suggests that a public attitudes shift on disfigurement is either impossible or unnecessary.

I am concerned by anecdotal reports suggesting that the main reason why some potential patients for a British transplant eventually decided not to go ahead was because they were not prepared to face the media exposure that is likely to follow them and their family for years to come. It's disturbing that fear of media intrusion may prevent some people exploring what could be a potentially life-changing operation – and indeed robbing medical science and hence other patients in the future of vital research evidence. I doubt that this problem is unique to the British media.

'Long-term media management' needs to be a resource available to a clinical team before a face transplant programme seeks to find its patients. There are many lessons to be learned from the reactions of people who have been injured or attacked and then caught up in a media frenzy. Some, like Katie Piper after her acid attack, are supported by their clinical team to rise above the media intrusion; but others find the whole experience intimidating and something they wish to avoid at all costs. Some patients and families are offered large sums to tell their stories.

In the ideal world, there would be a media agreement to leave people with new face transplants alone unless they explicitly give their permission – rather as the media held off coverage of the younger members of the British royal family when they were at school.

6. Donors and their needs

The interests of donors and their families have rightly received considerable attention since the first face transplant, after which the donor family's life was made difficult by local media and social media speculation.

It is of the utmost importance that donors' privacy and dignity is upheld to the greatest possible extent. The question as to whether the recipient should ever know or meet the donor's family is one which should be clarified in the ethical procedures of each transplant programme and prior to each transplant. What is most important is that the wishes of the donor's family be uppermost in this; but it might well be sensible to allow for a reappraisal of those wishes after a period of years.

CONCLUSION

So much for the face transplant story so far. It is still in its research phase. There needs to be an international consensus conference to assess it – and it is good to see a new seven-year project called 'About Face' focused on the 'emotional and cultural history of face transplants' starting up at York University in England, for which I recently wrote a blog post.[9]

One thing I should add. Anyone who decides to have a face transplant should only do so if they can honestly say that the information they received before consenting to the intervention was full, accurate and objective. It's all in the consenting. Expectations are set, requirements for compliance explained and all manner of uncertainty and anxiety allayed if things are done well.

I continue to support, as ever, research in basic medical science, clinical care, psychology and other subjects to tackle the problems posed by facial and other disfigurement, but I stress that it should always be done with the safety and interests of patients and families at the forefront of ethical concern.

I will also support any UK face transplant team in the future that meets all the Royal College of Surgeon's fifteen preconditions. But I still remain undecided about the risk–benefit balance in face transplantation and doubtful that, given its life-shortening effects, it is as psychologically beneficial as is claimed.

ADDENDUM 1:
FACE TRANSPLANTS SHOULD NOT BE DONE WITHOUT MORE RESEARCH

Zosia Kmietowicz, article as it appeared in the British Medical Journal[10]

Facial transplantation should not be performed until more research is done on the procedure and the risks that go with it, says an expert group of surgeons from England.

The advice, from a working party from the Royal College of Surgeons of England, has been issued after concern from the charity Changing Faces that speculation in the press earlier this year about the possibility of facial transplants has been unrealistic.

The college and the British Association of Plastic Surgeons were also concerned that sensationalist newspaper coverage and a 'media hunt' for the world's first patient to have had a facial transplantation could upset any such patient and his or her family.

In response to the charity's concerns, the college formed an expert group to examine the proposed procedure. The report that has resulted urges caution in experimenting with the procedure because of the need to take into account the psychological impact of such surgery, the long-term effects of immunosuppression and the ethics of facial transplantation.

Concern has also been expressed that surgeons will not be able to obtain acceptable and valid consent from patients because of the uncertainties about the risks and benefits of a procedure that remains highly experimental.

ANNEX 1

There have been no procedures like facial transplants, which are also called composite tissue allotransplantations, performed in the United Kingdom to date. However, since the first hand transplantation was carried out in France in 1998 there have been twenty more hand transplant operations, nine abdominal wall transplantations, a laryngeal transplantation and a tongue transplantation around the world.

In its conclusion the report says: 'The working party believes that until there is further research and the prospect of better control of these complications it would be unwise to proceed with human facial transplantations. Equally this conclusion does not underestimate the suffering of those patients who might be tempted by the prospect of facial transplantation.'

ADDENDUM 2:
THE RCS'S 15 PRECONDITIONS, NOVEMBER 2006[11]

The RCS's second report considers that a patient may wish to take what it calls a 'leap in the dark' and that this would be acceptable if a local Research Ethics Committee (REC) can be assured that fifteen minimum requirements are all satisfied:

1. The surgical unit has sufficient technical skill and experience to optimise the chances of a successful transplant.
2. An institutional structure exists within the hospital to ensure integrated clinical care between the transplant team and other surgical and medical units for both short- and long-term treatment.
3. A comprehensive and coherent protocol for the selection of suitable patients exists.
4. The hospital's or institution's Research Ethics Committee (REC) protocol provides potential patients with adequate information on the basis of which valid informed consent can be given.

5. The REC protocol provides adequate information for potential patients about how little is known about some of the risks associated with facial transplantation.
6. The surgical unit has integrated links with a team with appropriate psychological expertise to provide support adequate to ensure that prospective patients can give valid informed consent.
7. People in the process of acquiring informed consent are sufficiently independent from the transplant team to ensure that they are not influenced by any factors other than respect for and protection of the patient.
8. Sufficiently trained people are involved in the process of seeking the consent of appropriate donor relatives for the donation of facial tissue.
9. Confidence exists that the psychological team can provide effective long-term therapeutic support to the patient in the aftermath of both successful transplantation or potential and/or actual failure.
10. Mechanisms are in place to ensure satisfactory delivery of the duty of care towards the recipient's family.
11. Mechanisms are in place to ensure satisfactory delivery of the duty of care towards the donor's family that extends beyond obtaining their consent for donation.
12. Guarantees exist that the transplant and psychological teams and the hospital can provide the long-term funding required to ensure that all patients will continue to receive the care and support outlined in the protocol approved by the REC, whether the transplant has been successful or not.
13. Provision of the extra surgical, medical, psychological and social care resources that will be required for facial transplantation are in place without reducing the quality of care of other patients with facial disfigurements at the host hospital.
14. Equitable management in the care and support offered to the families of potential donors of facial tissue is planned both when they are approached to obtain consent and afterwards, in the event of subsequent distress.

15. Any body that considers an application for facial transplantation must include experts in reconstructive surgery, immunosuppression, psychological problems posed by severe facial disfigurement and a representative of one of the organisations that provides support for those with such disfigurement.

ADDENDUM 3:
LETTERS TO THE ROYAL COLLEGE OF SURGEONS

28th February 2003

Sir Peter Morris
The President
The Royal College of Surgeons
Lincoln Inn's Fields
London WC2A 3PN

Dear Sir Peter,

Face Transplantation

You may be aware that a story appeared in *The Sunday Times* on 23rd February 2003 (attached) in which Mr Peter Butler, the British surgeon from the Royal Free Hospital who is claiming to be nearly ready to undertake the first face transplant, was quoted as saying that a fourteen-year-old Irish woman and three others are being 'assessed' in the next few weeks to establish whether she is a suitable candidate. Since that day, the media has been seeking information from all sources, especially from Changing Faces, about the identity of this young person. An intense media frenzy is developing to be the first to gain her story.

Changing Faces believes that this is an entirely inappropriate and potentially exceedingly damaging way to proceed with the development of what might be an important technological innovation. Whilst in no way wishing to halt scientific advance, we are extremely concerned by the way in which what should be a completely private clinical issue subject to strict ethical and scientific processes, is being conducted through the media. Along with many other observers and experts, including surgeons themselves, we also have serious questions to pose about the technology being proposed – on technical, ethical and psychosocial grounds. I believe that these issues should be resolved in a careful and transparent fashion before any such transplantation trial is undertaken.

In the interests of all present and future patients with disfigurements, their parents and families, I call on you and the Royal College of Surgeons as a matter of the greatest urgency to attempt to create a Moratorium on further media coverage of the issue. We also urge that the College establishes a Committee, including scientists, surgeons, ethicists, psychologists and people with disfigurements, charged to investigate and report on all aspects of face transplantation prior to any experimentation whatsoever.

Yours faithfully,

James Partridge OBE, DSc
Founder and Chief Executive

ANNEX 1

3rd February 2006

Mr Bernard Ribeiro, FRCS
The President
The Royal College of Surgeons
Lincoln Inn's Fields
London WC2A 3PN

Dear Mr Ribeiro,

Face transplantation

You will have followed with interest, I am sure, as we and many others have, the recent developments in face transplant surgery. I am writing to you to suggest that the time is right for the Royal College to reconvene the Working Party on this subject to take stock of progress and develop pointers to the future.

Changing Faces was very pleased that your predecessor, Sir Peter Morris, responded so positively and promptly to our suggestion back in 2003 that he should set up the Working Party in the first place – and we were broadly supportive of the cautious approach taken in its Report in November 2003.

As we understand it, having tried to keep pace with French surgery developments and with Mr Butler's arguments (see, eg, the *BMJ* 10.12.2005), it is now argued that the all the reservations and research deficits identified by your Working Party have been answered and therefore approval should now be given for UK face transplantation research to be instigated.

Changing Faces has very important questions about some of the key issues that we would want the Working Party to address… In making this request, we would like to make it abundantly clear from the outset that we are not and have never been against face transplantation per se. Our position is that as a charity supporting and representing people with disfigurements of any kind, we wish to see improvements in the health care and other services available to them and to bring about changes in public attitudes and behaviours towards them. We fully recognise that many people with disfigurements have reason to be extremely grateful to surgeons – I certainly am myself. We therefore consider it inappropriate for some proponents of face transplantation to characterise Changing Faces as being against such potentially important scientific developments.

Our concern has always been and will continue to be that vulnerable patients should be able to make fully informed decisions about the choice of treatments available to them as individuals (to meet their physical, functional, aesthetic, psychological and social needs), as far as possible behind a veil of clinical privacy.

I hope that you will be able to draw these questions and our concerns to the attention of the Working Party...

We should also say that these are our chief concerns, but they are not an exhaustive list; others will pick up on different aspects.

Yours sincerely,

James Partridge OBE, DSc, FDSRCSEd (Hon)
Founder and Chief Executive

ANNEX 2

'At long last, a newsreader who made us face reality'[1]

Catherine Bennett's article in *The Observer*, Sunday 22 November 2009.

Broadcasters believe that looks are more important than the message. James Partridge proved them wrong

Considering its pioneering work for the rehabilitation of freak-shows, it was not immediately clear what Channel Five intended when it invited James Partridge, who has a disfigured face, to read its lunchtime news bulletins last week. Partridge, who founded the charity Changing Faces, wanted his appearances to be a contribution towards 'facial equality'. He hoped, he said, 'to challenge people to become aware of their culturally determined reflexes and thereby, if not break the mould, at least start the mould-breaking – be more informed, less quick to recoil – and ultimately, challenge "face-value judgments"'.

Perhaps it represented some sort of victory that this admirable experiment was staged by the people whose trademark shudderfests have included *The Man Whose Arms Exploded*, *The Woman With Giant Legs* and *Growing up Without a Face*. In routine Channel Five circumstances, Partridge himself would have been introduced as the

Man Who Lost His Looks, following an accident in which his car burst into flames.

Although it is hard to know how much Partridge's five, fleeting appearances will have done to change attitudes towards disfigured and other unusual-looking people, they must, surely, have raised some doubts about the attributes of more conventional newsreaders: the Presenters with Giant Egos Whose Vanity Exploded. Doesn't their extreme glossiness sometimes distract from what they are saying? Wouldn't you switch channels rather than watch the worst-affected ones? Perhaps they could learn something from Mr Partridge. What he lacked by way of big hair, mannerisms, and the singing and dancing skills that have become mandatory for newsreading professionals, was outweighed by a powerful impression of intelligence and decency.

Is it possible that reading aloud is less difficult than anyone thought or is Mr Partridge just a natural? Although, inevitably, his delivery was at first somewhat stilted and ponderous, it improved so much from bulletin to bulletin that you almost hoped for some ghastly newsflash to come his way, towards the end of the week, to see if he wouldn't be a more reassuring bearer of grim news than one of the Children in Need dancing girls. He may not be Walter Cronkite, but then again, neither is Natasha Kaplinsky.

With some startlingly vicious exceptions, responses to his appearances on various message boards suggested that many viewers are, as a *Five News* survey had found, tolerant about seeing disfigured faces on television. Or moderately disfigured ones. It was pointed out, perhaps reasonably enough, that Partridge, who must once have been very handsome, was not the most challenging case imaginable. Some viewers may even have responded to his performance in the way Jane Eyre did, to the spectacle of scarred Mr Rochester: 'One is in danger of loving you too well for all this; and making too much of you.' There is no knowing what the respondents had in mind when, questioned for a YouGov poll, 44% said they thought it would be a good idea for people with facial disfigurements to present television shows. More than half said they would not switch off if a disfigured person came on.

If the prospects for facial equality are so propitious, it is curious that there should be so few people on television with any visible differences (outside programmes that are actually about people who have some disfigurement or disability). Now that Mr Partridge has retired from his week-long career on Five, the only regulars on British television with a non-standard appearance would appear to be Frank Gardner and CBeebies' Cerrie Burnell, who was born with one hand. Last year, the BBC had to defend its appointment of Ms Burnell to angry parents, presumably irritated that she did not look more like Konnie Huq or Fearne Cotton.

For on children's programmes, as everywhere else in broadcasting, the tendency is towards ever-higher standards of presenter-perfection. People with noticeable disfigurements are not, as Fiona Bruce confirmed recently, the only people to suffer from facial inequality. The plain and homely, overweight and middle aged are equally unwelcome, particularly if they are women. 'If you look like the back end of a bus,' Bruce said, 'as a woman you won't get the job. If you look like the back end of a bus as a bloke, you might get the job.' It was to counter such charges that the BBC recently launched a quest for the Holy Grail: a woman newsreader in middle age whose plastic surgery still allows her some degree of facial movement. At the time of writing, the search continues.

The Corporation might have done better to stress, after it identified Arlene Phillips as a memento mori, that its prejudices are not unusual. After sex, most celebrity news focuses on physical perfection or, more gleefully, on its obverse: the veiny arms, wrinkled knees and up-skirt cellulite that condemn the once-flawless. The changes to Kate Moss's skin and abdominal region are charted with closer attention in the *Daily Mail* than the melting of the polar icecaps. But if parts of the media place a deranged and damaging emphasis on bodily perfection, that still doesn't account for the bias against plainness in careers where good looks confer no obvious professional advantage. Academic studies have calculated that the 'plainness penalty' is between 5% and 10% of earnings: more than the financial bonus for being beautiful.

Correspondingly, other studies of appearance find that vast numbers of women, perhaps as many as a quarter, would consider plastic surgery. Three-quarters of British girls dislike something about their appearance by the age of 12. A recent survey of Girl Guides confirmed, yet again, that independence has done nothing to liberate women from anxiety about their looks: 46% of these children, between the ages of 11 and 16, would like cosmetic surgery to make themselves prettier or thinner.

But then they spend their lives looking at Cheryl Cole instead of Valerie Singleton. It is hard to argue with academics, specialising in appearance, who say that the pressure to be beautiful is more relentless now than at any time in history. Some even think it's time diversity practice caught up: discrimination against the plain should be covered by equal opportunities legislation, along with sexism, ageism and racism. There is little, after all, that the truly homely can do to force themselves upon lookists. Other than cover themselves with a burka and claim religious discrimination.

Kate Moss's silly maxim – 'Nothing tastes as good as skinny feels' – was widely reported last week, along with many a sad reflection on fashion, size zero and the promotion of anorexia. But an obsession with thinness, surely, is just part of an exaltation of appearance that creates such unhappiness in the imperfect majority. If Moss is at fault for being such a poor role model, then so, and more so, are national broadcasters who believe that only beautiful people can read the news. Our thanks to James Partridge for proving them wrong.

ANNEX 3

The International Media Standard on Disfigurement (2020)

@FaceEqualityInt
faceequaliltyinternational.org

Creating a world where
everyone is treated fairly
whatever their face looks like

FACE IT

The International Media Standard supports responsible media organisations and professionals to show respect and care for individuals who live with a facial difference or disfigurement.

The media should avoid words or descriptions which could further stigmatisation and stereotyping. It should always:

VOCABULARY

- Use sensitive, non-stigmatising vocabulary.
- Name the condition or injury that causes a facial difference, and give an objective explanation of it.
- If in doubt about a generic phrase, 'a person with a disfigurement' or 'facial difference' tend to be preferred.

SENSATIONALISM

- Refrain from over-dramatising the condition or injury, and avoid parallels with non-human objects or characters from fiction or non-fiction who are defined adversely by their condition (ie: Joseph Merrick or Freddy Kreuger).

PERSONALITY

- Avoid portraying the person as passive, helpless, a victim, to be pitied or inept.
- Avoid words or phrases that suggest the person's facial appearance indicates anything to do with their personality (eg: that they may be a villain).
- Avoid asking readers or viewers to express an opinion on someone's face or attribute qualities to a person based on their appearance.

SYMPATHY

- Avoid evoking sympathy purely because someone has a facial difference or disfigurement; any sympathy should be warranted by the context — for example, if someone has been mistreated.

ANNEX 3

MORE ON LANGUAGE

- Face Equality International uses 'disfigurement' as a collective term for the visual effect that a congenital, skin or eye condition, a paralysis, a scar or the treatment of cancer or another condition can have on the appearance of a person's face, hands or body.
- The Alliance also respects the fact that some people dislike the term 'disfigurement' and so 'facial difference' may be more widely accepted. In some instances, 'visible difference' may be used when relating to a disfigurement that affects a person's face and body.

EDITING

- It is common to see editing that involves dramatic music, black and white or grey filters and other dramatic devices. Unless the subject matter justifies this, i.e hate crime or abuse, then the device creates sympathy without reason and further ostracises the person with a disfigurement. It's important to prioritise empathy over sympathy.

INTERVIEWING

- If conducting a live broadcast interview ask the individual to self-identify and provide you with their preferred term, i.e 'I have vitiligo and I prefer for it to be called a skin condition'.
- Speak to your interviewee first and have researchers/producers get to know them before the interview in order to figure out their preferred language, whilst ensuring everyone involved has read this Standard and understands the subject matter.
- Take the person's lead on how comfortable they are about their experience and how much they would like to share. If they would rather not share medical details or that of an accident or trauma, then try not to probe for details. Consider whether it's relevant to the feature to discuss anything that may create drama or sympathy without reason.

Face Equality International, an alliance of 30 NGOs/charities which work for people with facial differences, has produced this Standard to prevent poor media coverage given the success of standards from NGOs such as the Samaritans. Responsible media organisations should consult and accept the guidance of FEI's Member organisations in their country or region which will publish their own Media Guidelines, appropriate to their own culture(s), language(s) and subject area. Face Equality International will list these on its website

---

For further information visit: faceequalityinternational.org/mediastandard

Face Equality International is a charity registered in Guernsey, No. CH597, and a company limited by guarantee, No. 65374.

FACE EQUALITY
INTERNATIONAL

ANNEX 4

A Logo With Meaning

Face Equality International chose as its logo a symbol of wabi-sabi, the Japanese aesthetic which sees the beauty, profundity and authenticity in irregularity and imprecision.

According to Japanese legend, a young man named Sen no Rikyū sought to learn the elaborate set of customs known as the 'Way of Tea'. He went to tea master Takeno Jōō, who tested the younger man by asking him to tend the garden. Rikyu cleaned up debris and raked the ground until it was perfect, then scrutinised the immaculate garden. Before presenting his work to the master, he shook a cherry tree, causing a few flowers to spill randomly on to the ground.

To this day, the Japanese revere Rikyu as one who understood to his very core a deep cultural thread known as wabi-sabi. Emerging in the fifteenth century as a reaction to the prevailing aesthetic of lavishness, ornamentation and rich materials, wabi-sabi is the art of finding beauty and profundity in earthiness, of revering authenticity above all. In Japan, the concept is now so deeply ingrained that it's difficult to explain to Westerners; no direct translation exists.

Face Equality International campaigns for a global culture that sees the beauty, profundity and authenticity in distinctive and irregular faces and values every single human being equally, whatever their face looks like.

The beautiful, meaningful and profound logo symbolically reflects the aesthetic culture we aspire to create.

Wabi-sabi is particularly in evidence in pottery and art:

> While we may be tempted to throw away a broken plate or bowl, ceramics in Japan are mended using resin mixed with powdered gold, silver, or platinum. You can see the visible cracks, but the repaired pieces' quirky beauty somehow makes them even more covetable.
>
> And it's not just used with things that are broken. Artists in Japan often leave subtle fractures in the glaze when making a vase or bowl as a reminder of the wabi-sabi nature of life.[1]

The making of human faces is far subtler and more complex than the making of a vase or a portrait. The judgements we make about them should be, too — and not based on outdated or commercially inspired stereotypes.

We hope you will enjoy the logo in all its fullness!

ACKNOWLEDGEMENTS

Many people over the years – friends, professional allies and fellow campaigners – have encouraged and helped me to write this book and I cannot possibly thank them all. But there are some without whom it really wouldn't have turned out as it has.

The list starts with the surgeons, nurses and paramedical staff at what was then St Lawrence's Hospital, Chepstow and Queen Mary's, Roehampton. So, a big thank you to Kathy Chrystal, Jim Evans, Tim Milward, John Gowar and John Clarke, to Margaret Pooley, Joyce Broughton, Nurse Pottinger, Ruth Clarke, Maggie Kennedy, Carol Addison, Pat George and many more.

I would like to acknowledge the informed and ever-questioning help I had in developing the psychosocial empowerment programmes at Changing Faces: Nichola Rumsey, Jo Ouston and her team, Richard Lansdown, Kathy Lacy, Emma Robinson, Pat Blakeney, Walter Meyer, Alex Clarke, Veronica Kish, Berni Castle, Lorna Renooy, Nick Ambler, Liv Kleve, Lyn Maddern, Julia Cadogan, Natty Triskel, Carole Easton, Sam Cheatle, Elizabeth Noble, Wendy Eastwood, Orla Duncan and Alyson Bessell – and there are many more. Thank you!

Then I want to thank those whose great enthusiasm and commitment turned a drip-drip of public awareness effort into the full-blown campaign for face equality: Stephen Woodford, Dianne Thompson, Winnie Coutinho, Alison Rich, Henrietta Spalding, Jane Frances, Steve Taylor, Phyll Swift, Rehana Browne Chris Binding and Bill Simons –

and all the many champions who 'lent' their faces to the campaign like David Bird, Lucas Hayward, Kellie O'Farrell, Adam Pearson, Michelle Syms, Rebecca Vezey and her father, Chris, and Victoria Wright.

And I acknowledge the great support given to me by trustees in creating and steering Changing Faces and Face Equality International, notably Campbell Adamson, John Clarke, Juliet Campbell, Andrew Jarvis, Anthony Brown, Tony Cline, Maxine Whitton, David Clayton, Mark Landon, Jill Clark, Graham Beveridge, Tony Pickford and Karlene Wright.

None of that would have been possible without the transformational philanthropy of Greville and Lisa Mitchell, Geoff and Fiona Squire, Mary Perkins, Julian Richer, Hans and Märit Rausing, and the Garfield Weston family... and the gifts of many, many other generous people.

In writing the book, I thank Christopher Sinclair-Stevenson and Jonathan Mantle for never giving up on me, and John Bond, Chris Wold, Caroline McArthur and Miranda Ward at Whitefox for their great advice and help in making the book possible... and I am very grateful to all those who have given their stories and faces to this book: Bill Cooper, Marc Crank, Carly Findlay, Matthew Joffe, Kapil Kapur, Patricia Lefranc, Mike Okninski, Margaret Soars and Jennifer Wallace.

So many dear friends have been unwaveringly 'with me' through all this too... like Giles, Hugh, Douglas, Tina and Charles, Andrew, Cedric, Tina, Jerry, Bob, Tony, Francis, Michael, Keith, Nige and Fiona, Mark and Keri, William, Claire and Desmond, Geoff, Jonathan, Julia, Sam, Rob, Phil, Simon, Susan, Nigel and Geraldine, Kathleen, Hilary, Rita, Graham, Colin and Claire, Anthony and Gabrielle, Robin and Yvette... Thank you all!

Above all, my family has been such an immense source of strength – I am hugely grateful to my parents, David and Sue, Clare and Joel, Alison and Fenella and all theirs.

My children, Simon, Charlotte and Harriet, have all witnessed, probably been embarrassed at times by, and had to tolerate my crazy

ACKNOWLEDGEMENTS

life in pursuit of face equality and I love them, their partners and all their little ones to bits for their patience, perseverance and unconditional support.

Most of all, none of this would have happened without my wife, Carrie, and her amazing and multiple skills, her dedication to family-building and her colossal strength of purpose. She enabled me to find my voice and allowed me to try to make my dream a reality... It's impossible to thank her enough!

NOTES

9. Discovering *Stigma*

1. West, Nathanael. (1933). *Miss Lonelyhearts*, quoted in Goffman, E. (1963). *Stigma: Notes on the Management of Spoiled Identity*. London: Penguin (1990 reprint), 7.
2. Goffman, E. (1963). *Stigma: Notes on the Management of Spoiled Identity*. London: Penguin (1990 reprint), 11.
3. Ibid. 15.
4. Ibid. 15–16.
5. Ibid. 16.
6. Ibid. 17–18.
7. Ibid. 18.
8. Ibid. 19.
9. Ibid. 24.
10. Ibid. 25–26.
11. Ibid. 45.
12. Simpson, W. (1958). *I Burned My Fingers*. London: Pan Books.

10. Restarting Life

1. Williams, H.A. (1972). *True Resurrection*. London: Michael Beazley.
2. Ibid. 10.

12. Building a New Me

1. Partridge, J., 'A face from the flames: saluting Niki Lauda', (8 Sep 2013), https://jamespartridge.wordpress.com/2013/09/08/a-face-from-the-flames-saluting-niki-lauda (accessed 1 Apr. 2020).
2. Draper, P. et al. (1978). *The NHS in the next 30 years: A new perspective on the health of the British*. London: Unit for the Study of Health Policy.

13. Looking Back and Moving Foreward

1. Goffman, E. (1963). *Stigma: Notes on the Management of Spoiled Identity*. London: Penguin.

Mezzanine

1. Downie, P. (ed.) (1984). *Cash's Textbook of General and Surgical Conditions for Physiotherapists.* London; Boston: Faber & Faber.
2. Partridge, J. (1990). *Changing Faces: The Challenge of Facial Disfigurement.* London: Penguin. Available from https://jamespartridge.wordpress.com/books/.

14. Inventing Changing Faces

1. Bull, R., Rumsey, N. (1988). *The Social Psychology of Facial Appearance.* New York: Springer-Verlag.
2. Macgregor, F.C. (1990). 'Facial Disfigurement: Problems and Management of Social Interaction and Implications for Mental Health.' *Aesthetic Plastic Surgery*, 14:1, 249–257.
3. Rumsey, N., Bull, R. (1986). 'The effects of facial disfigurement on social interaction.' *Human Learning*, 5, 203–208.
4. *Guide to Major Trusts*, many editions. London: Directory of Social Change.
5. Robinson, E., Rumsey, N., Partridge, J. (1996). 'An evaluation of the impact of social interaction skills training for facially disfigured people.' *British Journal of Plastic Surgery*, 49:5, 281–289.
6. The self-help guides in their up-to-date form are available on the Changing Faces website here: www.changingfaces.org.uk/adviceandsupport/self-help-guides (accessed 1 Apr. 2020)

15. Faces: The Principles of Effective Psychosocial Care

1. Royal College of Surgeons of England, 'Facial Transplantation', Working Party Report (Nov. 2006), www.rcseng.ac.uk/-/media/files/rcs/library-and-publications/non-journal-publications/facial-transplantation-2006.pdf (accessed 3 Apr. 2020)
2. 'Building your resilience', first published by the American Psychological Association in 2008, https://www.apa.org/helpcenter/road-resilience (accessed 1 Apr. 2020)
3. Clarke, A. et al. (2014). *CBT for Appearance Concerns.* New Jersey: Wiley Blackwell.
4. Kübler-Ross, E. (1969). *On Death and Dying: What the Dying have to teach Doctors, Nurses, Clergy and their own Families.* New York: Scribner/Simon & Schuster.
5. Strauss, R.P., 'Blessings in Disguise: A New Paradigm for Thinking About Children with Craniofacial Conditions', Cleft Advocate (May 2002), www.cleftadvocate.org/keynote2002.html (accessed 1 Apr. 2020)
6. For an excellent review, see Fletcher, D., Sarkar, M. (2013). 'Psychological resilience: A review and critique of definitions, concepts and theory.' *European Psychologist*, 18:1, 12–23.
7. Macgregor, F.C. (1990). 'Facial Disfigurement: Problems and Management of Social Interaction and Implications for Mental Health.' *Aesthetic Plastic Surgery*, 14:1, 249–257.
8. Cole, J. (1997). *About Face.* Cambridge, MA: MIT Press.

NOTES

16. Making Faces Available to Everyone

1. NHS England, 'NHS commits to major transformation of mental health care with help for a million more people', (15 Feb. 2016), www.england.nhs.uk/2016/02/fyfv-mh/ (accessed 1 Apr. 2020)
2. Bessell, A., Brough, V., Clarke, A., Harcourt, D., Moss, T.P., Rumsey, N. (2012). 'Evaluation of the effectiveness of Face IT, a computer-based psychosocial intervention for disfigurement-related distress.' *Psychology, Health and Medicine*, 17:5, 565–577.
3. Williams, H.A. (1972). *True Resurrection*. London: Michael Beazley.

18. 'Face-ism' Unmasked

1. Bogdan, R., Biklen, D. (1977). 'Handicapism.' *Social Policy*, 7, 14–19.
2. Macgregor, F.C. (1990). 'Facial Disfigurement: Problems and Management of Social Interaction and Implications for Mental Health.' *Aesthetic Plastic Surgery*, 14:1, 249–257.
3. YMCA, 'Be Real: In Your Face', (Feb. 2018), www.ymca.org.uk/wp-content/uploads/2018/02/In-Your-Face-v1.0.pdf (accessed 1 Apr. 2020)
4. BAAPS, 'Cosmetic surgery stats: number of surgeries remains stable amid calls for greater regulation of quick fix solutions', (20 May 2019), https://baaps.org.uk/media/press_releases/1708/cosmetic_surgery_stats_number_of_surgeries_remains_stable_amid_calls_for_greater_regulation_of_quick_fix_solutions (accessed 1 Apr. 2020)

19. Where Does Face-ism Come From?

1. 'The Most Magical Airbrush Apps for Flawless Selfies', HudaBeauty (22 April 2017). https://hudabeauty.com/the-most-magical-airbrush-apps-for-flawless-selfies (accessed 9 Apr. 2020)
2. Modiface, www.modiface.com (accessed 13 Apr. 2020)
3. Bosker, B., 'New Selfie-Help Apps Are Airbrushing Us All Into Fake Instagram Perfection', HuffPost US (5 Dec. 2013), www.huffingtonpost.com/2013/12/05/selfie-instagram_n_4391220.html (accessed 1 Apr. 2020)
4. Rees, A., 'This Inspiring Fashion Campaign Features an Acid Attack Survivor', Cosmopolitan (14 Jan. 2016),: www.cosmopolitan.com/style-beauty/fashion/news/a52176/inspiring-fashion-campaign-features-acid-attack-survivor/ (accessed 1 Apr. 2020)
5. Changing Faces. 'Disfigurement in the UK', (May 2017), www.changingfaces.org.uk/wp-content/uploads/2017/05/DITUK.pdf (accessed 1 Apr. 2020)
6. Rumsey, N. & Harcourt, D. (Eds.) (2012). Oxford Library of Psychology. *The Oxford Handbook of the Psychology of Appearance*. Oxford: Oxford University Press.
7. Dion, K., Berscheid, E., Walster, E. (1972). 'What is beautiful is good.' *Journal of Personality and Social Psychology*, 24:3, 285–290.
8. 'A speech by HRH The Prince of Wales at the 150th anniversary of the Royal Institute of British Architects (RIBA), Royal Gala Evening at Hampton Court Palace' (30 May 1984), https://www.princeofwales.gov.uk/speech/speech-hrh-

prince-wales-150th-anniversary-royal-institute-british-architects-riba-royal-gala (accessed 9 Apr. 2020)
9. Wardle, C. & Boyce, T. 'Media Coverage and Audience Reception of Disfigurement on Television', (2009), www.researchgate.net/publication/265266990_Media_Coverage_and_Audience_Reception_of_Disfigurement_on_Television (accessed 13 Apr. 2020)
10. Widdows, H. (2018). *Perfect Me: Beauty as an Ethical Ideal*. New Jersey: Princeton University Press.
11. Department of Health, 'Government Response to the Review of the Regulations of Cosmetic Interventions', (Feb 2014), www.gov.uk/government/uploads/system/uploads/attachment_data/file/279431/Government_response_to_the_review_of_the_regulation_of_cosmetic_interventions.pdf (accessed 1 Apr. 2020)

20. The Vision of a World That Respects Face Equality

1. Changing Faces. 'The incidence and prevalence of disfigurement', (2016), www.changingfaces.org.uk/wp-content/uploads/2016/03/FE-Campaign-Epidemiology-2-pages.pdf (accessed 3 Apr. 2020)

21. The Campaign for Face Equality in the UK to Date

1. Wardle, C. & Boyce, T. 'Media Coverage and Audience Reception of Disfigurement on Television', (2009), www.researchgate.net/publication/265266990_Media_Coverage_and_Audience_Reception_of_Disfigurement_on_Television (accessed 13 Apr. 2020)
2. Gerard, J., Bingham, J., 'News reader with facial disfigurement is broadcasting phenomenon', *Telegraph* (20 Nov. 2009), www.telegraph.co.uk/finance/newsbysector/mediatechnologyandtelecoms/media/6615767/News-reader-with-facial-disfigurement-is-broadcasting-phenomenon.html (accessed 3 Apr. 2020). And 'James Partridge reading Five News 19 November', Changing Faces UK, YouTube (19 Nov. 2019) 2009 https://www.youtube.com/watch?v=TuJ12T7pFkA (accessed 9 Apr. 2020)
3. Strang. F., 'Who is Winnie Harlow? Lewis Hamilton's friend and model who's embraced vitiligo condition', *Sun* (7 Nov. 2018), www.thesun.co.uk/tvandshowbiz/1754421/winnie-harlow-lewis-hamilton-vitiligo/ (accessed 3 Apr. 2020)
4. Rees, A., 'This Inspiring Fashion Campaign Features an Acid Attack Survivor', *Cosmopolitan* (14 Jan. 2016), www.cosmopolitan.com/style-beauty/fashion/news/a52176/inspiring-fashion-campaign-features-acid-attack-survivor/ (accessed 3 Apr. 2020)
5. Changing Faces, '#PledgeToBeSeen', www.changingfaces.org.uk/campaign/pledgetobeseen (accessed 3 Apr. 2020)
6. 'Leo', Changing Faces UK, *YouTube* (11 Apr. 2012) http://www.youtube.com/watch?v=6va7WsWyWTM (accessed 9 Apr. 2020)
7. Changing Faces, 'I Am Not Your Villain - A Campaign to Challenge the Film Industry' (16 Nov. 2018), www.changingfaces.org.uk/i-am-not-your-villain-campaign-launches-today-in-the-telegraph

NOTES

8   Chatterjee, A., 'Scarring Your Children With The Lion King?', *Psychology Today* (5 Aug. 2019), www.psychologytoday.com/us/blog/brain-behavior-and-beauty/201908/scarring-your-children-the-lion-king (accessed 3 Apr. 2020)

9   Dowell, B.. 'Jeremy Clarkson's "Facial Growth" comment prompts complaints', *Guardian* (10 Feb 2012), www.theguardian.com/media/2012/feb/10/jeremy-clarkson-facial-growth-comment-complaints (accessed 3 Apr. 2020) and Sweney, M., 'Top Gear: Jeremy Clarkson's Elephant Man joke ruled offensive', *Guardian* (1 Oct. 2012), www.theguardian.com/media/2012/oct/01/top-gear-jeremy-clarkson-elephant-man (accessed 3 Apr. 2020)

10 Newsbeat, 'People with facial burns criticise "offensive" advert' (2 Feb. 2015), www.bbc.co.uk/newsbeat/article/31100039/people-with-facial-burns-criticise-offensive-advert (accessed 3 Apr. 2020)

11 Nuffield Council on Bioethics, 'Cosmetic procedures: ethical issues', (22 Jun. 2017), nuffieldbioethics.org/publications/cosmetic-procedures (accessed 3 Apr. 2020)

12 UNICEF, 'The Right to an Education', https://www.unicef.org.uk/rights-respecting-schools/the-right-to-education (accessed 3 Apr. 2020)

13 Rosenthal, R., Jacobson., L. (1992). *Pygmalion in the classroom*. Expanded edition. New York: Irvington; Schrank, W. (1968). 'The labeling effect of ability grouping.' *Journal of Educational Research*, 62, 51–52; Brophy, J. E. (1985). 'Teachers' expectations, motives and goals for working with problem students.' In Ames, C. and Ames, R. (eds) *Research on motivation in education: The classroom milieu*. Orlando, FL: Academic Press, 175–221.

14 De Young, A.C., Hendrikz, J., Kenardy, J.A., Cobham, V.E., Kimble, R.M. (2014). 'Prospective Evaluation of Parent Distress Following Pediatric Burns and Identification of Risk Factors for Young Child and Parent Posttraumatic Stress Disorder', *Journal of Child and Adolescent Psychopharmacology*, 24:1, https://doi.org/10.1089/cap.2013.0066 (accessed 3 Apr. 2020)

Nelson, L.P., Gold, J.I. (2012). 'Posttraumatic stress disorder in children and their parents following admission to the pediatric intensive care unit: A review.' *Pediatric Critical Care Medicine*, 13:3, 338–347, doi: 10.1097/PCC.0b013e3182196a8f (accessed 3 Apr. 2020)

McDermott, B.M., Cvitanovich, A. (2000). 'Posttraumatic Stress Disorder and Emotional Problems in Children Following Motor Vehicle Accidents: An Extended Case Series.' *Australia & New Zealand Journal of Psychiatry* https://doi.org/10.1080/j.1440-1614.2000.00753.x (accessed 3 Apr. 2020)

Diseth, T.H. (2006). 'Dissociation following traumatic medical treatment procedures in childhood: A longitudinal follow-up.' *Development and Psychopathology*, 18:1, 233–251.

15 Department for Education, research report 2016, https://assets.publishing.service.gov.uk/government/uploads/system/uploads/attachment_data/file/509679/The-link-between-absence-and-attainment-at-KS2-and-KS4-2013-to-2014-academic-year.pdf (accessed 3 Apr. 2020). This is not a long report but see especially p15-16.

16 Vandell, D.L., Anderson, L, D., Ehrhardt, G., Wilson, K.S. (1982). 'Integrating Hearing and Deaf Preschoolers: An Attempt to Enhance Hearing Children's Interactions with Deaf Peers.' *Child Development*, 53:5, 1354–1363.

17. Nabors, L. A., Lehmkuhl, H.D., Warm, J.S. (2004). 'Children's Acceptance Ratings of a Child with a Facial Scar: The Impact of Positive Scripts.' *Early Education & Development,* 15:1, 79–92.
18. Cline, T., Proto, A., Raval, P., Di Paolo, T. (1998). 'The effects of brief exposure and of classroom teaching on attitudes children express towards facial disfigurement in peers.' *Educational Research,* 40, 55–68.
Frances, J. (2000). 'Providing effective support in school when a child has a disfigured appearance: The work of the Changing Faces school service.' *Support for Learning,* 15, 177–182.
Kish, V., Lansdown, R. (2000). 'Meeting the psychosocial impact of facial disfigurement: Developing a clinical service for children and families.' *Clinical Child Psychology and Psychiatry,* 5, 497–512.
Speltz, M. L., Richman, L. (1997). 'Editorial: Progress and limitations in the psychological study of craniofacial anomalies.' *Journal of Pediatric Psychology,* 22, 433–438.
19. Mojon-Azzi, S.M., Kunz, K., Mojon, D.S. (2010). 'Strabismus and discrimination in children: are children with strabismus invited to fewer birthday parties?' *British Journal of Ophthalmology,* 95:4, http://bjo.bmj.com/content/early/2010/07/30/bjo.2010.185793 (accessed 3 Apr. 2020)
20. Harper, D.C. (1999). 'Social psychology of difference: stigma, spread and stereotypes.' *Childhood, Rehabilitation Psychology,* 44:2, 131–144.
21. Ibid, 139.
22. Ibid, 139.
23. Kish, V., Lansdown, R. (2000). 'Meeting the psychosocial impact of facial disfigurement: Developing a clinical service for children and families.' *Clinical Child Psychology and Psychiatry,* 5, 497–512.
24. Bronfenbrenner, U. (1979). *The ecology of human development: Experiments by nature and design.* Cambridge, MA: Harvard University Press, 58
25. See more at Inclusive Solutions, 'Circle of Friends', https://inclusive-solutions.com/circles/circle-of-friends (accessed 3 Apr. 2020)
26. Changing Faces (2017). Disfigurement in the UK', www.changingfaces.org.uk/wp-content/uploads/2017/05/DITUK.pdf (accessed 3 Apr. 2020)
27. Changing Faces, 'Faces of Equality', faceequalityinternational.org/shop
28. Saunders, H. (2018). 'The Invisible Law of Visible Difference: Disfigurement in the Workplace.' *Industrial Law Journal,* 48:4, 487–514.
29. Face Equality International, 'A logo with meaning', (31 Oct. 2018), https://faceequalityinternational.org/a-logo-with-meaning (accessed 3 Apr. 2020)

22. What Can We All Do to Create Face Equality?

1. Gladwell, M. (2000). *The Tipping Point: How Little Things Can Make a Big Difference.* London: Little, Brown and Company.
2. Whittle, S., 'A brief history of transgender issues', *Guardian* (2 Jan. 2010), www.theguardian.com/lifeandstyle/2010/jun/02/brief-history-transgender-issues (accessed 3 Apr. 2020)

NOTES

3. Singer, P., 'The abuse of animals won't stop until we stop eating meat', *Guardian* (11 Feb. 2015), www.theguardian.com/commentisfree/2015/feb/11/abuse-animals-meat-eating-industry-liberation-speciesism (accessed 3 Apr. 2020)
4. European Commission, 'Internal Market, Industry, Entrepreneurship and SMEs', https://ec.europa.eu/growth/sectors/cosmetics/legislation_en (accessed 3 Apr. 2020)
5. Personal communication: Nigel Mercer.
6. Griffiths, D., Mullock, A. (2018). 'Cosmetic Surgery: Regulatory Challenges in a Global Beauty Market'. *Health Care Analysis* 26, 220. https://link.springer.com/article/10.1007/s10728-017-0339-5 (accessed 3 Apr. 2020)
7. Ibid.
8. Tikunova, P., 'Acid Attack Survivor Becomes Face of Fashion Brand in India', Bored Panda, www.boredpanda.com/acid-attack-survivor-laxmi-fashion-model-india/ (accessed 3 Apr. 2020)
9. Illamsqua, www.illamasqua.com/shop/collections/imperfection (accessed 3 Apr. 2020)
10. Rivett-Carnac, M.R., 'Face value: portraiture and facial disfigurement', Art UK (27 Feb 2014), https://artuk.org/discover/stories/face-value-portraiture-and-facial-disfigurement (accessed 3 Apr. 2020)
11. Gladwell, M. (2013). *David and Goliath*: Underdogs, Misfits, and the Art of Battling Giants. London: Little, Brown and Company.

Annex 1

1. Shanmugarajah, K., Hettiaratchy, S., Clarke, A., Butler, P.E. (2011). 'Clinical outcomes of facial transplantation: a review'. *International Journal of Surgery*, 9:8, 600–607.
2. Tasigiorgos, S. et al. (2019). 'Five-Year Follow-up after Face Transplantation'. *New England Journal of Medicine*, 380, 2579–2581.
3. Lantieri, L. et al (2016). 'Face transplant: long-term follow-up and results of a prospective open study'. *The Lancet*, 388:10052, 1398–1407.
4. Butler, P.E., Hettiaratchy, S. (2002). 'Face transplantation – fantasy or the future?' *The Lancet*, 360:9326, 5–6.
5. Royal College of Surgeons of England (2006). 'Working Party on Face Transplantation report', www.rcseng.ac.uk/library-and-publications/rcs-publications/docs/facial-transplantation-working-party-report/
6. Winter, G.F. (2016). '"Social anonymity": The ethics of facial transplantation'. *The Bulletin of the Royal College of Surgeons of England.* 98: 7, 288–292.
7. www.washingtonpost.com/health/2019/09/23/her-body-is-rejecting-transplanted-face-one-solution-is-unthinkable/
8. Clarke, A, Butler, P.E. (2009). 'The psychological management of facial transplantation'. *Expert Review of Neurotherapeutics*, 9:7, 1087+.
9. Partridge, J., 'Framing the face: history, emotion, transplantation', About Face (30 Oct. 2019), https://aboutfaceyork.com/framing-the-face-history-emotion-transplantation/ (accessed 3 Apr. 2020)

10 Kmietowicz, Z., 'Face transplants should not be done without more research', *BMJ* (22 Nov. 2003), https://www.ncbi.nlm.nih.gov/pmc/articles/PMC274081/ (accessed 3 Apr. 2020)
11 The Royal College of Surgeons of England, 'Facial Transplantation', Working Party Report (Nov. 2006), https://www.rcseng.ac.uk/-/media/files/rcs/library-and-publications/non-journal-publications/facial-transplantation-2006.pdf (accessed 3 Apr. 2020)

Annex 2

1 Bennett, C., 'At long last, a newsreader who made us face reality', *Guardian* (22 Nov. 2009), www.theguardian.com/commentisfree/2009/nov/22/james-partridge-tv- newsreaders (accessed 3 Apr. 2020)

Annex 4

1 Brownlees, J. '"Wabi-Sabi" is the Latest Wellness Trend to Impact the Internet', *The Thirty* (4 Jan. 2018) https://thethirty.byrdie.co.uk/wabi-sabi (accessed 9 Apr. 2020)

CREDITS

Photographs: p129 Brian Green, Guernsey Press; p234 Harriet Saddington; p264 Justin Downing for Sky TV; p297 Mazz Image; p330 Teri Blythe; p331 Leigh Partridge.

Articles and quotes: Changing Faces for many projects etc.; Penguin Random House for Goffman's *Stigma: Notes on the Management of Spoiled Identity*, published by Penguin in 1963; p102 The Orion Publishing Group for Colin Wilson's *The Outsider* published by Dell Publishing Co. Inc in 1956; P198 Bryan Appleyard; p344 The *British Medical Journal* for an article about the Royal College of Surgeons of England's 2003 report on face transplantation; p351 The Guardian News & Media Limited for an article in the *Observer* in November 2009; p263 The Telegraph Media Group Limited for an article about my reading of the news on Channel 5 in 2009.